Forging Democracy from Below

The transition to democracy in both El Salvador and South Africa poses two puzzles. Why did the powerful and fervently antidemocratic elites of these countries abandon death squads, apartheid, and other tools of political repression and take a chance on democracy? And why did these two protracted civil conflicts prove amenable to resolution via negotiated transitions to democracy, in contrast to other civil wars whose resolution through negotiation appears so elusive? *Forging Democracy from Below* shows how popular mobilization – in El Salvador led by an effective guerrilla army supported by peasant collaboration and in South Africa led by a powerful alliance of labor unions and poor urban dwellers – transformed elite economic interests, thereby forcing elites to the bargaining table, and why both a durable settlement and democratic government were the result. Using interviews with both insurgent and elite actors as well as analysis of macroeconomic data, Elisabeth Wood documents an "insurgent path to democracy" and challenges the view that democracy is the result of compromise among elite factions or the modernizing influence of economic development.

Elisabeth Jean Wood teaches comparative politics and political economy at New York University. She has done fieldwork for many years in rural El Salvador as well as in South Africa. Her research in El Salvador was supported by the U.S. Institute of Peace and the MacArthur Foundation. Her South Africa research was carried out as a Scholar of the Harvard Academy of International and Area Studies. Professor Wood's next book is an ethnographic account of peasant insurgency in Usulután and Tenancingo, El Salvador.

Cambridge Studies in Comparative Politics

General Editor

Margaret Levi   *University of Washington, Seattle*

Associate Editors

Robert H. Bates   *Harvard University*
Ellen Comisso   *University of California, San Diego*
Peter Hall   *Harvard University*
Joel Migdal   *University of Washington*
Helen Milner   *Columbia University*
Ronald Rogowski   *University of California, Los Angeles*
Sidney Tarrow   *Cornell University*

Other Books in the Series

Stefano Bartolini, *The Class Cleavage: The Political Mobilization of the European Left, 1860–1980*

Carles Boix, *Political Parties, Growth and Equality: Conservative and Social Democratic Economic Strategies in the World Economy*

Catherine Boone, *Merchant Capital and the Roots of State Power in Senegal, 1930–1985*

Michael Bratton and Nicolas van de Walle, *Democratic Experiments in Africa: Regime Transitions in Comparative Perspective*

Valerie Bunce, *Subversive Institutions: The Design and Destruction of Socialism and the State*

Ruth Berins Collier, *Paths Toward Democracy: The Working Class and Elites in Western Europe and South America*

Donatella della Porta, *Social Movements, Political Violence, and the State*

Gerald Easter, *Reconstructing the State: Personal Networks and Elite Identity*

Roberto Franzosi, *The Puzzle of Strikes: Class and State Strategies in Postwar Italy*

Geoffrey Garrett, *Partisan Politics in the Global Economy*

Miriam Golden, *Heroic Defeats: The Politics of Job Loss*

Frances Hagopian, *Traditional Politics and Regime Change in Brazil*

J. Rogers Hollingsworth and Robert Boyer, eds., *Contemporary Capitalism: The Embeddedness of Institutions*

Ellen Immergut, *Health Politics: Interests and Institutions in Western Europe*

Series list continues on the page following the Index.

Forging Democracy from Below

INSURGENT TRANSITIONS IN SOUTH AFRICA AND EL SALVADOR

ELISABETH JEAN WOOD

New York University

CAMBRIDGE
UNIVERSITY PRESS

CAMBRIDGE UNIVERSITY PRESS
Cambridge, New York, Melbourne, Madrid, Cape Town, Singapore,
São Paulo, Delhi, Dubai, Tokyo, Mexico City

Cambridge University Press
The Edinburgh Building, Cambridge CB2 8RU, UK

Published in the United States of America by Cambridge University Press, New York

www.cambridge.org
Information on this title: www.cambridge.org/9780521788878

First published 2000

A catalogue record for this publication is available from the British Library

Library of Congress Cataloguing in Publication Data

Wood, Elisabeth Jean, 1957–
    Forging democracy from below: insurgent transitions in South Africa and El Salvador/
Elisabeth Jean Wood.
        p.   cm. – (Cambridge studies in comparative politics)
    Includes bibliographical references and index.
    ISBN 0-521-78323-2 – ISBN 0-521-78887-0 (pbk.)
    1. Political participation – South Africa.   2. Political participation – El Salvador.   3.
Democracy – South Africa.   4. Democracy – El Salvador.   I. Title.   II. Series.

JQ1981. W66 2000
320.968–dc21   00-023018

ISBN 978-0-521-78323-1 Hardback
ISBN 978-0-521-78887-8 Paperback

To my parents

Contents

Illustrations and Tables

Illustrations

Photographs

Tables

Preface

Forging Democracy from Below is about how the sustained mobilization by poor people in both El Salvador and South Africa transformed the political economy of their countries and convinced hitherto recalcitrant elites to negotiate an end not only to civil conflict but also to authoritarian rule. I argue that this enduring insurgency was the principal reason for the political pacts that led to democracy in these two unequal societies. Evidence supporting the argument draws on methods from both political economy and ethnography.

I began this book as an investigation of El Salvador's unusual insurgent path to democracy. But if El Salvador were the only polity whose transition to democracy followed this route, the argument would be of limited interest and, indeed, less persuasive for that reason. My explanation of democratic transition in El Salvador would be more compelling if other cases had followed a similar path. Moreover, if forging democracy from below is to stand as a particular mode of transition, other cases should populate the category.

I therefore took up a perhaps unlikely case for comparison, that of South Africa. If the transition to democracy in South Africa, a country different from El Salvador in many respects, was nonetheless similar in its principal features to that of El Salvador, the argument for a path to democracy from below would be much more persuasive than if a more similar country followed a similar route. In the latter case, a similar path to democracy could be the result of any of a large number of similarities not stressed by the democracy-from-below interpretation proposed here. Testing the argument against such an apparently different country would help to distinguish between general features of the path from below and its local variations.

My argument concerning El Salvador focuses on two key claims. First, largely as a result of the sustained support of insurgent peasants that undergirded the military capacity of the Frente Farabundo Martí para la Liberación Nacional (FMLN), the guerrilla force became a necessary party to any enduring resolution of the civil war. Second, ongoing unrest and the counterinsurgency reforms that attempted to counter it together reshaped elite interests, perceptions, and opportunities, with the result that elites long resistant to even mild reform decided to negotiate an end to the war and to take their chances on the vagaries of electoral competition. In the years before the civil war, no one would have imagined the Salvadoran elite sitting down at the bargaining table with representatives of subordinate classes to negotiate a transition to democracy.

South Africa offers striking parallels. First, mobilization, particularly by labor unions but also by township residents, sustained a deepening political crisis for well over a decade, bringing into existence an insurgent counter-elite, the African National Congress (ANC), without whose agreement there would have been no political settlement. Second, as unrest continued, economic elites pressed for fundamental political reform and negotiations with the ANC, a defection from the ruling alliance that crucially undermined continued support for apartheid.

Note to the Reader

Given the substantial degree of political tension and uncertainty surrounding the themes of this study – political mobilization and violence, coercive labor relations, the distribution of property rights, and clandestine collaboration with the FMLN – most of the Salvadorans interviewed for this study preferred to remain anonymous. For this reason, in characterizing interviewees I list only their status (government official, peasant organization leader, etc.) and the year the conversation occurred. Although interviews with South Africans were much less sensitive, I follow the same procedure for those interviewees.

Throughout this book, my interviews with informants are italicized; quotations from other sources are not. In addition, the Spanish *campesino* (literally, of the countryside, *campo*, frequently translated as "peasant") is used to refer to residents engaged in agricultural activities (except, of course, landlords of substantial property who hire significant numbers of wage laborers) or (when used as an adjective) to organizations in which they participate. Thus a *campesino* may be a landless day-laborer, a permanent wage employee, or a farmer working a smallholding. This usage reflects the residents' own vocabulary and, more important, their nearly universal aspiration to work their own land. When distinctions between those agriculturalists who engage primarily in work on their own plots, on those of others, or on a mix of employment are necessary for the argument, I make them explicitly.

Acknowledgments

This book reflects a decade-long political and economic study of the civil war in El Salvador. The work began in 1987, when I visited the town of Tenancingo to research the return of residents displaced by violence. I made a number of subsequent brief trips to follow that community's evolution. Beginning in September 1991, I carried out sixteen months of fieldwork in the war-torn province of Usulután, followed by a series of short trips to document later events. While detailed analysis of peasant insurgency in El Salvador based on those years of fieldwork is reserved for a separate book (Wood 2000), I draw as needed on that material for the argument presented here.

My investigation took me to South Africa on three trips of varying duration. In 1997 I spent several months there during my initial exploration of the comparison with El Salvador that resulted in this book. I returned to South Africa briefly in 1998 and for three months in 1999 to gather further material and present my initial findings to South African researchers.

One accumulates many debts in ten years of research. Principal among these debts is that to the residents of the field sites in El Salvador for their willingness to describe their history and that of their communities through the years of the civil war. Such fieldwork in the midst and immediate aftermath of civil war is difficult; I am especially grateful to the shelter and counsel provided by Sister Elena Jaramillo of the parish of Jiquilisco, by Ana Karlslund in Santiago de Maria, by the staff members of COMUS in San Francisco Javier, and by Madre Ivonne and the staff members of FUNDASAL in Tenancingo. Their experience and wisdom saved me many an error (or worse) and made both possible and pleasurable my stays in the contested communities of El Salvador.

I am also grateful to the many persons interviewed in San Salvador and other urban areas, particularly the landlords of Usulután and Tenancingo for sharing their experiences and perceptions of the war. My thanks also go to government officials in the various reconstruction, land reform, and land-transfer agencies, to several officers of the Salvadoran Armed Forces, to the field commanders of the Popular Revolutionary Army (the guerrilla force active in the Usulután field sites) and to those of the Popular Liberation Forces (the force active in Tenancingo), to the members and staff of the FMLN working on land transfer and reconstruction, to the staff members of the United Nations Mission in El Salvador, to Michael Wise, Ana Luz de Mena, and María Latino of the United States Agency for International Development, and to the directors and staff of the Salvadoran Foundation for Development and Low-Income Housing.

I am grateful as well to those I interviewed in South Africa, who ranged from trade union officials to business executives, leaders of business organizations, academics, representatives of various political parties, and government officials.

The individuals interviewed chose to share their perceptions and data with an academic researcher in the hope of collaborating in a work that would document and analyze troubled periods of their national histories. I can only hope this book proves worthy of their trust and aspirations.

Many individuals and families in South Africa extended to me not only their collegial collaboration but also the hospitality of their homes. I am particularly grateful to David Lewis, Terry Kurgan, Jillian and Christopher Nicholson, Lael Bethlehem, Emilia Potenza, Charles Meth, and Francis and Lindy Wilson. For hospitality in San Salvador, I thank David Holiday, Corina Dufka, Tom Gibb, Melinda DeLashmutt, and Francisco Altschul.

For comments on all or parts of the manuscript, I would like to thank James Boyce, Chuck Call, Ruth Collier, Raphael De Kadt, George Downs, Richard Fagen, Johannes Fedderke, Michael Foley, Jeffrey Goodwin, James Heintz, Jeffrey Herbst, Stathis Kalyvas, Terry Karl, Roy Licklider, Cynthia McClintock, Kevin Middlebrook, Christopher Mitchell, Barrington Moore Jr., Mike Morris, Nicoli Nattrass, Jillian Nicholson, Daniel Posner, Adam Pzreworski, Kenneth Roberts, Donald Rothchild, Philippe Schmitter, Jeremy Seekings, Mary Simons, George Vickers, Michael Watts, Richard Wood, and particularly Charles Meth, David Lewis, Jack Spence, and William Stanley.

I would also like to express my appreciation to the Institute for Economic and Social Research of the José Simeón Cañas Central American

Acknowledgments

University, which provided invaluable institutional support during my fieldwork in Usulután, and to FUNDASAL for logistical and other help during my fieldwork in Tenancingo. Particular thanks go as well to the researchers and staff of the Development Policy Research Unit and the South African Labour and Development Research Unit, both of the University of Cape Town, for their institutional support and warm hospitality.

I am fortunate to have worked with Alex Holzman and the outstanding editorial team at Cambridge University Press; they have made this a better book. Thanks also to Peter Lange, who was editor of the series when the book was under review. His insightful comments helped to improve the book. Research assistance from Ethel Brooks, Stephen Brown, Catalin Cretu, Matt Golder, Bridget Longridge, and Rodrigo Mardones was invaluable.

Funding for this research project came from the United States Institute of Peace, the Academy for International and Area Studies of Harvard University, the MacArthur Foundation through the Stanford Center for Arms Control, the Tinker Foundation, the Institute for the Study of World Politics, and New York University. I am grateful to all of them for their support.

Finally, a most heartfelt thank you to Sam for everything.

Abbreviations

AHI	Afrikaner Commercial Institute
AIFLD	American Institute for Free Labor Development
ANC	African National Congress
ANSESAL	Salvadoran National Special Services Agency
ANSP	National Academy of Public Security
ARENA	National Republican Alliance
AZAPO	Azanian People's Organization
BCM	Black Consciousness Movement
BPR	Popular Revolutionary Block
CBM	Consultative Business Movement
CEA-COPAZ	Special Agrarian Commission to COPAZ
CODECOSTA	Coordinator for Development of Cooperatives
CODESA	Convention for a Democratic South Africa
COMUS	United Municipalities and Communities of Usulután
CONARA	Commission for the Restoration of Areas
CONFRAS	National Confederation of Federations of Agrarian Reform Cooperatives
COPAZ	National Commission for the Consolidation of Peace
COSAG	Concerned South Africans Group
COSATU	Congress of South African Trade Unions
CUSA	Council of Unions of South Africa
DNA	Department of Native Affairs
ERP	Popular Revolutionary Army
FAN	National Anti-Communist Front
FAPU	United Popular Action Front
FECCAS	Christian Federation of Salvadoran Peasants
FENACOA	National Federation of Agrarian Cooperatives

FMLN	Farabundo Martí Front for National Liberation
FOSATU	Federation of South African Trade Unions
FPL	Popular Liberation Forces
FUSADES	Salvadoran Foundation for Economic and Social Development
IFP	Inkatha Freedom Party
INCAFE	National Coffee Institute
ISTA	Salvadoran Institute of Agrarian Transformation
MEA	Municipalities in Action Program
MIPLAN	Ministry of Planning and Coordination of Economic and Social Development
MK	Spear of the Nation, the armed force of the ANC Alliance
MPNP	Multiparty Negotiating Process
NEDLAC	National Economic Development and Labour Council
NEF	National Economic Forum
NMC	National Manpower Commission
NUM	National Union of Mineworkers
ONUSAL	United Nations Observer Mission in El Salvador
ORDEN	National Democratic Republican Order
PAC	Pan-Africanist Congress
PCN	National Conciliation Party
PDC	Christian Democratic Party
PNC	National Civilian Police
PRN	National Reconstruction Plan
PRUD	Revolutionary Party of Democratic Unification
RENAMO	National Resistance of Mozambique
SACOB	South African Chamber of Business
SACP	South African Communist Party
SACTU	South African Congress of Trade Unions
SASM	South African Students Movement
SASO	South African Students Organization
SASOL	South African Synthetic Oil Limited
SRN	Secretariat of National Reconstruction
SSC	State Security Council
UCS	Salvadoran Communal Union
UDF	United Democratic Front
UNDP	United Nations Development Programme

Abbreviations

UNITA	National Union for the Total Independence of Angola
USAID	United States Agency for International Development
WNLA	Witwatersrand Native Labour Association
WPGWU	Western Province General Workers Union

Introduction

1

From Civil War to Democracy

Knaves will tell you that it is because you have no property that you are unrepresented. I tell you, on the contrary, that it is because you are unrepresented that
you have no property.

— English Chartist Bronterre O'Brien, 1846[1]

From [the proletariat, peasants, and petty bourgeois], this [republican] constitution demands they should not go forward from political to social emancipation,
from [the bourgeoisie] that they should not go back from social to political
restoration.

— Karl Marx, 1850[2]

As the civil war in El Salvador drew to a close, peasants allied with the
Frente Farabundo Martí para la Liberación Nacional (Farabundo Martí
Front for National Liberation, FMLN) throughout the province of
Usulután raced to consolidate their claims to de facto property rights,
enclosing occupied properties with barbed wire, taking over additional
properties, and patrolling boundaries against the return of the erstwhile
landlords. On January 29, 1992, thirteen days after the signing of the peace
agreement that ended more than a decade of civil war, government forces
arrested peasant leaders of the Cooperativa California in an effort to repos-
sess the Hacienda California, a large and valuable property on the coastal
plain that the cooperative had forcibly occupied six months earlier. Two
days earlier, militant peasants occupying a nearby property had been
evicted and twelve leaders arrested. In addition, two were hospitalized
(as a result of excessive force by government troops, according to United
Nations observers). In response to the arrests, FMLN field commanders

[1] Plummer 1971: 177.   [2] Marx 1964: 69–70.

3

slowed the movement of their forces to the designated cease-fire areas in several areas of Usulután – an action that posed a significant threat to the closely choreographed separation of armies under way at the time – until arrested peasant leaders were released and further eviction attempts suspended. Undeterred by arrests and evictions, peasants continued to occupy further properties.

With the military and logistical support of many peasants through the years of the civil war, the FMLN had fought government forces to a stalemate. Beginning in 1990, government and guerrilla negotiators hammered out the terms of a peace agreement to end the war and to found a democratic regime, which included the legalization of the FMLN as a political party, civilian control of state security forces, and electoral reform. On March 20, 1994, members of the Cooperativa California voted in the nation's first inclusive elections, marking the country's transition to political democracy.

Similarly in South Africa, decades-long political mobilization by black workers and the unemployed demanding political rights and economic resources forced recalcitrant elites to negotiate a transition to democracy in order to end civil strife. A wave of unprecedented strikes by black workers in the early 1970s and the spread of protest by township residents after the shooting of schoolchildren in Soweto in 1976 had been met with repression as well as measures to reform apartheid without extending universal suffrage. Trade unionists took advantage of reform measures to build a militant trade union movement that demanded political emancipation as well as economic concessions. From mid-1984 to mid-1986, the townships again erupted in a wave of protest; only the imposition of a severe state of emergency in 1986 and the arrest of tens of thousands of activists of the United Democratic Front (UDF) quelled the uprising. As a result of the repression, increasingly restrictive international economic sanctions were imposed. As the government appeared unable or unwilling to address the crisis, growing numbers of business executives and Afrikaner intellectuals initiated contact with the African National Congress (ANC) to discuss transition scenarios. After President F. W. de Klerk released ANC political prisoner Nelson Mandela and revoked the banning of the ANC and the allied South African Communist Party (SACP) in 1990, negotiations between the ANC, the governing National Party, and other political parties led to the first inclusive elections in April 1994.

In these unequal societies, elites long opposed democratization not only for the usual reason – that the many might expropriate or heavily tax the

4

wealth of the few – but because the economic privileges of the elite depended on state-enforced procedures unlikely to be sustainable under democratic rule. In South Africa, these measures included strict controls on the mobility of labor, reliance on highly regulated foreign migrant labor, fiscal priorities that sharply favored elite interests, and the exclusion of the majority from suffrage; in El Salvador, they included the torture and disappearance of labor activists and sometimes their families by death squads allied to state security forces and paramilitary groups, coercive workplace practices that long prevented any labor organizing, and close local alliances between landlords and representatives of the state that pre-empted political organization in the countryside. Elite recalcitrance in the face of rising political and economic claims by workers for effective polit-ical inclusion and adequate economic participation brought El Salvador to civil war and South Africa to its brink.

This book addresses two related puzzles. What accounts for the tran-sition to democracy in South Africa and El Salvador after decades of elite opposition to democratic participation and electoral contestation by sub-ordinate classes? And why were these civil conflicts amenable to negoti-ated resolution, in contrast to other civil wars whose resolution through negotiation appears so elusive?

The answer to the first puzzle, I argue, is that democracy in both coun-tries was forged from below by the sustained insurgency of lower-class actors. Once-unyielding elites in South Africa and El Salvador conceded democracy because popular insurgency, although containable militarily, could not be ended, and the persisting mobilization eventually made com-promise preferable to continued resistance. In contrast to the transitions in many countries where mobilization by the poor played a lesser role – Spain, Brazil, and many others – in South Africa and El Salvador the timing of the transitions, the split among elite factions between those supporting and those opposing the transition, the political actors who negotiated the transition, and the nature of the compromises that led to democracy were all forged through insurgent mobilization. My central claim in response to the first question then is that the transition to democracy would not have taken place in either country when it did, as it did, and with the same con-sequences in the absence of sustained popular mobilization.

Two processes together make up this *insurgent path* to democracy. First, sustained mobilization eventually constituted the leadership of the popular opposition as an *insurgent counter-elite*, by which I mean representatives of economically subordinate and socially marginalized actors that are a necessary party to negotiations to resolve an enduring crisis of the political regime. This insurgent counter-elite is "elite" only in the strictly limited sense of being a necessary party to the negotiations if the ongoing conflict is to be durably resolved. Second, the accumulating costs of the insurgency (and the various counterinsurgency measures) transformed the core interests of economic elites, eventually convincing substantial segments that their interests could be more successfully pursued by democratizing compromise than by continued authoritarian recalcitrance. As a result, these economic elites pressed regime elites to negotiate, changing the balance of power within the regime between those willing to consider compromise and those resolutely opposed.

In answer to the second puzzle, together these two processes forged the political and structural bases of compromise, with the result that the two conflicts proved amenable to negotiated resolution via a transition to democracy. These class-based conflicts differed from many civil wars in that the contending forces were economically interdependent. Even in South Africa, where racial and ethnic identities were extremely salient, class and race coincided to a remarkable degree because of decades of apartheid policies. Once insurgency transformed elite interests away from their reliance on coercive institutions, the economic interdependence of key antagonists enhanced the returns to resolution of the civil strife: income from joint production would no longer be lost due to strikes, boycotts, sabotage, sanctions, and guerrilla attacks. As a result of the economically unequal and politically exclusive nature of Salvadoran and South African societies, a particular political bargain was possible. If institutions credibly promising a mutually satisfactory distribution of the benefits of compromise could be fashioned, insurgents would accept political inclusion at the cost of economic moderation (principally a commitment to economic liberalism), while economic elites gained constitutional protection of the status quo distribution of wealth in return for accepting electoral and other forms of democratic competition as the terrain on which they would henceforth pursue their interests.

Labor-Repressive Institutions and Recalcitrant Elites in Oligarchic Societies

Both South Africa and El Salvador were what I term *oligarchic societies*: societies in which economic elites rely on extra-economic coercion of labor by the state for the realization of incomes superior to those possible under more liberal, market-based arrangements. Thus oligarchic societies are those in which the dominant labor relations are what Barrington Moore Jr. (1966) termed "labor-repressive." By *economic elites* I mean those individuals who by virtue of their control of the means of production attain significant income and social status. By *regime elites*, I mean those individuals whose power depends on their occupation of state (and government) offices. *Extra-economic coercion* may be contrasted with the market discipline of labor: in a market-based economy, a worker who demands too much pay or does too little work runs the risk of becoming unemployed or unable to pay freely contracted debts. Excess supply in labor markets and limited borrowing opportunities in credit markets induce compliance with the economic interests of the wealthy. Discipline by market forces requires the state's enforcement of property rights of course, but little other direct state intervention is involved. Thus in liberal economies employers rely on markets and especially glutted labor markets to discipline labor.[3] In contrast, by *extra-economic coercion*, I mean directly coercive labor relations such as slavery; coercive restrictions on the mobility of labor such as serfdom, debt peonage, criminal vagrancy laws, and laws that prohibit residency in some areas without a state-issued pass; and coercive practices in the workplace that repress nascent attempts by laborers to organize. Extra-economic coercion thus entails gross violations of fundamental liberal rights of association, speech, free movement, self-ownership, due process, and equality before the law.

The reliance of economic elites on coercion by regime elites in oligarchic societies leads to an enduring alliance between them, with economic elites supporting authoritarian political structures that secure the extra-economic coercion of labor on which their economic position depends. The result may be extreme racially coded inequality, as in South Africa, or moderate inequality, as in El Salvador. However, it is not inequality per se that explains the characteristic politics of oligarchic societies but the way it is generated and sustained. Because the processes determining the distribution of income and wealth are underwritten by the political control of labor, the structure of these societies precludes fully democratic rule: in oligarchic societies these processes are such that the historical dread among elites – that rule by the many would threaten the privileges of the few – cannot easily be allayed by Madisonian reassurances. In oligarchic societies, the link – or more precisely, the presumed link –

---

[3] Stiglitz and Shapiro 1984.

between political democracy and egalitarian redistribution must be severed if a democracy is to emerge.

Hence if electoral contestation occurs, it is severely restricted in terms of suffrage or political competition, or both, with the result that the oligarchic alliance is not challenged through democratic procedures. Whether civilians or military officers rule and whether or not significant cleavages exist among the elite, the state protects the core interests of the economic elite (a cheap and hard-working labor force and the existing distribution of property) to the advantage of both regime and economic elites. Moreover, while the reliance of economic elites on labor-repressive practices may erode as markets expand, the alliance between economic and regime elites endures, limiting the autonomy of the state. Although regime elites act with autonomy in some areas, reformist factions within the state do not compromise the foundations of the alliance by instituting changes in the electoral regime that would threaten the interests of economic elites.

Of course, the interests of regime elites and economic elites do differ: economic elites prefer to retain the largest possible share of their profits for private consumption or investment, whereas regime elites prefer to tax those profits to capture resources for the state. Regime elites – as in El Salvador and South Africa – often favor interventionist economic policies over the more laissez-faire preferences of some of the economic elite. These and other differences may lead to significant strain within the alliance in times of labor acquiescence, particularly if regime elites and economic elites are largely drawn from ethnically distinct populations, as in South Africa. But in oligarchic societies, as the following chapters demonstrate, elites join forces to defend their common interests against mobilization by subordinant social actors who might threaten the political control of labor or the stability of the polity – and thus the existing distribution of wealth, political power, and social status.

The distinction between extra-economic coercion and market discipline of labor is not always sharp, as Moore and subsequent authors have recognized.[4] Some workplace practices discourage worker organizing efforts yet

---

[4] Moore 1966: 434. For example, Rueschemeyer, Stephens, and Stephens weaken Moore's definition of labor repression to include merely labor-intensive agriculture in order to capture the full range of landlord reliance on political control of labor, arguing that agrarian elites in labor-intensive regions oppose democracy because the accompanying freedom of association for workers would force them to pay higher wages (1992: 163–5, 288).

would not strike most observers as directly repressive, and some forms of nonmarket control of labor are not in the interests of the economic elite. For example, state corporatism, as in Brazil, was surely a form of political control of labor, yet the unionization and incorporation of labor occurred under the auspices of a significantly more autonomous state, and the economic elite probably would have done better without corporatist labor relations (workers' wages were probably *higher* as a result of corporatist inclusion, as in Juan Peron's Argentina). Although the distinction between market and political forms of labor discipline is not particularly salient in nonmarket societies, certainly in communist countries political, not market, forces determined working conditions and wages. However, economic elites (plant managers, for example) would probably have done better under market-based labor regulations, as their recent economic success in some of the former communist countries suggests. So neither communist nor corporatist countries count as oligarchic in the relevant sense.

In contrast, both El Salvador and South Africa were oligarchic societies: economic elites long relied on extra-economic coercion of labor for the realization of their income. In El Salvador, labor-repressive agriculture led to a long-standing alliance between economic elites and the military that maintained a highly unequal distribution of land.[5] When the military did not rule directly, electoral contestation was limited to an exceedingly narrow spectrum of political parties dominated by the official military party. Occasional attempts at reform by modernizing factions of the regime elite were swiftly brought to a halt by coups of hardline elements of the military encouraged by the economic elite.

In South Africa, labor-repressive agriculture and mining laid the foundations for a racial oligarchy in which effective suffrage was limited to the white population; all others could not vote to determine the leadership of the polity, and most could not own property, could not live in urban areas without an approved pass, and could not move between areas without the approval of white authorities and employers.[6] Of course not all white South Africans controlled significant means of production; some were workers or civil servants, and some were unemployed. Nonetheless, the relative wealth and social status of whites versus that of nonwhites in South

---

[5] See Weeks 1986 and Rueschemeyer, Stephens, and Stephens 1992: 226–68.
[6] On the oligarchic nature of South African society and the associated obstacles to democratization, see Adam 1971; Greenberg 1980; Lipton 1985; Price 1991: 6; Friedman 1995 and 1997; and Bratton and van de Walle 1997.

Africa and the provision of generous public services to less fortunate whites depended on the political control of labor and would be undermined by the political enfranchising of the black majority.[7] For its white citizens, the South African regime was significantly more democratic than the Salvadoran regime. Civilians ruled through regular elections, and the state was significantly more autonomous from economic elites as it promoted Afrikaner economic and political interests at the expense of the interests of the mostly "English" economic elite. Nonetheless, Afrikaner ideology and interests converged with English business interests on the maintenance of influx controls on African labor, the illegality of black trade unions, and the political disenfranchisement of Africans. In particular, the dispossession of African farmers and the banishing of black workers fired for shirking or union activism to nonwhite areas by the confiscation of the pass lowered the cost of labor for economic elites.

The Insurgent Path to Democracy in Oligarchic Societies

The transition to democracy generally takes one of four routes. The first pattern, defeat in war followed by the imposition of democracy by occupying forces, as in Germany and Japan in the aftermath of World War II, is not relevant for the set of countries of concern here. Second, a faction of moderate elements may emerge within an authoritarian regime and initiate a period of political liberalization, which may be followed by democratization, a process in some cases impelled by an upsurge of political mobilization after liberalization and sometimes involving a political pact with opposition leaders. This second path was followed in much of Latin America and southern Europe, as well as in Russia. Third, political mobilization by a cross-class alliance of those excluded from power, if successful in forcing regime elites from office, may bring about a democratic regime, as in the Philippines, Nicaragua, Czechoslovakia, and many African countries. Finally, sustained political mobilization from below by working-class actors may force regime elites to negotiate a transition to democracy, as in South Africa and El Salvador, I argue. In the concluding

---

[7] The analysis of South African politics must draw on the racial terminology of the apartheid state as it shaped the politics of the country as well as the life course of all. I use "African," "Afrikaner," "English," "Indian," and "Coloured" for that reason. "White" refers to "Africaner" and "English" people as a group. I use "black" to mean "nonwhite," a term embraced by opposition movements as a way of rejecting the manipulation of identities by the state.

chapter of this volume, I consider other possible examples of this fourth insurgent path: Poland and Guatemala.

Because of the cohesiveness of economic and regime elites and their unity when challenged from below, regimes in oligarchic societies are not vulnerable to overthrow by cross-class alliances of rebellious social forces. In contrast, the personalist regimes of Nicaragua, the Philippines, and much of Africa were vulnerable to regime transition by insurrection because of the availability of allies from the upper stratum excluded from state power, with the result that cross-class coalitions overthrew the regime.[8] Such outright victory by insurgent forces is unlikely in oligarchic societies: because democratic rule poses a threat to the political control of labor, economic elites unite with regime elites against the threat posed from below. For the same reason, regime elites are unlikely to initiate liberalization and democratization except under unusual circumstances – they too have much to lose under democratic rule.

The insurgent path to democracy in oligarchic societies is thus one whereby working-class and other insurgent forces prove strong enough to force hitherto recalcitrant elites to compromise but not so strong as to overthrow the regime militarily.[9] The distinctive feature of the path stems from the fact that the key *dramatis personae* are not contending elite factions, ethnic groups whose economic interests are separable, or simply "insiders" versus "outsiders," but representatives of distinct classes, whose conflicts of interests propelled the conflict and whose interdependence shaped its democratizing resolution.

In oligarchic societies, the exclusivist ideology of economic and regime elites (whether racially coded or not) toward subordinates (indeed, its explicit disdain for members of subordinate groups), together with the experience of repression, fuels deep resentments that can be mobilized by an insurgent group, providing a collective identity based on their claim to common citizenship that lessens the costs of collective action and contributes to the emergence of its leadership as an insurgent counter-elite.[10] Rather than simply responding to new political opportunities extended by

---

[8] See Goodwin and Skocpol 1989; Price 1991; Snyder 1992; Bratton and van de Walle 1997; and Geddes 1999.

[9] See also Price 1991: 7–12 and Paige 1997: 332–3.

[10] Marx 1992 and 1998; see also Price 1991 and Seidman 1994. Because of the experienced intensity of this disdain, once mobilization begins in oligarchic societies, the experience of rebellion may provide affective rewards that further fuel rebellion (see Wood 2000 for development of this claim in the Salvadoran case).

the state, the insurgent social movements create and expand the structure of political opportunity through their interim victories and ongoing struggles.[11]

The transition to democracy in oligarchic societies thus occurs via a negotiated settlement and appears at first glance similar to negotiated transitions in Latin America and southern Europe. However, the agreements in El Salvador and South Africa were not pacts between elites. Although small groups of representatives of the government and the insurgency did negotiate pacts – indeed, few transitions were as tightly choreographed with as certain an electoral outcome as the South African case – the opposition representatives sitting across the bargaining table from government elites were representatives of lower-class and marginalized social actors (workers, the unemployed, and in El Salvador, poor peasants) long excluded from political and economic participation. For example, the principal negotiator for the ANC had been the chief official of the formerly illegal mineworkers union. The presence at the bargaining table of representatives of organizations such as the FMLN and the ANC needs to be explained, not conflated with the type of elite or cross-class oppositions that played a central role in other transitions.

To parry an initial objection to this categorization, it is both incontrovertible and irrelevant that insurgent leaders are typically well-educated people who have significantly wider economic opportunities than the workers and peasants they represent. Although members of the black middle class supported the ANC (and would be the chief beneficiaries of the transition), the principal protagonists of the unrest that propelled the transition were organized workers and poor township residents. Similarly, though many FMLN leaders were well-educated sons (and a few daughters) of middle-class families, the insurgency was sustained by land-poor and landless *campesinos*. The ANC and the FMLN were insurgent organizations whose representatives were long-standing, well-recognized leaders who spoke authoritatively for those organizations during the formal negotiations; but these leaders were elite *only* by virtue of their leadership of powerful insurgent organizations. One indication of the degree to which the leaders of both the ANC and the FMLN represented their organizations is that although the compromises they made during negotiations led to intense controversy within their organizations as the concrete terms of the pacts became known to constituents, those terms held. That some of

---

[11] Brockett 1995: 132; Goodwin and Jasper 1999: 39.

the insurgent counter-elite subsequently became regime elites or economic elites in the aftermath of the transitions to democracy should not be confused with their role as a counter-elite representing economically marginalized actors in the negotiations that led to those transitions.

The emergence of a sustained popular insurgency does not by itself explain the transition to democratic rule in El Salvador or South Africa of course. Why then did democratic rule emerge in these inegalitarian and repressive polities? Consider the Salvadoran case. Whether one ascribes to gradualist, structuralist, or elite-bargaining theories of political development, El Salvador on the eve of its civil war was an unlikely candidate for transition to democracy. El Salvador had few of the "social requisites of democracy"[12] or the attributes of "civic culture"[13] thought by some to be essential to the emergence of democracy. That the class structure and repressive political regime reflected the historical dominance of coercive agrarian labor systems was even less auspicious for the emergence of democracy.[14] Nor was the transition the consequence of the gradual emergence of a more diversified economic elite based on manufacturing or a growing professional middle class, as the literature on modernization would lead one to expect. Rather, the traditional agro-export sector – the core of the labor repression economy of the old regime – had fared very well during the decade before the war, while manufacturing declined. And given the oligarchic alliance, El Salvador was notable for the absence of competing groups of elites whose relatively equal power or legitimacy could be institutionalized via a pacted transition to democracy.[15] Moreover, revolutionary peasant mobilization of the type that sustained the Salvadoran civil war is not thought to result in democratic regimes.[16] Similar challenges are posed by the recent transition to democratic rule in South Africa; indeed, many observers thought an escalation into civil war more likely in South Africa than a negotiated transition to democracy.

Why, then, did the political and economic elite of these oligarchic societies abandon their implacable opposition to democratic rule and eventually negotiate with the insurgent counter-elite? Why did the Salvadoran elite – one of the most conservative in the hemisphere, whose principal party had been founded by the mastermind of the country's notorious death squads – accommodate to a liberal constitution including the prin-

---

[12] Lipset 1960.   [13] Almond and Verba 1963.
[14] Moore 1966; Weeks 1986; Stephens 1989.
[15] Rustow 1970; O'Donnell and Schmitter 1986.   [16] Moore 1966; Karl 1990.

13

ciple of democratic accountability of the security forces? In South Africa, why did regime elites long committed to racial exclusion and anti-communism finally abandon their attempts to construct a moderate black opposition and negotiate with Nelson Mandela, the ANC, and its ally the South African Communist Party (SACP)?

Along the insurgent path to democracy, popular mobilization is sustained long enough to create the structural conditions for the resolution of conflict: insurgency reshapes the economic interests and opportunities of the economic elites (and perhaps of some regime elites) sufficiently for them to judge the foreseeable returns to continued recalcitrance as less than the returns to compromise with the insurgents. In oligarchic societies, this eventual willingness of economic elites to compromise is particularly consequential: the unprecedented break in the oligarchic alliance makes possible the split within the regime between regime hardliners and reformists that culminates eventually in a negotiated transition to an inclusive regime.

The mechanism by which insurgency altered elite perceptions and interests was different in the two cases. In El Salvador, prolonged rebellion together with counterinsurgency measures taken to undercut mobilization reshaped the political economy, transforming elite economic interests (as well as elites' perceptions of their core interests) and thereby inducing hitherto recalcitrant elites to negotiate a democratic compromise with the insurgents. In particular, the civil war led to a dramatic transformation of the structure of the economy, as the commercial sector fueled by migrants' remittances boomed and the export agriculture sector declined. In South Africa, sustained mobilization by trade unions and to a lesser extent by township organizations – despite repressive measures by the apartheid state and repeated National Party efforts to develop a moderate black opposition – contributed to a climate of general uncertainty, declining investment, and a gathering perception that apartheid rule was not sustainable.

However, whether the returns to the economic elite of compromise exceed those of recalcitrance depends on the distributional terms of the transition. Although this is a consideration in any transition to democracy, in oligarchic societies it is particularly acute as elite income and status have historically depended on nondemocratic means. Crucial to this outcome is not only the "structural dependence of the state on capital"[17] usual in

[17] Przeworski and Wallerstein 1988.

14

capitalist societies but also the economic interdependence between the working-class insurgents and the economic elites, as this interdependence generates returns to cooperation that make compromise eventually more attractive than the returns to recalcitrance. Insurgency dampens the usual returns for the elite – assets are destroyed, costly strikes occur, security costs rise, investment is suspended, and taxes increase. If sustained long enough, expected returns under democracy look attractive in comparison – if the distributional terms of the transition do not greatly threaten the status quo distribution of property rights (see the Appendix for a formal model of these issues).

The politically exclusive nature of oligarchic societies makes the fundamental political bargain in capitalist democracies acceptable to insurgents despite their past rhetoric of socialist transformation. Insurgents value the realization of political democracy: leaders in part because they anticipate post-transition roles of power and status (particularly in the case of the ANC) and their constituents because they value democratic participation per se. Moreover, like the economic elite, insurgents anticipate the enactment of at least some redistributive policies in a democratic polity as even rightist parties would be forced to make some appeal to the poor.

The transition to democracy in both El Salvador and South Africa followed this insurgent path. However, other factors played a role as well. The fall of the Communist regimes of Eastern Europe reduced the likelihood that socialist policies would be implemented while also making elite opposition to democratic rule increasingly difficult to justify. Moreover, the growing hegemony of neoliberal economic policies made it unlikely that postconflict states would have the capacity to implement confiscatory redistributive policies that would threaten elite interests. Deviation from the neoliberal model would be punished by capital movements that would threaten any alternative model of development. As a result of both the fall of communism and the rise of neoliberalism, the set of possible long-term outcomes was truncated in ways that facilitated compromise. In South Africa, the erosion of the governing National Party's coalition also contributed to this outcome. Even so, it was sustained insurgency that forged the two conditions necessary for the transition to democracy in these two countries – namely, the emergence of an insurgent counter-elite and the erosion of elite economic interests – to occur when and as they did.

These transitions are therefore unusual. Whereas most transitions involve elements of protest from below, these transitions were *driven* from below: the erosion of elite support for the regime, the split within the regime, the timing of the transition, the parties that negotiate the terms of the transitions, and the eventual terms themselves all result from the sustained insurgency. My argument thus combines "structuralist" and "process-oriented" approaches to democratic transitions[18] and thus bridges the divide between structure and agency by analyzing how the antecedent regime and society led to sustained mobilization, which then established the political and structural conditions for compromise through the constitution of a new political actor and the evolving structure of elite economic interests.

Such insurgent-driven negotiated transitions are often conflated with elite-initiated transitions involving explicit political pacts, particularly in the early literature on the "third wave" of democratization. There are three related reasons for this. First, the initial cases in the "third wave" occurred in Latin America and southern Europe in the wake of military rule and were largely cases of elite-led democratization, in contrast to later transitions in Eastern Europe and Africa, where popular protest played a much more significant role.[19] This led to an initial emphasis on elite bargaining not borne out by the later expanded universe of cases.

Second, this initial emphasis on political pacts between contending elites led to a confounding of distinct types of transitions (for example, as "transplacements")[20] by treating all negotiators as similarly "elite." By failing to distinguish leaders of previously powerful political parties and the leaders of previously excluded and marginalized groups, this approach confuses transitions in which negotiations reflect the weakness of the regime in relation to the traditional (and usually elite) political opposition and those in which a previously subordinate group has forced its way to the bargaining table through sustained popular mobilization.[21] As a result, the transitions in El Salvador and South Africa are sometimes confused with those in which negotiations took place between very different kinds of opposition elites and government representatives.[22]

Third, the beginning of the transition to democracy was often *defined* as the start of political liberalization, overlooking the possibility that polit-

---

[18] Kitschelt 1992.
[19] Bratton and van de Walle 1997; Geddes 1999; Collier forthcoming.
[20] Huntington 1991: 151–63.
[21] Throughout her book, Collier similarly stresses the importance of distinguishing between various elites in the sense of class, political incumbents, and political leadership in explaining diverse paths to democracy (see, in particular, 1999: 17–19).
[22] See, e.g., Huntington 1991 and Herbst 1997–8.

ical liberalization and hence democratization were both caused by a previous factor, be it political mobilization, economic crisis, or both.[23] As a result, some analysts overlook the increasingly well-documented argument that nearly all transitions combine elements "from above" with elements "from below." For example, some argue that the transition to democracy in El Salvador began with the 1979 split in the military regime that led to political liberalization and the holding of increasingly competitive elections, but this suggestion neglects the previous mobilization that led to the split within the military. A decade later, civil war rather than the consolidation of democracy was under way as FMLN troops occupied parts of the capital city.

Not all analyses emphasize the role of elites in the Salvadoran and South African transitions. Glenn Adler and Eddie Webster (1995) make the case that labor mobilization pushed the South African transition along when negotiations stalled. Robert Price (1991), writing at the time of Mandela's release from prison, argued that the combination of insurrection and economic crisis might be sufficient to force a negotiated settlement. Jeffrey Paige (1997) interprets the Salvadoran transition as a revolutionary transition from below and traces the evolution of the dominant ideology among Salvadoran elites toward compromise. The analysis presented here extends these arguments by providing the causal mechanisms by which mobilization from below impacted on elite economic interests, brought the relevant parties to the table, shaped the evolution of the transition process, and structured the resulting settlement.[24]

In contrast to the early literature on transitions, the subsequent literature emphasizes the role of class actors, the nature of the antecedent regime, and the potential for cross-class opposition coalitions in order to account for the variety of recent transitions, as well as the historical cases.[25] In analyzing the relation between class conflict and democratization, many recent studies revisit the work of Barrington Moore Jr. (1966) and Goran Therborn (1979). Moore argues that the structure of agrarian labor relations, the relative power of the agrarian and urban dominant classes, the structure of state-class relations, and the availability of resources for

---

[23] Collier and Mahoney 1997: 287. See also Haggard and Kaufman 1995; Bratton and van de Walle 1997.

[24] However, Adler and Webster do not account for how mobilization led to negotiations in the first place, while Paige gives little attention to how the war reshaped the macroeconomic structure of the Salvadoran economy.

[25] Collier forthcoming.

17

peasant collective action shape political regimes and that agrarian elites reliant on labor-repressive institutions pose an enduring obstacle to democratization. In his analysis of the emergence of democracy in seventeen OECD countries, Therborn (1979) concludes that the working classes played an important (although nowhere sufficient) role in the extension of universal suffrage. In these countries capitalism had laid conditions propitious for democracy, creating a large working class and a diversified elite increasingly reliant on institutionalized contestation. War played a role in approximately half of his cases, either because victorious opponents imposed democracy or because "industrialized" labor-intensive war required massive conscription of all classes.

Working with a more restricted definition of democracy (roughly, nearly all adult males rather than universal suffrage), Dietrich Rueschemeyer, Evelyne Huber Stephens, and John D. Stephens (1992) follow Therborn in emphasizing both the role of working-class actors in forcing elites to extend suffrage and the availability of urban bourgeois or petty rural groups for alliance with these actors as a result of capitalist development. Haggard and Kaufman (1995) similarly stress the role of economic interests, particularly the importance of economic crisis in provoking transitions. Michael Bratton and Nicolas van de Walle (1997) identify a particular pattern of democratic transition in Africa and trace its causal origins to the antecedent regime, neopatrimonial rule. Barbara Geddes (1999) argues that the preferences and incentives of regime actors depend on the nature of the antecedent regime with the result that democratic transitions occur for different reasons in military, personalist, and one-party regimes. In contrast, Ruth Berins Collier emphasizes both the antecedent regime and society, identifying three dimensions of democratization: the distinction between the working class and the middle class, whether each class was previously included in the antecedent regime, and whether the "arena of action" is mobilization or negotiation.[26] Both Collier and Nancy Bermeo argue that political mobilization may impel rather than derail the process of democratic transition, as has often been argued.[27]

The argument presented here extends this recent literature and its emphasis on antecedent regime and class actors by explicitly addressing *how* political mobilization brought about democratic transitions to these

---

[26] Collier 1999: 19–22.   [27] Bermeo 1997; Collier 1999.

two oligarchic societies. In my cases, however, mobilization by lower-class actors was sustained over a much longer period and played a significantly greater role than in other cases, and elites were significantly more reluctant to compromise. It was not, as Moore and Rueschemeyer et al., argue, the slow penetration of commercial agriculture that dissolved elite opposition to democracy; rather, sustained insurgency outran this more gradual process, directly altering hitherto inert elite preferences in the space of a decade.

The argument is closest to Collier's path of "destabilization/extrication," whereby working-class unrest destabilizes the authoritarian regime, initiating processes eventually leading to transitions.[28] The causal role played by working-class actors is significantly greater in El Salvador and South Africa than in Collier's cases in two ways. First, not only does the insurgent counter-elite sit at the bargaining table (as do labor representatives in some of her cases), but no other party to the negotiations (except for the government) was remotely as important to the success of any resulting agreement. Second, insurgent mobilization so threatened elite interests that their core interests were transformed from coercive agriculture to the commercial and service sectors in the Salvadoran case, and from reliance on the political control of labor to an accommodation with the market discipline of labor in the South African case.

Overview

The transition to democracy in South Africa and El Salvador, I argue, followed a similar logic despite the many obvious differences between the two cases, including the level of development, the degree of racial cleavage, the class structure, the size and complexity of the country, and the degree of electoral success by the insurgents after the transition. The argument thus rests on what is termed a most dissimilar research design: should the argument prove persuasive for two societies that were so distinct in all but their common history of elite reliance on political more than market control of labor, the consequent elite opposition to liberal democracy, their sustained insurgencies, and their subsequent path to democracy, it should be the more compelling for their differences.

My argument relies on both political economic and ethnographic evidence. I draw on statistical series and primary documents of government,

---

[28] Collier 1999: 114–32. See also Collier and Mahoney 1997.

international, business and insurgent organizations, as well as on interviews conducted in El Salvador over nearly a decade during and after the civil war and in South Africa between 1997 and 1999. The analysis of the Salvadoran case relies on interviews with peasant leaders, landlords, members of peasant political organizations, church officials, government officials, Salvadoran military officers, FMLN field commanders, nongovernmental staff members, and development specialists and staff members of the United Nations mission and the U.S. Embassy. In many cases those interviews were repeated over the years of field research in El Salvador.[29] The South African argument draws on interviews with business, labor, government leaders, and academics, some of them key participants in the transition.

Part One focuses on El Salvador, beginning in Chapter 2 with the origins of El Salvador's oligarchic society in labor-repressive export agriculture. I chart the emergence of its rigid class structure and authoritarian regime, the failure of conservative modernization, the emergence of social movements and the repressive response of the state, and the descent into civil war by 1980. I then analyze the emergence of the FMLN as an insurgent counter-elite and argue that peasant collaboration was crucial to the FMLN's military and political capacity. I draw on interviews with *campesinos*, landlords, and FMLN field commanders in the municipality of Tenancingo between 1987 and 1991 and in several municipalities in the province of Usulután between 1991 and 1996. Both sites were heavily contested militarily throughout the war: peasant political mobilization in the 1970s was followed by a wave of repression by government forces, guerrilla organizations were active before and throughout the war, nearly all landlords of commercial scale left the area, many outlying hamlets were abandoned by *campesinos* as well as landlords, and neither the guerrillas nor the military were able to dominate the area. In both field sites, a few peasants initially supported the insurgents; by the war's end, a great many did so actively but loyalties remained deeply divided.

In Chapter 3, I turn to the question of elite interests and show how they evolved during the course of the civil war, shifting away from coercive agriculture toward commerce, a sector not dependent on labor-repressive institutions. I argue that this shift, along with the change in elite political

---

[29] Elsewhere (Wood 2000), I analyze insurgent mobilization in two areas of El Salvador, drawing in much greater depth on material collected during these years of field research.

representation occasioned by the measures taken to counter the insurgency, was key to bringing the elite to the negotiating table.

In Chapter 4, I analyze the logic of the negotiated end to the Salvadoran civil war, exploring how the changes wrought by the war and the peace agreement together led to an enduring peace and a democratic political regime. I emphasize the main bargains struck, particularly in regard to land redistribution and combatant reintegration, drawing on interviews with key participants representing the government, the FMLN, agricultural business associations, and peasant organizations, as well as working documents from the bargaining process.

Part Two is about the South African transition. The analysis here draws on interviews with political, business, and labor leaders in 1997 and 1998 and on secondary sources, statistical series, and primary documents. In Chapter 5, I describe the foundations of South Africa's oligarchic society in labor-repressive agriculture and mining and the further extension of those institutions throughout the economy under the National Party beginning in 1948. I then analyze the emergence of a broad social movement demanding a range of political and economic rights and the eventual constitution of the leadership of the ANC as its insurgent counter-elite.

I open Chapter 6 with a discussion of the economic logic of apartheid as a set of institutions designed to discipline labor by raising the cost of job loss to shirking or militant workers. I then explain how sustained insurgency undermined this logic, threatening elite economic interests and leading to the suspension of investment and eventually the decision by key business groups to support full political inclusion of blacks and negotiation with the ANC. I also consider alternative explanations for the suspension of investment that emphasize the costs of distortions to markets under apartheid rather than insurgent mobilization and argue that the latter better accounts for the evidence.

In Chapter 7, I argue that an extraordinary series of political initiatives by prominent businessmen was crucial to the decision by the National Party to negotiate with the ANC, as was the erosion of the party's basis of support. I then analyze the political pact that resulted in the 1994 elections.

In the conclusion, I return to the comparative perspective. I first summarize the two transition processes, highlighting differences as well as similarities. I then discuss the characteristics of the civil conflicts in El

Salvador and South Africa that rendered them amenable to negotiated resolution via a democratizing political pact, in contrast to many other civil wars. In the Epilogue, I briefly assess the challenges to consolidation of democracy and economic reform in oligarchic societies after democratic transitions.

PART ONE

El Salvador's Path to Democracy

2

From Conservative Modernization to Civil War

To maintain order on my farm, I built my house on a hill overlooking the fields and congregated the workers in a settlement directly below. It was my observation point, and my private police told me everything. If a stranger arrived, he was delivered back across the river and warned not to return. Before the agrarian reform, there was discipline!

– Former landlord, San Salvador, October 1991

The civil war in El Salvador broke a pattern of development whose origins go back more than a century to the expansion of coffee cultivation in the late 1880s, and indeed farther back to earlier agro-export cultivation. Central to the evolution of the country's political economy was a class structure based on the extra-economic coercion of agrarian labor. State elites enforced repressive labor conditions and highly concentrated property rights on behalf of the small economic elite, the well-defended "bottom line" of state-society relations. Despite a degree of economic diversification and modernization after World War II and despite several attempts at reform by regime moderates, coalitions of economic elites and military hardliners defended labor-repressive institutions and practices until the civil war.

Salvadoran history is thus characterized by elite resistance to change. The fundamental logic of the polity – an economy based on export agriculture, elite reliance on the political control of labor, and the consequent elite opposition to political reform – changed little until the civil war. Nothing about the economy's dependence on coffee made this configuration of classes and labor-repressive institutions inevitable; coffee flourishes under a variety of class structures. Rather, the coalition of the economic and regime elites at the turn of the century forged a pattern of repressive labor relations and concentrated property rights that left a legacy of class relations whose enforcement and reproduction depended on the strong arm of an authoritarian state. In the aftermath of a communist-led uprising in 1932, the fervently anticommunist elites identified any progressive social policy as a threat; as a result, they worked with hardline elements of the military to defeat reformist efforts.

From the 1950s through the 1970s modernizing members of both the regime and economic elite sought greater integration of the Salvadoran economy with its Central American neighbors, a diversification of economic interests via the growth of manufacturing, and a limited liberalization of the political regime. Had these efforts come to fruition, the Salvadoran economy and social structure might have evolved in ways favorable to an eventual elite-guided transition to democratic rule. The essential condition for such an evolution was the displacement of the elite's reliance on labor-repressive export agriculture and the growth of profit-making opportunities in sectors of the economy less dependent on the coercive apparatus of the state, notably manufacturing. International comparative evidence suggests that a sustained increase in per capita income would also have contributed to a democratic transition and consolidation.

But conservative modernization failed. Manufacturing stagnated and the small middle class did not develop as an autonomous political force. The owners of manufacturing and financial concerns were from the traditional coffee elite rather than a new class of employers and professionals with interests distinct from the coffee oligarchy. Indeed, the decade preceding the outbreak of the civil war saw an intensification of collaboration between regime and economic elites, and of the dependence on export agriculture. As a result of ongoing political and economic exclusion, by the end of the 1970s El Salvador was not at the doorstep of democracy but on the brink of civil war.

The origins of labor-repressive export agriculture, the consolidation of a repressive polity, the culmination of this pattern of political and economic exclusion in civil war, and the emergence of the FMLN as an insurgent counter-elite are the themes of this chapter.

Land, Labor, and the State

The war originated in the social injustice of this country, a pattern dating from the colonial period and characterized by a few people controlling great wealth while the great majority remained poor. There were never structural reforms. What aggravated the sit-

uation was the violation of human rights of innocent people. The people cried out ever louder for justice.

– Salvadoran Catholic bishop *whose destiny,* he
said, *was to live through the war in difficult areas,*
June 1993

The control of land and labor are at the heart of El Salvador's historical development from the Spanish conquest in the fifteenth century until the civil war. During the colonial period, securing a cooperative labor force was more difficult than securing access to land, which was both abundant and could be readily obtained by superior force. The control of labor proved a more daunting challenge. First the cacao merchants, then the indigo growers, and later the coffee planters tried to reshape the indigenous communities into a labor force that would produce commodities for exchange, initially with the Guatemalan merchant elite and, after independence, directly with the international market. But the communities had their own forms of cultivation and organization that resisted any easy "solution" to the labor question.

After the mid–nineteenth century, coffee cultivation expanded rapidly. By the 1850s and 1860s, pressure for the sale of national, municipal, and communal lands intensified as all readily available land was planted. Urban professionals and state officials were the usual initial developers as they had the connections to secure the necessary property titles and outlay of credit. To promote the expansion, the state offered a range of incentives, including tax breaks and registration of titles for land planted with coffee.

Labor shortages proved a difficult challenge to this expansion given the high labor requirements of coffee.[1] One strategy used to address this problem was to increase overall control of the population. The police force was centralized in 1848 and a rural force founded in 1855. In addition to protecting the now-private properties, the police had increasing responsibility for the enforcement of vagrancy laws, which helped maintain an adequate supply of labor on estates. But the practices of the indigenous communities in the volcanic highlands and the reluctance of many villagers to labor on coffee estates continued to impede coffee expansion. That reluctance was overridden by force.[2]

Under the justification that "backward" customs posed obstacles to progress, the government abolished communal forms of tenure in 1881

---

[1] Browning 1971: 167.   [2] Lindo-Fuentes 1990: 64–5.

and 1882.[3] Municipal and communal officials, placed in charge of distributing land to private persons, rarely defended community interests in the confusion that followed: most Indians and poor ladinos (people of mixed parentage and Indians who no longer identified as Indian) were without the contacts, the cash, and the knowledge to file claims properly and rapidly.[4] Urban professionals and government officials proved much more adept at the legalization of claims, and the indigenous communities were effectively dispossessed. Military service emerged as a link between politics and the economy: coffee planters became military officers, military officers discovered the possibilities of coffee – and some (Generals Gerardo Barrios, Francisco Menéndez, and Tomás Regalado) became president.[5]

Land was therefore secured and labor mobilized for coffee production – not by the gradual workings of a land market or the lure of wages, but by the sudden redefinition of property rights and direct coercion. That labor might be obtained by increasing wages was never seriously considered.[6] This strategy of accumulation by force paid off for the elite and the state: after these reforms, labor was adequate, real wages declined to levels below those of the 1850s, and coffee exports boomed. Increasing coffee profitability contributed directly to the era of political stability (for the wealthy) as increased tax revenues paid for the expanding police forces.

Both indigenous and ladinized communities bore the costs. Many Indian communities resisted and some revolted: Izalco and Atiquizaya in 1884, and Cojutepeque in 1885 and 1889.[7] As a result, the government founded a new mounted police force for the western highlands in 1889 to evict squatters and enforce vagrancy laws, financed by a tax on coffee estates. Some of the dispossessed went to settlements within the large estates, administratively controlled by the estate owner, not the town government. Forbidden to grow foodstuffs, the dispossessed became the *colonato*, an institution that effectively bound workers and their families to particular estates, thereby ensuring a permanent labor force. Although

---

[3] *Tierras comunales* were abolished on February 26, 1881, and *ejidos* in March of 1882 (Browning 1971: 204–5).
[4] However, more small and medium farms nevertheless emerged than in the Guatemalan case. Williams attributes this difference to the decentralized process and the lesser development of the coercive capacity of the state in El Salvador (1994: 76–7).
[5] Williams 1994: 75.
[6] Bulmer-Thomas 1987: 12.   [7] Lindo-Fuentes 1990: 133; Williams 1994: 75.

only the male officially counted as being employed, the women and children were expected to work during peak periods as well. This "hidden dimension" of family labor was a key feature of labor organization[8] and was still widespread as late as 1961, when *colonos* accounted for 25 percent of the rural labor force.[9]

Other dispossessed community members joined the ranks of migrant labor and still others squatted on smallholdings at the periphery of the coffee zone and in the northern departments. The migrants and squatters were regulated under a number of laws (codified in the Agrarian Code of 1907) designed to curtail their enduring subsistence practices of gleaning, shifting cultivation, and claims to de facto possession.[10] Estate workers were also subject to other legal measures: agricultural judges compiled lists of available workers, visited estates to ascertain labor-supply needs, and "arranged for the capture of those who left estates before fulfilling their obligations."[11] As communities were dispersed, indigenous identification gradually declined.

This pattern of coffee expansion in areas of relatively dense indigenous settlement, resulting in the widespread displacement and expropriation of indigenous property, was unique in Latin America.[12] This reorganization of the political economy led to a particular pattern of state-society relations as the required policing of land and labor fostered close cooperation between local landlords and the military. The National Guard, founded in 1912 as a reorganization of the rural police in the coffee zones, was not only the principal body used to enforce property rights and labor law in the countryside but was also the most powerful agency of the state until 1948. These close landlord-military ties at the local level were to have long-standing consequences: "Local units were called on by local elites to evict squatters or to jail workers who were viewed as troublemakers; this tradition put Salvadoran public institutions at the service of individual economic elites for no other reason than their elite status."[13] National Guardsmen were frequently billeted on large estates, particularly during the coffee harvest. Although the Army displaced the National Guard as the principal national military institution in 1948, this pattern of close local cooperation between elites and representatives of the coercive apparatus of the state (which included the National

---

[8] Stolcke 1995: 76.   [9] Weeks 1986: 39.   [10] Browning 1971: 217–19; Stolcke 1995: 84.
[11] Browning 1971: 271.   [12] Roseberry 1991: 359; Stolcke 1995: 84.
[13] Williams 1994: 245.

Guard as well as large numbers of ex-soldiers organized into reserves under army command) endured until the armed insurrection of the 1980s forced the abandonment of some parts of the countryside by both landlords and the state.[14]

The rapid expansion of coffee cultivation had consequences beyond the concentration of land ownership and the reorganization of labor. Coffee planters and their allies in state office also moved to institutionalize favorable access to credit, an important development given coffee's substantial capital requirements. From 1880 to the end of the century, seven banks were founded by different groups of planters.[15]

In the first quarter of the new century, the ranks of the elite were swelled by European immigrants who contributed significantly to the expansion of coffee and the development of infrastructure. Lured by the growing coffee trade, immigrants with capital typically started an export concern (either with initial capital or through capital acquired after administering some governmental or private concern), gradually acquiring processing facilities and eventually estates as well. Perhaps because they came from various countries, the immigrants did not form ethnic enclaves (as did the Germans in Guatemala) but joined the elite as social equals.[16] The exception was the immigrants from the Middle East (*los arabes* or *los turcos*), who established urban commercial firms based on long family traditions as merchants and who remained a separate group of the upper class.[17]

By 1920, the elite had begun to coalesce into the oligarchy that would direct the country's economy until the reforms of 1980.[18] Of the Central American countries, only Guatemala had a more concentrated coffee sector. This "power pyramid"[19] or "magic square"[20] of coffee production,

---

[14] Walter and Williams 1993: 34.

[15] Bulmer-Thomas 1987: 5; Lindo-Fuentes 1990: 161.

[16] Williams 1994: 155, 182–3. Nor was immigration subsidized by the state, as in Brazil. The labor shortage in El Salvador was met by the coercive creation of a dispossessed labor force, not through the immigration of labor.

[17] Lindo-Fuentes 1990: 184.

[18] Lindo-Fuentes 1990: 184. The founding of the coffee producers' association La Cafetelera in 1929 is a key benchmark. Stanley (1996) argues against characterizing the elite as an oligarchy at this early date, claiming that the elite were as yet too regionalized and unconsolidated. Nonetheless, given their political cohesion and later consolidation as an oligarchy, I refer to the elite as an oligarchy during this period as well as later. See Vilas 1995: 72–4.

[19] Paige 1987: 179.   [20] de Sebastian 1979.

of agricultural workers remained formally illegal until the end of the civil war.

This combination of paternalism and coercion in the discipline of rural labor changed little despite the expansion of cotton and sugar production after World War II. To police the labor forces, the military expanded paramilitary networks in the countryside to some 40,000 members by 1960.[29] Elites continued to rely on close mercenary ties to local officials, particularly the National Guard, and to billet National Guardsmen on their estates. Together, these measures were quite successful in maintaining favorable conditions for coffee production. At the beginning of the 1950s, Salvadoran coffee yields per hectare were the highest in the world, and from 1950 to 1961 they *increased* 57 percent.[30]

A fourth legacy of the *matanza* was a fifty-year political arrangement in which the military ruled directly, while economic elites directed economic policy from various cabinet posts.[31] The arrangement evolved from the personalistic rule of the Hernandez Martinez government (1931–44) to more institutional forms of rule after 1950 and came to include contested municipal and legislative elections in the 1960s, but the principal features of the regime exhibited more continuity than change. Although presidential elections were held, the Army invariably ruled at the national level, through *oficialista* parties after 1950 (the Partido Revolucionario de Unificación Democrática, PRUD, from 1950 to 1961 and the Partido de Conciliación Nacional, PCN, from 1961 to 1979) and by fraud if necessary (as in 1972). According to William Stanley (1996), this enduring relationship was a "protection racket" in which the military exaggerated the extent of "communist" threats to elite interests in order to maintain military prerogatives and to justify the expansion of the coercive apparatus of the state.[32] One such prerogative was the regularized practice of graft by the most senior officers, which gave them an incentive to retain power and encouraged junior officers to assert their own.

This form of rule precluded the development of an adequate justice system; instead, it spawned a tradition of impunity for violence committed by the elite and state forces against opposition activists. According to the Commission on the Truth, a body empowered by the peace agreement

---

[29] Walter and Williams 1993: 42–8.   [30] Bulmer-Thomas 1987: 154.
[31] Johnson 1993; Walters and Williams 1993; Stanley 1996.
[32] On protection rackets generally, see Tilly 1985.

and appointed by the United Nations secretary general to investigate acts of violence that occurred during the civil war,

A kind of complicity developed between businessmen and landowners, who entered into a close relationship with the army and intelligence and security forces. The aim was to ferret out alleged subversives among the civilian population in order to defend the country against the threat of an alleged foreign conspiracy.[33]

As a result, violence was "a part of everyday life."[34]

Conservative Modernization and the Failure of Reform from Above

Economic modernization in El Salvador in the years after World War II took the form of an authoritarian capitalist model of development, which Barrington Moore called conservative modernization. The vulnerability of a mono-export economy had been demonstrated during the Great Depression as international demand for coffee fell, causing domestic revenues and income to deteriorate. Coffee earnings recovered during World War II, but the fragility of the country's dependence on coffee was clear and opportunities for diversification were readily available as the war had disrupted world trade in textiles, displacing suppliers and creating new opportunities, which deepened as reconstruction and the Korean War spurred renewed growth.

With an existing artisanal base and an abundance of investment resources from the ongoing coffee boom, El Salvador was well placed to respond: cotton production began to expand from the early 1940s, repeating the highly concentrated pattern of coffee. But the subsequent diversification of agricultural production did little to expand the membership of the economic elite: of the 26 largest family groups producing coffee, 23 were also among the top 24 coffee processors, 12 were among the 14 largest cotton producers, and 9 were among the 10 largest sugar producers.[35] Of the 16 family groups producing more than 1,000 bales of cotton in 1972–3, 14 were also among the top 50 coffee families; at least half held diverse cotton investments, including insecticide and textile firms; most had other industrial and commercial investments; all but 1 were principal stockholders in the commercial banks; and 3 individual members of these families held half of the private sector directorships of the Central Reserve Bank.[36]

[33] Commission on the Truth for El Salvador 1993: 358.
[34] Commission on the Truth for El Salvador 1993: 357.
[35] Baloyra-Herp 1982: 25f. [36] Williams 1986: 47.

Peasant smallholders and laborers were once again displaced by the expansion of export agriculture. Before the expansion of cotton, the coastal plain was cultivated only sporadically by large haciendas that combined extensive cattle grazing with smallholder tenancy. The expansion of cotton led to the expulsion of tenants from smallholdings to squatter settlements along right-of-ways, or out of the zone altogether to search for work elsewhere.[37] Credit policies favored mechanization, and there was little need for permanent labor aside from mechanics and drivers. On a typical large farm, only 35 semiskilled workers might be employed year-round, supplemented by 800 cotton pickers at harvest.[38] The development of sugar production followed a pattern similar to that of coffee and cotton, including state promotion, the displacement of peasant tenancy on estates, and increasing concentration of land ownership. Sugar also spurred the development of food processing, the largest sector of Salvadoran industry.

As a result, landlessness increased among the rural population. Population growth also contributed, but William Durham concluded from census data that the principal factor was the concentration of land ownership after World War II.[39] Because of this extremely rapid "competitive exclusion," the excluded population (the landless and the land-poor with less than a hectare) increased dramatically in the two decades following midcentury. Ironically, the abolishing of the *colonato* and the establishment of a rural minimum wage in 1965 may have contributed to the diaspora, as some landlords responded by evicting tenants.[40] Another contributing factor was the return of hundreds of thousands of Salvadorans from Honduras after the brief "Soccer War" between the two countries in 1969.

In the 1960s, these factors quickened the evolution of the class composition of the countryside (Figure 2.1). Most strikingly, the percentage of economic active rural residents who were temporary day laborers grew from 28 to 38 percent between 1961 and 1971. The fraction of the total with access to more than 1 hectare of land declined in relative terms from 28.5 to 14.4 percent. When the temporary wage workers and the land-poor are combined to estimate the workers that relied on seasonal employment, the seasonal workers increased from 51 to 60 percent as a fraction of the total. The high degree of landlessness in 1971 reflected the increased concentration of property holdings: the smallest 49 percent of farms accounted for only 4 percent of the farmland, while the 0.5 percent of

[37] Browning 1971: 236; Bulmer-Thomas 1987: 161.
[38] Browning 1971: 236.   [39] Durham 1979: 47–8.   [40] Browning 1971: 261.

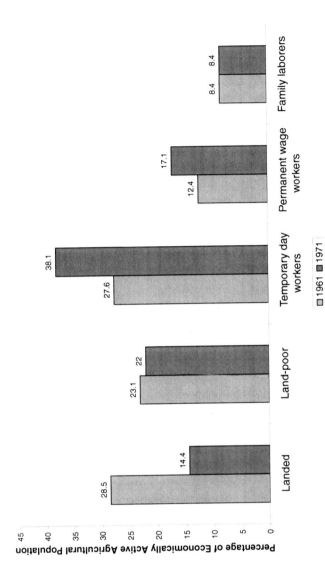

Figure 2.1 Agrarian structure in El Salvador, 1961–1971. In 1961 the economically active agricultural population was 416,728 people; in 1971, it was 581,661 people. *Source:* Data from Mitchell A. Seligson, 1995, "Thirty Years of Transformation in the Agrarian Structure of El Salvador, 1961–1991," *Latin American Research Review*, Volume 30, Number 3, pp. 43–74, Table 5: 62, based on data from the 1961 and 1971 agricultural censuses.

36

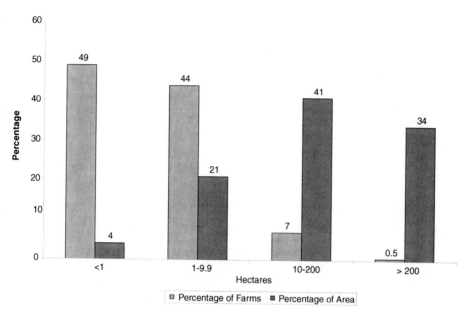

Figure 2.2 Size distribution of farms in El Salvador, 1971. *Source*: Dirección General de Estadística y Censos 1974, vol. 2, p. 1.

farms over 200 hectares accounted for 34 percent (Figure 2.2). In 1960, only Guatemala, Ecuador, Brazil, Peru, Venezuela, and Iraq had higher levels of inequality in the distribution of land ownership.[41] As landlessness increased, real wages stagnated.[42]

The logic of the export agriculture sector posed formidable obstacles to industrialization. As price takers in the world coffee market, Salvadoran coffee growers depended on containing labor costs for their profitability, with the result that the internal market for mass consumption goods was small, and it was therefore difficult to exploit economies of scale in industrial production. Although a substantial demand for luxuries existed, these took the form of imports and personal services (e.g., ser-

---

[41] The area in farms did not expand between 1961 and 1971: with the development of the coastal plain, the agricultural frontier had closed. The Gini coefficients for the distribution of land in approximately 1960 were the following: for El Salvador 82.7, for Guatemala 86.0, for Ecuador 86.4, for Brazil 84.5, for Peru 93.3, for Venezuela 90.0, and for Iraq 88.2. Data compiled in Taylor and Hudson 1972 and Taylor and Jodice 1983, summarized by Persson and Tabellini 1992.

[42] Bulmer-Thomas 1987: 162.

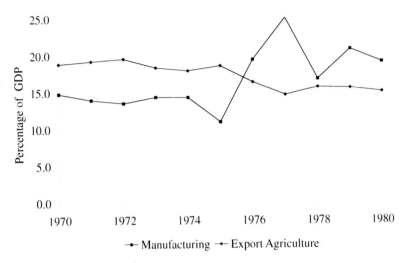

Figure 2.3 Manufacturing and export agriculture in El Salvador, 1970–1980

vants) for the most part. In line with the development model prevalent in Latin America at the time, government advisers argued that a Central American Common Market would attenuate this problem, as the market for Salvadoran industrial products could expand without compromising the low rural wages on which coffee profits relied.

The Salvadoran economy continued to grow steadily from 1970 until 1978, thanks to a boom in the agro-export sector. Real gross domestic product (GDP) grew at an annual average rate of 5.5 percent, and real GDP per capita also increased. As world commodity prices steadily increased in the mid-1970s, the agro-export sector was the principal source of growth (see Figure 2.3, but note that the figure understates the sector's importance as its contribution to value added in food processing and other nonagricultural sectors is not included). The purchasing power of Salvadoran exports grew through the 1970s, owing to the steep increase in world coffee prices: the purchasing power of exports in 1979 was almost double that of 1970.[43]

Although manufacturing continued to expand slightly in real terms, its share in current-price GDP fell from 19.0 percent in 1970 to 15.8 percent in 1978. Whereas manufacturing exports to other Central American coun-

[43] Bulmer-Thomas 1987: Table A.15.

38

tries grew throughout the 1970s, the sector's share of total exports stagnated, as did the much smaller volume of manufacturing exports outside the region.

Not only did the halting rise of manufacturing fail to dislodge agro-exports from their premier position in the Salvadoran economy, the sector was controlled by the usual economic elites: in 1971, the largest 36 landlords controlled 66 percent of the capital of the 1,429 largest firms.[44] Of the twenty family groups who in 1979 controlled the largest quantity of nonagricultural investments, only four were *not* rooted in the agro-export sector.[45] The manufacturing sector that emerged mirrored the agro-export sector in its highly concentrated distribution, with 1 percent of the businesses controlling 69 percent of production.[46] Indeed, during the 1970s, concentration of manufacturing increased as smaller firms proved unable to compete in a context of rising prices for imported inputs: the number of industrial establishments with five or more employees decreased from 2,670 in 1961 to 1,128 in 1978.[47]

By the 1970s, three groups constituted economic elites. Two of them, although distinct, were tightly linked: the agrarian-financial group and the agrarian-financial-industrial group, to use the terms coined by Salvadoran scholar Italo López Vallecillos.[48] The first group originated in coffee growing (and in some cases large-scale cattle ranching) in the late 1890s, moving into finance and controlling the four oldest banks.[49] In general, this group was more conservative and opposed to all changes in land tenure or wages, with its interests closely tied to the plantation economy.[50] The second group – largely immigrants in the first half of the century that had expanded export concerns into processing (and some into coffee cultivation as well) – had more diversified interests and were more open to political modernization.[51] The first group tended to dominate the second, particularly during economic downturns through their greater control of foreign exchange and credit. Though distinct, both groups remained firmly rooted in the agro-export economy through the 1970s.

---

[44] Dunkerley 1988: 344.   [45] Montgomery 1995: 71.   [46] Sevilla 1985: 17.
[47] Bulmer-Thomas 1987: 210.
[48] López Vallecillos 1979: 558. Three classic studies are the principal sources for nearly all analyses of the Salvadoran oligarchy before the civil war. Eduardo Colindres contributed two studies of the structure of the political economy as a whole (Colindres 1976 and 1977); Manuel Sevilla (1985) analyzed the concentration of income in the hands of 116 families. Robert Aubey identified thirty families as the Salvadoran oligarchy in the late 1960s; the fortunes of two-thirds were based on coffee production and export (Aubey 1969; see also Paige 1987: 184).
[49] Colindres 1977; Paige 1997.   [50] López Vallecillos 1979.   [51] López Vallecillos 1979.

The third group, descendants of the Middle Eastern immigrants, was also a major actor in urban economic activity, by the 1970s owning approximately a quarter of the assets of the commerce sector, a third of the service and construction sectors, and less than a fifth of manufacturing.[52] The group's distinguishing feature was the absence of significant holdings in agro-export production or processing.

Thus despite the diversification of agricultural production and the emergence of some manufacturing, the families of the traditional agro-export elite continued to control an extraordinary fraction of the nation's economic activity.[53] Of the 34,000 people declaring capital holdings in 1979, a mere 1,753 persons held 56.4 percent of the 10 billion colones declared. The *declared* income at the top of this grouping was extremely high: the wealthiest 116 had an average reported income of US$9 million in 1979. The wealthiest comprised a closely knit class: the 1,309 people declaring capital holdings over 1 million colones can be grouped into 114 family groups that owned 84.5 percent of the capital held by corporations in 1979.

The limited "modernization" of the economic interests of elites and of the policy rhetoric of the state was not matched by political modernization: economic diversification was not accompanied by political tolerance, and the same exclusionary political model prevailed.[54] Modernization of agriculture due to the expansion of cotton and sugar cultivation was not accompanied by liberalization of labor policy: though wage labor became more common, the political control of labor through local collaboration of state agents and landlords continued, and the fruits were no more widely shared than those of coffee production had been. The security forces responded to the challenge of increased landlessness by intensifying their paramilitary networks. Under the Alliance for Progress rubric and with U.S. assistance, the military further extended the paramilitary networks with the founding of the National Democratic Republican Order (ORDEN), whose peasant members, many of them clients of powerful patrons, supplied intelligence on rural troublemakers in exchange for loans, access to health services, immunity from any consequences of their paramilitary activities, and agricultural inputs such as land and fertilizer.[55] The military also expanded its rural reserves and village patrols.[56]

Thus although the military had embraced a rhetoric of developmental-

---

[52] Dunkerley 1988: 345.   [53] Sevilla 1985: 24–6.
[54] Bulmer-Thomas 1983.   [55] Stanley 1996.   [56] Walter and Williams 1993: 51.

ism and modernization beginning in the 1940s, political change was to be strictly controlled. Relations between the military and economic elites were at times uneasy: the military had its own interests to pursue, which often led them to support reformist measures not in the apparent interest of elites, such as increased regulation of *colonato* relationships in 1942 and literacy drives after the reformist coup of 1948. But reformist as well as hardline elements in the military protected the traditional bottom line, control of the countryside through paramilitary networks and no change in the structure of the rural labor force.[57] Thus the core interests of economic elites – control of land and labor, particularly agrarian labor – were never compromised.

Although military leaders preferred "electoralism over dictatorship," it was an electoral procedure strictly controlled from above: no members of parties unallied with the military held congressional seats until the 1960s.[58] Only after the introduction of proportional representation for the 1964 election were opposition parties allowed to occupy seats in the national legislature and some mayoral offices, including that in San Salvador. A few minor parties with little organization or appeal had been tolerated since the 1940s, but the first serious electoral competition at the municipal and legislative levels was provided by the Christian Democratic Party (PDC) in 1964.[59] The PDC built up a significant party apparatus through Napoleon Duarte's three terms as mayor of San Salvador. The party's philosophy drew on Catholic social thought and even appealed to some military officers. However, when press reports indicated that Duarte, the presidential candidate for a coalition of parties including the PDC, was developing a lead in the 1972 presidential elections, the military suspended press coverage and in short order proclaimed the candidate of the ruling PCN the victor.

Thus the five decades following the 1932 *matanza* saw a process of slowly increasing (but fundamentally circumscribed) political liberalization. However, this process was interrupted by a series of coups by reformist officers, followed by countercoups led by conservative groups. The military faced a dilemma of increasing magnitude: on the one hand, given the de facto restrictions on political participation, the regime's legit-

---

[57] Johnson 1993: 97; Walter and Williams 1993: 41.
[58] Dunkerley 1988: 356; Walter and Williams 1993: 47.
[59] For analysis of the history and ideology of the PDC, see Karl 1985 and Eguizábal 1992.

imacy was limited, which led to a periodic impulse to broaden its political base.[60] On the other hand, reforms that went too far in the eyes of the elite prompted its hardliners to collaborate with regime hardliners. Three distinct currents within the military – hardliners willing to crack down on even moderate opposition, based principally in the security forces and rural army bases; reformists who nonetheless sought continued military rule, principally junior army officers from lower-middle- and middle-class backgrounds based in urban bases; and democratic reformists willing to cede rule to civilians (of which there appear to have been very few) – both reflected and reinforced this dilemma.

In response, agrarian elites fomented divisions within the military and the security forces and cultivated close ties to the security forces at the national level as well as locally, "knocking at the doors of the barracks" to undermine reformist initiatives.[61] As a result of this coalition between hardline regime and economic elites, as well as the unity of agrarian elites, countercoups followed close on the heels of reformist coups in 1944, 1960, 1972 (when the reformist effort was defeated early and never proclaimed a government), and 1979. In 1944, for example, a coup deposed General Andrés Menéndez when his announcement of free elections led to the articulation of ambitious reforms by new opposition figures. In 1948, a more institutionalized form of military rule began but failed to challenge the agrarian elite. In 1960, reformist officers staged a coup and accepted the demands of civilian members of the subsequent junta to hold free elections; but a countercoup led by Colonel Julio Rivera displaced the reformists three months after the initial coup.[62]

Most dramatic of the many instances of hardline coalitions defeating reformist efforts was the national mobilization by economic elites to defeat the military regime's effort at limited agrarian reform in 1976. In response to the announcement of the initiative, business organizations led a campaign that mixed vitriol in speeches and in advertisements with lethal intimidation in the countryside. Pressure for land reform had been growing steadily in the 1970s after the broad First Congress of Agrarian Reform was held in 1970; even the army held seminars in 1973 on the topic.[63] In 1975, the Salvadoran Institute of Agrarian Transformation

---

[60] William Stanley provides the best analysis of the military regime; my analysis is heavily indebted to his work (Stanley 1996, especially 75ff.).
[61] Walter and Williams 1993; Stanley 1996.   [62] Dunkerley 1988: 354.
[63] Browning 1983.

(ISTA) was founded, and enabling legislation passed the following year. The reform specifically targeted large estates in Usulután and San Miguel, particularly the large farms planted in cotton along the coast. Despite assurances of compensation from the U.S. Agency for International Development (USAID), landlords throughout the targeted area together with the national business organizations defeated the initiative.[64] President Arturo Armando Molina had sworn that the government would not allow even a single backward step away from the reform measure, but – according to a deputy leader of ISTA – the government took "*fourteen steps to the right*," a reference to the mythical fourteen families of the oligarchy.[65]

Thus conservative modernization did not lead to the gradual emergence of democracy but merely diversified the sources of income of the traditional economic elite.

From Political Mobilization to Civil War

Although the renewal of the alliance between hardline elements of the regime and economic elite defeated reformist efforts when necessary, repression and intimidation failed to quell unrest in the 1970s. The quiescence of the economically and politically excluded gave way to protest as urban youth found little opportunity for upward mobility and as new social actors began to contest economic and political exclusion in the countryside. Some elements of the Catholic Church began developing new pastoral practices, particularly in rural areas such as Aguilares, north of the capital, where Father Rutilio Grande led a team of Jesuits that encouraged *campesinos* to reflect on the implications of the Bible for contemporary issues of social justice.[66] There, and elsewhere, many *campesinos* participated in Bible study groups, then in overtly political organizations such as the Christian Federation of Salvadoran Peasants (FECCAS), demanding land and better working conditions. In addition, the Christian Democrats extended their party organization to the countryside from its origins among urban professionals, a few progressive business elements, and urban residents. PDC leadership and USAID funding contributed to the organizing of *campesinos* in associations such as the Salvadoran Communal Union (UCS), founded in 1968 after several years of USAID training and funding through the American Institute for Free Labor Development (AIFLD).[67] After splits within

---

[64] Brockett 1988: 147–8.   [65] Interview with ISTA official, 1991.
[66] Cabarrus 1983; Cardenal 1985.
[67] See Bollinger n.d. for a detailed history of the labor movement.

the electoralist Communist Party, armed revolutionary organizations such as the Popular Liberation Forces (FPL) and the Popular Revolutionary Army (ERP) began clandestine organizing and military training in the early 1970s. Although their numbers remained quite small throughout the 1970s, they maintained close ties to some popular organizations. According to a wealthy landlord, "It was like a plague that kept advancing because they obtained the support of the parish priest then in Tenancingo, and that's where was born the god of the poor and the god of the rich."[68]

As networks of activists developed and coordination between various groups improved, mobilization became national once peasant activists joined student and union groups in protests sponsored by organizations such as the Popular Revolutionary Block (BPR) and the United Popular Action Front (FAPU).[69] Coordination between organizations by members of guerrilla groups contributed to mobilization at the national level.[70]

As already mentioned, however, the dominant response of the state was not to compromise but to exercise its coercive power. The military, particularly the security forces, poured increasing resources into various coercive agencies, including the presidential security agency (ANSESAL), which coordinated the gathering of intelligence. Landlords and local military commanders further built up already extensive political and intelligence networks in the countryside, particularly ORDEN.

As political mobilization continued, repression escalated from intimidation to the arbitrary detention and torture of those thought to be militants, then to assassination. In November 1974, six peasants were killed and thirteen disappeared in La Cayetana after a land invasion there. Some three dozen students were killed when security forces fired on a march protesting the Miss Universe pageant in July 1975. In a few months in 1977, two priests were killed, ten exiled, eight expelled, and several tortured.[71] On February 28, 1977, security forces opened fire on a midnight vigil following a political rally, leaving dozens dead.[72] Later in the year, repression deepened after constitutional protections were suspended. Violence against progressive Catholics escalated as well: between 1977 and 1979, six priests were killed.[73]

---

[68] From "Datos Sobre la Destruccion of Tenancingo," a typewritten statement given to me by a family that left Tenancingo for San Salvador during the civil war.
[69] For a discussion and analysis of the mobilization of the 1970s, see Lernoux 1980; Cabarrus 1983; Cardenal 1985; Pearce 1986; Brockett 1988; and Montgomery 1995.
[70] Gordon 1983; Byrne 1994; Montgomery 1995.
[71] Brockett 1988: 152.   [72] Stanley 1996: 109–10.   [73] Peterson 1997: 63–5.

Demonstration calling for release of political prisoners, San Salvador, 1980. Photograph by Tommie Sue Montgomery.

Intensifying repression led to the founding of an organization of junior officers, the Juventud Militar (Military Youth). Opposed to the increasing brutality of the military regime, the group carried out a coup in October 1979. Although senior officers soon displaced the reformist junior officers, the escalating mobilization made significant change necessary for the first time since the 1940s: opposition politicians were brought into the government, and agrarian reform was carried out.

After the civilian members of the first junta resigned to protest the ongoing violence, a new governing alliance was constituted, which for the first time included a non-*oficialista* political party. The Christian Democratic Party entered the government under an explicit agreement with the Armed Forces that the socioeconomic reforms announced by the young officers would be carried out.[74] The high command, faced with the threat of renewed rebellion by the junior officers, needed some legitimizing partner in the government. The PDC provided a substantial set of resources for that role: a party organization, international ties, and the active support of

[74] Stanley 1996: 183–4.

45

the United States. The PDC agreed to join the junta in exchange for a public commitment that the reforms announced by the junior officers would be carried out and human rights practices would improve. The United States, whose assistance was increasingly important after 1983 and nominally conditioned on support for agrarian reform and restraint of human rights violations, attempted to reinforce this commitment.

However, regime elites did not compromise their core interests: although ORDEN was formally abolished, its networks and militants remained in place, the legal "cover" for repression was steadily expanded throughout 1980, and the military continued to control key state institutions.[75] Indeed, in some respects the autonomy of the military *increased* during the PDC years in power, as the military consolidated its presence in various state agencies, developed a degree of independence from economic elites, and institutionalized its autonomy in the 1983 Constitution.[76]

The new governing alliance moved quickly to implement the reforms. In March 1980, in an unprecedented move against economic elites, the Armed Forces expropriated hundreds of properties, including many of the largest estates, as the first measure of what was to be an extensive agrarian reform.

The right reacted to the pact with ferocity and a clear strategy: block the agrarian reform by attacking the PDC's constituency.[77] Military forces carried out the first phase of the land reform but left a trail of dead and disappeared in their wake as they moved against both activists and the estates. Despite the military's formal alliance with the PDC, the extreme right under the leadership of Roberto d'Aubuisson rapidly built up a network of death squads within the hardline security forces and the intelligence divisions of the army to carry out a deadly mixture of targeted assassinations, interrogations, and generalized violence.[78]

Thus the pact between the PDC and the military did not displace a more fundamental and long-standing dynamic *within* the military: the high command would protect those responsible for human rights violations in return for their support against reformist junior officers.[79] The involvement of the security forces in profound human rights violations was so

---

[75] Acevedo 1991: 23; Walter and Williams 1993: 54.   [76] Walter and Williams 1993: 57.
[77] Stanley 1996.
[78] There is abundant documentation of human rights abuses by death squads and their ties to government forces. See particularly Joint Group 1994 and the annual reports on El Salvador issued by Americas Watch in the 1980s.
[79] Stanley 1996: 136–7.

pervasive that in an April 11, 1981, cable, the State Department declared the Treasury Police "beyond all possibility of recuperation."[80]

The Emergence of the FMLN as an Insurgent Counter-Elite

The brutal response by regime elites to increasing political mobilization by peasants, workers, and students in the 1970s had various consequences, some unintended. First, despite enduring differences in ideology and strategy, the armed revolutionary groups unified their political representation in 1980 to form the FMLN. After the failure of the 1981 offensive, the FMLN turned to a longer-run strategy of building a guerrilla army in the countryside.[81]

Second, repression led many people active in peasant or student organizations to support the previously inconsequential Salvadoran guerrilla forces. In interviews, several FMLN members stated that they joined the guerrillas out of outrage at the actions of the security forces against family members or neighbors. Many former student activists and urban professionals joined the guerrilla forces in response to the killing of priests, particularly the assassination of Archbishop Oscar Romero in 1980 (on the orders of Roberto D'Aubuisson).[82] As the violence deepened, some participants in Christian base communities reinterpreted traditional teachings and refashioned sacramental rituals, finding meaning in the accumulating deaths (particularly that of Archbishop Romero) as those of martyrs whose exemplary dedication renewed their own commitment to activism.[83]

Others joined because they felt they had no choice, some because they had been identified as activists in opposition organizations and were therefore likely targets of the government forces, and others because they were reputed to be such activists even if they were not. According to one resident of Usulután,

Some armed themselves, others fled. We were all seen as guerrillas. Every time we went to the coast, we were searched at the intersection with the coastal highway; 1982 was a year of desperation, almost everyone left. My brother disappeared in 1982, one of hundreds who disappeared in 1982-3. Every day there were two or three bodies at the intersection. After all these years of war, the dead weigh heavily. (Resident, Comunidad La Peña, April 1992)

[80] Cited by the Joint Group 1994: 18.
[81] See Byrne 1996 for a comprehensive analysis of the evolution of FMLN strategy.
[82] Vilas 1995: 33, 175; McClintock 1998: 267-9. The authoritative account of Romero's assassination is that of the Commission on the Truth for El Salvador 1993: 142.
[83] Peterson 1997.

Others saw the emerging guerrilla organization as an opportunity to act on long-held resentments against local landlords or ORDEN members:

Before the war, we were despised by the rich. We were seen as animals, working from 7:00 to 4:00 and without even enough to put the kids in school. This is the origin of the war: there was no alternative. The only alternative was the madness of desperation. (Member of the Cooperativa Los Ensayos, March 1992)

Third, because repression affected other organizations more than it did the armed FMLN, it had the unintended consequence of unifying opposition under the umbrella of the FMLN. According to one lay catechist,

Thanks to persecution, the campesinos had to be quiet. It was necessary to always coordinate with the armed [guerrilla] forces, as a guarantee. The foundational work of liberation could not be expressed. (Member of the Land Defense Committee, Las Marías, May 1992)

While coercion by the guerrillas also contributed to the growing support for the FMLN, extensive interviews in areas of FMLN strength suggest it played a distinctly minor role compared with repression by the state. With the exception of the assassination of some rural mayors by one faction (the ERP) between 1985 and 1989, it was generally limited to the expulsion of suspected informants from guerrilla-held areas, short detentions of potential recruits, and the extortion of supplies. According to interviews in the province of Usulután, residents could remain in the area as long as they did not collaborate with government forces and provided a biweekly quota of supplies. Indeed, residents felt they had to contribute to both armed groups:

In order to survive, you had to give to both sides, even though you belong more to the revolution, you had to give to both. They asked for beans, water, tortillas; sometimes they would pay you. (Leader of Cooperative Los Tres Postes, 1992)

The most immediate effect of the emergence of the FMLN was the ever-deepening involvement of the United States in the conflict. In the reluctant view of the military, the ongoing insurgency made U.S. assistance necessary, and as a result, political liberalization as well. The United States developed programs ranging from support for centrist labor organizations allied to the PDC, financial contributions to the PDC's electoral campaigns, military training, and economic assistance to underwrite the country's faltering economy, to the gathering of intelligence that was then passed on to the military.

After its initial strategy proved militarily unsustainable, the FMLN decided to emphasize the building of political as well as military capacity.[84] In Usulután, the ERP promoted the founding of peasant cooperatives and other organizations. ERP commanders reported in interviews that areas where the Catholic Church had been active were particularly propitious areas for recruiting members for these organizations, because organizers could draw on networks of activists in the previous mobilization. In the mid-1980s, when government forces emphasized winning the hearts and minds of rural residents more than direct repression, these organizations began to operate more publicly, some even applying for formal legal status. Although some leaders were detained and a few killed, many such organizations functioned partly aboveground while continuing clandestine activities in support of the FMLN. By this period the FMLN was able to coordinate actions across a broad range of organizations, much beyond the more limited coordination it contributed to the mobilization of the late 1970s, which depended on more autonomous networks of activists.

Key to this capacity was the diversity of relations between the FMLN and various organizations – more precisely, between each of the five guerrilla organizations making up the FMLN and their particular affiliated organizations. Examples from Usulután illustrate this range.[85] The leadership of some organizations was directly integrated into the hierarchy of the ERP (the most active group in the area), as in the case of the National Federation of Agrarian Cooperatives (FENACOA), whose key leaders were political officers of the ERP. While this relationship was covert, many militant activists were well aware that their organization, while nominally autonomous, in fact responded to strategy and tactics decided by the ERP (usually but not always coordinated with other guerrilla organizations). And they knew which of the leadership were political cadre. The leadership of other organizations was not directly integrated into the ERP's hierarchy but consulted extensively and routinely with its local commanders, as in the case of the United Municipalities and Communities of Usulután (COMUS) and Coordinator for the Development of Cooperatives (CODECOSTA), two regional organizations in southwestern Usulután. Leaders (and some members) of the cooperatives in both organizations were generally aware of and supported this relationship. Other organizations, such as the National Confederation of Agrarian Reform

---

[84] Byrne 1996: 132–6.   [85] This and the following paragraph draw on Wood 2000.

Cooperatives (CONFRAS), were vaguely allied with, but much more autonomous from, the ERP: though individual leaders might consult with the ERP, they did so covertly and only on issues of overall strategy and analysis.

These relationships imposed both opportunities and costs on the organizations. On the one hand, coordination and affiliation contributed to their very existence. Domestic and international networks supporting the FMLN raised the cost to the state of repressive action as moves against affiliated organizations were denounced in San Salvador, Washington, and various European capitals. Moreover, because participating in the organizations also meant participating in a greater movement, the experience of effective agency against the landlords and the state appealed to many activists: it undermined any self-perception that the disdain of the landlords had a basis in fact. On the other hand, the organizations sacrificed their autonomy to the party (in varying degrees), which undermined their appeal to potential members not willing to take on wider affiliation with the FMLN. Moreover, a large fraction of funds donated by European and American solidarity groups to opposition organizations went to the FMLN whatever their intended destination.

Partly as a result of this network of organizations, as well as widespread individual collaboration in the countryside, the FMLN developed a significant military capacity, one sufficient to support a military stalemate by the mid-1980s, despite more than $5 billion of U.S. assistance to the government. Also contributing to this military capacity was the training of some guerrilla commanders in Cuba and Eastern Europe and the FMLN's ability to operate with few constraints in Sandinista Nicaragua. According to a 1988 analysis by four U.S. Army colonels, the central element of that capacity was the extent and accuracy of their domestic intelligence networks, which were much better than those of the Salvadoran regime.[86] Any illusion that changes in the Soviet Union would erode that capacity were quickly belied by the FMLN's dramatic 1989 offensive, during which the guerrillas attacked San Salvador and occupied a number of wealthy neighborhoods for a few days.[87]

---

[86] On the inability of the government forces to defeat the FMLN, see the analyses by four U.S. military officers (Bacevich, Hallums, White, and Young 1988), by RAND's National Defense Research Institute (Schwarz 1991), and by three congressmen (Hatfield, Leach, and Miller 1990).

[87] Gibb and Smythe 1990.

Conclusion

The strong opposition of economic elites and dominant factions of the military to economic and political reform, the enduring dependence of economic elites on export agriculture, the regular recourse to repression rather than compromise, and the declining access to land by poor farmers pushed El Salvador toward civil war in the late 1970s. As repression closed the political space for nonviolent political mobilization, the FMLN emerged to challenge the oligarchic alliance of economic and regime elites on the only remaining terrain, that of military conflict. Extensive peasant support and the resulting military capacity, together with repression of other opposition groups, eventually turned the FMLN into an insurgent counter-elite, whose participation in negotiations would be required for a durable end to the war. Thus the failure of reform from above set the stage for rebellion from below.

The ongoing mobilization and the emergence of the guerrilla organizations that would make up the FMLN meant that many of the reforms initiated by the leaders of the 1979 coup were carried out, in contrast to previous efforts by reformist officers. In response to this unprecedented attack on economic elite interests, some economic elites, with the help of some military officers, formed a political party to contest elections. This was the first time economic elites had founded a political party to represent their interests directly, a theme to which I return in Chapter 3. While the counterinsurgency measures were thus to have far-reaching effects, their origins lay in the need to contain the wave of popular mobilization that preceded the war.

Given the long-standing record of collaboration between regime and economic elites against threats from below – of countercoups following reformist coups, of collaboration between hardline elements of the economic elite and the military to defeat reformist policies, of the ready deployment of state violence in defense of elite economic interests – it is extremely doubtful that the counterinsurgency measures would have been carried out and sustained without the threat posed by the ongoing insurgency. The insurgent threat prevented the usual countercoup, making possible reforms that hitherto had been quickly annulled. The civil war was thus the product of varying processes of insurgency and counterinsurgency, processes whose unintended as well as intended consequences eventually laid the foundations for political compromise.

3

The Structural Foundation of a Pact

THE TRANSFORMATION OF ELITE INTERESTS

What if the landowners had formed a united front [to resist the provisions of the peace agreement]? No one has organized to promote it, no one is willing to, no one is even attempting it. On our side, there's nothing. People are discouraged, disillusioned, and disappointed.

– Prominent Usulután landlord, December 1992

What then accounts for the acquiescence of Salvadoran elites? I show that the civil war forged a structural transformation of the country's political economy, reshaping core elite economic interests and consolidating a new form of elite political representation. Elites acquiesced in a democratic transition for two reasons. First, elites no longer depended on a highly repressive state because the economy had been transformed from one in which workers are "disciplined" by extra-economic coercion to accept low wages to one in which market forces, particularly urban unemployment, disciplined labor. Second, the war-induced transformation of the economy shifted the balance of power within economic elites toward those who came to favor compromise over recalcitrance, a shift reinforced by the initial electoral and other successes of their new form of representation. The argument thus traces the changing economic conditions, which after a decade of war provided the structural underpinnings for the pact that led to the first inclusive elections.

The civil war transformed elite interests in three ways. First, those interests were threatened by the new governing alliance between the Armed Forces, the Christian Democrats, and the United States in 1980, formed in response to the escalating social mobilization and armed conflict described in Chapter 2. Under that alliance, a series of reforms were

52

carried out to undermine the social bases of the insurgency and to undercut the economic and political power of the country's agrarian elites. Second, the initial degree of unrest, the ability of the FMLN to continue to mobilize substantial military capability despite ongoing repression, and the reforms themselves together created extreme uncertainty for economic elites. In response, elites exported capital, deferred investment in coffee plantations, and developed new enterprises less vulnerable to the vagaries of the war. Third, extraordinary inflows of foreign exchange from the United States – remittances from the hundreds of thousands of Salvadorans who had fled El Salvador along with the official transfer of billions of dollars in economic and military aid – presented new opportunities for gain not tied to coffee.[1]

Together, these forces reshaped the interests, identity, and political representation of the economic elites of El Salvador. Many families abandoned (often literally) their traditional agrarian interests as a result of the conflict, the loss of their properties under the agrarian reform, or the general uncertainty in the country. For those families who had diversified interests before the war, the war altered the balance between agricultural and other holdings. Even landlords of properties in areas not directly affected by the conflict (for example, the coffee-rich lands in the west) shifted their investments away from agriculture. Output and yields per hectare declined as investment was curtailed, marketing became uncertain, and fiscal policies grew less favorable. The civil war would not have transformed the political economy to such an extent had these three forces not been sustained for more than a decade.

The civil war also transformed the political representation of the elite in El Salvador. In response to the alliance between the centrist Christian Democrats, the military and the United States, rightist hardliners founded death squads to deter widening political participation and the National Republican Alliance Party (ARENA) to represent directly elite interests in elections, breaking the historical pattern of delegating governance to the military. By 1987, more moderate elements representing diversified

---

[1] See Johnson 1993; Paige 1993 and 1997; and Stanley 1996. They note similarly that elite economic interests had significantly changed during the civil war. However, neither Johnson, Paige, nor Stanley present more than minimal economic evidence to support this claim, subsidiary to their respective emphases on the changing composition of business organizations, the ideologies of the coffee elite, and the internal dynamics of the military and their evolving relation to the elite. Lungo Uclés's analysis of the economic transformation does not include data for the late 1980s.

economic interests controlled the party. The party's appeal to a wide range of voters culminated in the victory of ARENA candidate Alfredo Cristiani in the 1989 presidential election. The chapter thus documents the macroeconomic underpinnings for the emergence of ARENA, thereby extending the analysis of elite ideological evolution by Jeffrey Paige in his *Coffee and Power: Revolution and the Rise of Democracy in Central America* (1997).

I first document the shift in economic structure through the years of the civil war. I then analyze the transformation of elite interests. Interviews with (erstwhile) landlords of large properties and leaders of agrarian business associations confirm that this structural transformation was accompanied by a shift in the perceived interests of individual elites. I then discuss the evolution of elite political representation during the war and the ARENA party's rise to power.

Civil War and Economic Transformation

The structure of capital has changed. The big capitalists have left agriculture, they've left the countryside – broken up by the agrarian reform. There are still some in agro-industry and exporting, in coffee mills and cotton gins. Medium capitalists have also changed their way of thinking and of investing quite a bit; they're diversifying as they recapitalize the country.

– Member of the Executive Council of the
Coffee Growers Association, December 1992

As the nation slid into open civil war, economic production rapidly declined from its 1978 peak: between 1978 and 1982 GDP per capita fell almost 28 percent in real terms (Figure 3.1). One reason was capital flight, as elites sent increasing amounts of capital abroad in response to the reformist rhetoric of the junior officers who led the 1979 coup, the expropriation of more than three hundred of the largest estates, and the nationalization of agricultural-export marketing and the financial sector. Analysts concur that the flight was considerable. Funkhauser (1992: 136) estimates that capital equivalent to 6.3 percent of GDP in 1979 and 11.4 percent of GDP in 1980 was sent out of the country. Although a further decline was arrested (in part by international assistance), per capita domestic production stagnated between 1982 and 1989.[2]

---

[2] I rely principally on the national accounts data published by the Central Reserve Bank in the quarterly *Revista Trimestral*, compiled in the Statistical Appendix of Wood 1995. The

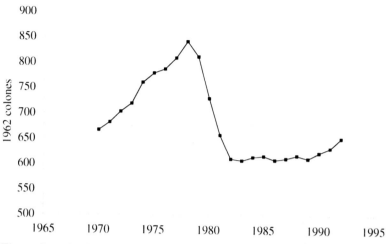

Figure 3.1 Real GDP per capita in El Salvador, 1970–1992

A significant shift in the relative contributions of various sectors to GDP underlay the economic crisis. The contribution of export agriculture to domestic production fell sharply: in the early 1970s, export agriculture accounted for 13 or 14 percent of GDP, increased to almost 25 percent in 1977, and declined to well below 5 percent by the end of the war (Figure 3.2).[3] The commercial sector, not manufacturing, surged as agriculture declined, increasing from prewar levels of 20 to 25 percent of GDP to more than 36 percent. This sectoral reshaping was in part due to movements in relative prices: although the agricultural price index increased by a factor of 6 from the early 1970s to the end of the war, that of commerce increased by a factor of 34 and that of manufacturing by 15.[4]

Export agriculture declined dramatically during the 1980s for four

figures draw on this data, as well as on additional data calculated from it, except where noted. However, analysis is severely constrained by the absence of census data: the last agricultural census was conducted in 1971. To keep in mind the prewar patterns, most figures in this chapter begin in 1970. Data to trace evolving elite investments by family do not exist; such information is extremely closely guarded, even within families.

[3] Export agriculture is defined here as the sum of the value added contributed to GDP by the production of coffee, cotton, and sugar, including initial processing of coffee and sugar, but not coffee roasting, beverage production, or other food processing.

[4] Wood 1995: Table 8.3.

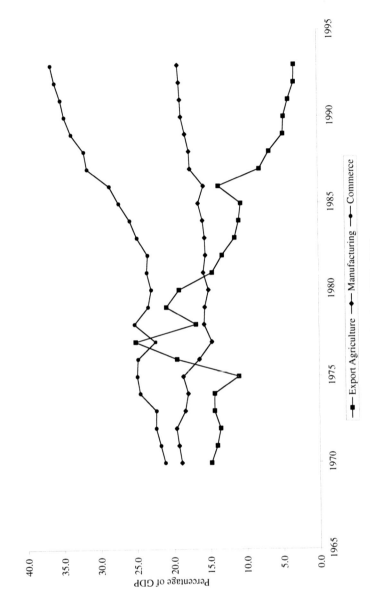

Figure 3.2 Sectoral composition of GDP in El Salvador, 1970–1993

56

principal reasons. First, elites became increasingly uncertain about the security of their property and investments in the wake of the various economic reform measures, notably, the expropriation in March 1980 of more than three hundred properties under phase 1 of the agrarian reform by the Armed Forces that included a number of large estates and coffee mills owned by elite families. In response, investment dropped precipitously and capital flight increased. To add to elite insecurity, the extent of the expropriations under way was not entirely clear: not all phase 1 expropriations conformed to the letter of the law (not all exceeded 500 hectares), and phase 2 (the expropriation of farms between 100 and 500 hectares) was promulgated at the same time. Phase 2 was not implemented, but landlords remained uncertain of their tenure until the ceiling of landholding was raised to 245 hectares in the 1983 Constitution. Guerrilla sabotage of infrastructure also undermined the confidence of the coffee sector.[5]

Second, the expropriations included properties with significant export production: 12 percent of land planted in coffee, 28 percent of land planted in cotton, and 11 percent of that in sugar were nationalized under phase 1.[6] More consequentially for elites, the expropriated coffee area was roughly 38 percent of the land planted in coffee on farms of 100 hectares or more.[7] However, the elite continued to dominate processing. Some sixty coffee mills with 83 percent of the country's installed capacity remained in the hands of forty-eight private holders.[8]

Third, to further undermine economic elites' dominance of the economy, the junta nationalized the financial and export-marketing sectors. The commercial banks were nationalized and the owners compensated, more generously and expeditiously than the owners of expropriated lands. The new National Coffee Institute (INCAFE) controlled all

---

[5] Pelupessey 1991: 147–52.

[6] Calculated from Wise 1986: Tables V and VI.

[7] Calculated from Wise 1986: Table VI and the 1971 agricultural census. This is only a rough approximation, as the census is based on a survey of farms, not landlords, who often owned several small to medium coffee estates.

[8] Only a handful of coffee mills were nationalized: agrarian reform cooperatives controlled four mills (less than 5 percent of installed processing capacity) and INCAFE four more (approximately 12 percent). Cotton processing remained entirely in private hands (through the cooperative of private growers, COPAL, dominated by large farmers). But cotton production collapsed in El Salvador when world prices declined, the costs of importing pesticides increased, and the guerrillas found the low-flying crop dusters and piles of harvested cotton easy targets. See Pelupessey 1991: 154–7.

coffee marketing, set processing rates, and directly controlled the foreign exchange earned.

Fourth, from 1980 to 1989 the counterinsurgency alliance of Christian Democrats, the military, and the United States maintained foreign exchange and tariff policies that transferred resources from agro-exports to other sectors of the economy. For example, the dual exchange rate penalized the export sector directly, and the duties on imported inputs for agriculture kept production costs high.

All these factors worked to make the agro-export sector much less profitable for elites during the war. In the late 1980s revenues exceeded costs on only the most productive coffee estates. As a result, investment in coffee plunged, with many planters saving on labor costs by ordering only minimal care of the coffee groves. The quality of the coffee – once a source of great pride among Salvadoran producers – declined as well.

Agro-export production would have declined even more had it not been for the labor policies maintained throughout the war: between 1980 and 1991 real wages for agricultural workers declined by 63 percent (Figure 3.3).[9] The decline was particularly important in coffee, where labor costs make up more than 70 percent of the annual production costs.

Compounding these factors was a sharp decline in world commodity prices (coffee prices, for example, were 73 percent higher in 1980 than in 1990). However, that decline does not explain the decline in the Salvadoran coffee sector, as is clear from a comparison with neighboring countries: the world market share of all four of the other Meso-American countries increased whereas El Salvador's fell, even though all faced the same decline in world prices and experienced similar climates and transportation conditions. Before the war, El Salvador ranked fifth among developing countries in the share of coffee exports: with 4.5 percent in 1967, it was of course far behind the giant producers Brazil and Colombia (with 33.2 and 14.6 percent, respectively) and close behind two African producers, Côte d'Ivoire and Angola (with 4.8 and 5.6 percent, respectively).[10] By 1992, El Salvador had fallen to the eighth position with 3.3 percent of the share: Costa Rica, Guatemala, and Mexico had outstripped

---

[9] Average wage data are not generally available: with one exception, the wage series underlying the graph is the minimum, not average, real wage. However, wages above minimum are rarely paid in agriculture. Wage data are from Paus 1996: Table 12.4.
[10] Talbot 1995: 157.

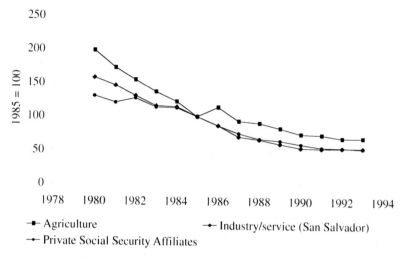

Figure 3.3 Real wages in El Salvador, 1980–1993

El Salvador, and Honduras was rapidly catching up as well.[11] Whereas the area planted in coffee expanded by 31 percent in Costa Rica and 24 percent in Honduras, in El Salvador it posted a 3 percent decline (Table 3.1). Moreover, yields in El Salvador fell by 13 percent, even as they increased significantly in all of the other countries, particularly in Honduras. World prices, although a contributing factor, do not therefore account for the decline in coffee production and exports in El Salvador: the civil war and the related social and political processes prevented the kind of adjustment to the changing external environment that took place in neighboring countries.[12]

Investment in other sectors also fell during the war. During the 1970s, total investment (private plus public) averaged 19.1 percent of GDP and was financed largely out of national domestic savings. In the 1980s, the average fell to only 12.9 percent (further decline was prevented by the increase in foreign transfers).[13] In particular, private investment fell sharply

---

[11] Calculated from UNCTAD 1992: 293, as a percentage of developing world exports.

[12] According to one study of the coffee sector, real prices to producers *increased* by 69 percent in Honduras and by 60 percent in Guatemala between the 1980/1 season and the 1986/7 season whereas they decreased in El Salvador by 24 percent over the same period (FUSADES 1989).

[13] Calculated from Boyce 1996: Table 6.1.

Table 3.1. *Coffee production in Central America, 1979–1992 (percent change, average 1979–81 to average 1990–92)*

Country	Yield	Area	Production
El Salvador	−12.9	−3.1	−15.8
Guatemala	19.4	−3.9	14.3
Costa Rica	14.4	31.3	50.0
Honduras	27.6	24.2	57.7

Source: Calculated from FAO 1992: Table 78 (1990 figures) and FAO 1995: Table 78 (all other data).

between 1978 and 1980, and despite some increases it remained low until 1990, when it began to rise, presumably because of Cristiani's election and the prospects of peace. Moreover, the composition of private investment shifted between sectors. Real private investment in agriculture was quite low in the 1980s compared with the 1970s. During the war, real private investment in industry fell precipitously and then remained low until 1990, with only a gradual increase. After 1990, industrial investment rose fairly steeply (particularly in the *maquila* sector, which registered increases from $10.0 million in 1990 to $25.6 million in 1993). In real terms, however, industrial investment in 1992 was only about three-quarters of its real value before the war.[14] Nor had private investment in agriculture recovered: in 1992, it was less than half of its real value before the war.[15]

Yet it is surprising that the decline of the agro-export sector did not occasion a more continuous slide in real GDP, which leveled off in 1982 and began to grow again in the late 1980s. As export earnings declined, the impact was mitigated by increasing flows of foreign exchange from two principal sources: by 1991, foreign aid from the United States and remittances sent home by Salvadorans together exceeded export earnings.[16] A conservative estimate of these inflows is presented in Figure 3.4.[17]

---

[14] Boyce 1996: Tables 12.2 and A.2b.
[15] Calculated from Central Bank figures compiled in Wood 1995: Table 8.8.
[16] Wood 1995: Table 8.4.
[17] The figures for U.S. aid are from the *Statistical Abstract of Latin America*, vol. 30, Table A2, except for 1991–3, which is from Overseas Development Council 1994: 77. A third new source of foreign exchange has been the rapidly expanding *maquila* sector, largely clothing exports to the United States. However, the net foreign exchange earnings in 1993

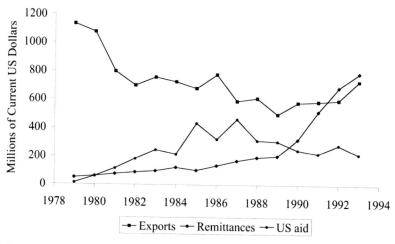

Figure 3.4 Inflows of foreign exchange to El Salvador, 1979–1993

These inflows contributed to a negative trade balance (more than 16 percent of GDP in 1992), ongoing and deepening deficits in the current account.[18]

This extraordinary inflow of remittances and international aid exerted strong pressure on the value of the colon.[19] Despite the devaluation of the official rate to the parallel rate in 1986, the liberalization of the foreign exchange market under Cristiani, and attempts to "sterilize" the inflow by expanding the Central Bank's holdings of international reserves, the colon was consistently overvalued throughout the war. As in the case of other types of "Dutch disease" in countries undergoing foreign exchange booms, the relative prices of goods in the service and commerce sectors increased over the price of tradables. As a result, the competitiveness of Salvadoran exports declined, further impelling elites out of agriculture toward more profitable sectors.

were only 8.6 percent of the value of merchandise exports (PRIDEX, cited in Boyce 1996: Table 12.1), so *maquila* earnings are not shown here.

[18] The decline in export earnings would have been still steeper were it not for the recovery of exports to the Central American Common Market after 1990, which by 1993 made up 42.4 percent of merchandise exports (Boyce 1996: Table A.9).

[19] This unprecedented flow of remittances is on a scale similar to that to southern Europe from the EEC in the 1960s and 1970s and to the Philippines, Sri Lanka, and Egypt from the Gulf Oil states before the Persian Gulf conflict. For additional discussion of the impact of aid and remittances, see Wood and Segovia 1995 and Kaimowitz 1990.

By the end of the 1980s, Salvadoran economic elites were doing remarkably well in the nonagricultural sectors. According to Arnold Harberger (1993), by 1990 the rate of return to capital (excluding agriculture and real estate) was more than 50 percent *greater* than the highest returns in the 1970s. One reason was the decline in wages, across all sectors.[20] Seasonal agricultural laborers were hardest hit of all, with coffee harvest wages declining by 84 percent, those in sugar by 80 percent, and in cotton by 80 percent. For workers in industry, service, and commerce, the minimum wage fell by 66 percent. Nor were the workers of sectors affiliated with the Salvadoran Institute for Social Security (roughly, the formal labor market) spared: their average monthly wage fell 60 percent. As a result of these wage declines as well as rising unemployment, poverty increased from 68 to 74 percent between 1980 and 1990, and extreme poverty increased from 51 to 56 percent.[21] Such a dramatic decline in wages means that not ending the war carried great opportunity costs for the elite: given the profits possible at such low wage rates, it made less sense to forgo investment because of the war.

Civil War and the Evolution of Elite Interests

Now it's the Arabs who are the strong capitalists. They've little in land, but they have the assets in the biggest textile factories and in fast food – in MacDonald's, Biggest, Mr. Donut, and Wendy's.

– Member of the Executive Council of the
Coffee Growers Association, December 1992,
referring to businessmen of
Middle Eastern origins

By the late 1980s the political economy was driven not by export agriculture and its processing but by international assistance and remittances from Salvadoran workers in Los Angeles, New York, and Chicago. This structural transformation of the economy reforged the interests of the economic elites as the balance in their portfolio shifted sharply to the booming sectors more dependent on consumer demand than on coercive labor relations. By the end of the 1980s, economic elites were well aware of these new interests.

[20] Paus 1996: Table 12.4.
[21] ECLAC 1993: 6; see also the analysis by the World Bank (1994a: 9–13).

Ideally, one would advance this claim on the basis of the sectoral composition of the wealth-holding of elites; however, no data concerning individual portfolios during the war (or in its immediate aftermath) are available. Nonetheless, the evidence for this shift in elite interests is compelling. First, a significant fraction of elite landholdings had been seized during the land reform or abandoned during the course of the war. Second, the value of the remaining holdings in the agro-export sector – that is, the present value of their future streams of profits – had fallen as a result of the control of agro-export marketing by the government, sabotage by guerrilla forces, and anticipation of further possible reverses. As a result of both, the restructuring of elite interests is almost surely understated by the sectoral shift in the composition of GDP.[22]

The obvious "winners" were those who controlled significant shares in the booming sectors: the courier companies that transferred remittances, the financial intermediaries that exchanged colones for dollars, the retail sector where they were spent, the import houses that provided the goods, and the real estate and construction companies. The commercial interests of many economic elites rapidly expanded, as the proliferation in the late 1980s of fast-food restaurants, gas stations, and shopping malls attests. For most elite families, these interests – whether already established (as in the case of the agrarian-financial-industrial group) or just developing – perpetuated their command of significant economic resources.[23]

Thus, hardest hit was the agrarian-financial group; with few commercial interests, many left the country entirely (a few, however, funded death squads from Miami in the early 1980s, as explained later in the chapter). Less hard hit was the agrarian-financial-industrial group, with its relatively diverse interests. The commercial group was least affected as its interests were not tied directly to the agro-export sector; indeed,

---

[22] The precise degree of remaining elite control over the agro-export sector (at least 30 percent of coffee production, probably 90 percent of coffee processing, but a significantly lesser fraction of cotton or sugar) has been a subject of some debate (see Baloyra 1982; Bulmer-Thomas 1987; Dunkerley 1988; and Pelupessy 1991). In any case, it is a declining share of a shrinking pie; the continued influence of large producers, whatever the degree, is not evidence for unchanging elite interests.

[23] There are ongoing reports, difficult to confirm, that a "golden ring" made up of a handful of capitalists now controls the reprivatized banks (Salazar Candell 1993: 259; Murray, Coletti, and Spence 1994; Spence, Vickers, and Dye 1995: 29).

this group was best situated to benefit from the boom in commerce and services.

The prospect of hemispheric free trade agreements also contributed to the shift in elite interests. Free trade was a central part of U.S. policy toward Latin America at the turn of the decade, and the idea gathered momentum after concrete negotiations over the terms of NAFTA began. However, El Salvador and other Central American countries feared that such agreements world divert trade and investment to Mexico.[24] Fourteen of the nineteen export-zone assembly plants in El Salvador were owned by foreign investors (eight by U.S. interests and six by Korean and Taiwanese interests)[25]; the possibility of such diversion was a principal worry for the Salvadorans. Faced with these changing terms of competition, El Salvador and the other Central American countries signed an agreement with Mexico to create a free trade zone by 1996. The gathering urgency to participate in regional integration was probably an important factor motivating business interests to support the peace negotiations.

Interviews with economic elites confirm this restructuring of their interests. Attitudes toward the war and the changes it brought varied significantly, as indicated in interviews with (erstwhile) landlords of the contested department of Usulután and the municipality of Tenancingo and with leaders of business organizations. Landlords who tried to maintain some cultivation on their properties during the war reported having to contend with the frequent presence of the FMLN, ongoing violence, and the hostility of some *campesinos*. Harvests were destroyed by sabotage, profits extorted in the form of "war taxes," and occasional direct redistribution to local workers and peasants by the FMLN. As a result, most landlords were heavily burdened by debt. In some areas, landlords tried to rent their properties commercially, but tenants leasing the farms also found the conditions too difficult. A number of landlords reported both veiled and explicit threats against their life when they tried to visit their property, some even after the signing of the peace agreement. At the war's end, landlords were well aware that if they decided to return to their properties, they would face a labor force distinctly different from that of the prewar era.

The stories of three landlords illustrate the varying accommodations made to these changing social and economic conditions. The first is that of an oligarchic family with widely diverse interests that decided to

[24] Paus 1996: 270.   [25] U.S. GAO 1993: 44.

abandon export agriculture after the war. Before the war, the family owned one of the largest cotton and cattle haciendas in the province of Usulután. In the interview quoted at the opening of this chapter, a leading family member reflected that if elites of the area had been less recalcitrant in the 1970s the war could have been avoided. He expressed his willingness to collaborate in the peace process:

We have to be positive, not a single shot has been fired [during the cease-fire] and every-body has to pay a quota of sacrifice. Let me not sound as though I favor either the FMLN or the army. (Usulután landlord, December 1992)

After a long struggle with the difficult wartime conditions, he had decided to sell the property:

I am absolutely willing to sell. It's been a nightmare, trying to work it individually, collectively, or to rent it. We are convinced we have to sell, at market prices or not. It's going to kill us. Why must we sell? First, if we want to work the property, they [the FMLN-allied campesinos occupying the property] are not going to let us. Second, we do want to cooperate with the peace process; we're conscious of that. Third, we need to pay the bank. With the losses and the strikes, we lost the working capital. So it's a distress sale.

This man, despite his family's traditional influence in the area, found it difficult to visit the property and reported that

I felt they were so closed – I haven't visited for months, nobody talks to me when I go.

A similar process of political learning – about the desirability of a bargained instead of a coerced resolution to conflict, and of the dangers to elites of predatory state institutions – was evident in a number of other interviews as well.[26]

Another landlord described a difficult struggle to survive economically after being forced to leave a group of properties in the coffee area of Usulután. Before the war, he had owned more than 350 hectares of coffee and a small mill. At first, he failed to understand why the FMLN had forced him to leave:

They didn't explain it to me. I was one of the smallest enterprises of the zone. We're middle class, we work ourselves, not like the oligarchy. We did good works, we constructed schools, clinics, a church, a well; we would take people to the doctor. I never paid less than the minimum wage, I paid at least that. I was a medium producer and a small processor. I know everyone not by number but by name. If they had so much hatred, why didn't they

[26] See also Johnson 1993 and Paige 1997.

pick on the great ones? Afterwards, I understood: it was a strategic area for them.
(Usulután landlord, December 1992)

With more than 350 hectares of coffee and their own mill, this family held significant wealth, although not by oligarchic standards, as he pointed out. After being forced out of the area, the couple constructed a small house on a piece of land belonging to the wife's family and lived from the profits of a gasoline station. He later became an executive in an electronics company in San Salvador. As his children had little interest in agriculture after spending their teen years exclusively in the city, he decided to sell the now-occupied properties, asking,

How could I work it again, with ex-combatants at my shoulder?

With great nostalgia, he described how his grandfather and father built the enterprise:

I was born on the property; now it's a museum of weapons for the FMLN. And upstairs in the coffee-drying patios is the United Nations.

However, not all the landlords blended nostalgia for the past with an acceptance of the changes brought by the war. One woman recalled her good works of the bygone days with great emotion:

We lived on the property, unlike so many others. The social relations were intimate, we were appreciated. I helped with birth control projects, through the Demographic Association. The Cotton Producers Association lent us two cars to travel around to give talks. Children were dying from pure ignorance, women were dying in labor. It was hard work. I brought some women here for the operation – sterilization. There are other methods but the truth is that they were so ignorant that you had to sterilize them. It was a nice project. With my friends from the other haciendas, I traveled around. We had equipment, nurses, we took down names, physical data. (Wife of Usulután landlord, November 1992)

For this woman and her husband, a lingering bitterness seemed to preclude a reflective assessment of the past decade as they recounted wild rumors whose constant theme was the role of the United States in losing the conflict. They argued bitterly that the United States had imposed too many restraints on the military:

The war here, it was an arranged thing, all sides avoiding contact. It wasn't like World War II, so much disorder and noise. It was a "low-intensity conflict," an invention – you're either at war or not.

66

They attributed the successful conclusion of the negotiation process to external pressure on President Cristiani. For them, the accords were "no more than a gift to the guerrillas."

As a result of the organized occupation of properties, the prospect of difficult labor relations, and the general decline of the sector, many landlords sought to sell their properties. Some benefited by selling their land through the land-transfer program under the peace agreement, as described in Chapter 4. Many of those lucky enough to have properties near urban areas subdivided their holdings and sold them through companies operating in Los Angeles and other U.S. cities with large concentrations of Salvadoran migrants. While those economic elites whose property was concentrated in western El Salvador were less affected by the conflict itself, the various counterinsurgency measures of the new governing alliance lessened the value of their agricultural holdings even as the dollar-driven boom in commerce and services increased other parts of their portfolio. While reshuffling their portfolios to protect their economic interests in a new economic environment, many economic elites came to recognize the need for more effective aggregation, articulation, and pursuit of these interests in the new political environment.

The Evolution of Elite Political Representation

The evolution of the political representation of economic elites during the years of the civil war was no less dramatic. As a powerful vehicle capable of articulating the interests of economic elites and of winning elections, ARENA would prove essential to the eventual willingness of the economic elite to compromise with the FMLN.

In the early 1980s, the extreme right responded to the escalating political mobilization and the counterinsurgency reforms with a "two-pronged" strategy (*doble vertiente*) that combined the terrorizing of activists with the founding of a political party to contest elections.[27] But in the aftermath of the reformist coup of October 1979, hardliners – both civilian and military – faced an organization problem. Before the coup, violence against activists, unionists, and demonstrators had been carried out largely by the security forces, drawing on intelligence from ANSESAL and ORDEN. In the aftermath of the coup, some hardline officers were dismissed, and both organizations disbanded. While decentralized violence by security forces

---

[27] FLACSO 1995: 61.

continued, particularly in rural areas, some new coordination was necessary if the right was to continue repressive violence against the popular movement. The "new" organizations (some were the same security units active in repressing opposition groups before the coup) were "death squads," which integrated military intelligence, civilian funding, and state security personnel for ongoing violence. Some of the key founders of ARENA helped direct, coordinate, and fund these coordinated agencies of coercion.[28]

According to the Commission on the Truth, the death squads represented the collaboration of three groups: former military officers led by Roberto D'Aubuisson, a number of elites who provided funding and logistical support, and the intelligence units of the military and the security forces. Former Major D'Aubuisson provided the leadership, organization, and intelligence files garnered from his years in ANSESAL. For example, D'Aubuisson's Frente Anti-comunista Nacional (FAN), a semi-clandestine group, sponsored the "Secret Anti-Communist Army," a death squad responsible for a wide range of violations during the 1980s. State forces killed more than one thousand civilians each month from September through December of 1980.[29] The death squads relied on the formally outlawed ORDEN as well as the intelligence units of the military for intelligence, accusations, and labor. Not all death squads were composed exclusively of members of the military, but the civilian groups were supported by state security forces with intelligence. As seen in Chapter 2, advocates of participants in the argrarian reform were particularly targeted. Nor was the church spared: a group of conspirators headed by D'Aubuisson assassinated Archbishop Oscar Romero on March 24, 1980.[30]

D'Aubuisson helped coordinate the civilians and the military, setting up meetings and transferring funds from the civilians to the death squads:

The Commission on the Truth obtained testimony from many sources that some of the richest landowners and businessmen inside and outside the country offered their estates, homes, vehicles and bodyguards to help the death squads. They also provided the funds used to organize and maintain the squads, especially those directed by former Major D'Aubuisson.[31]

---

[28] There is abundant documentation of human rights abuses by death squads and their ties to government forces. See Commission on the Truth for El Salvador 1993; Joint Group 1994; Stanley 1996; and the annual reports on El Salvador issued by Americas Watch in the 1980s.

[29] Stanley 1996: 206.   [30] Commission on the Truth for El Salvador 1993: 354.

[31] Commission on the Truth for El Salvador 1993: 358.

68

Much of the funding came from wealthy Salvadorans in Miami and Guatemala. According to a recently declassified U.S. Embassy cable, massive funding for the death squads came from "six enormously wealthy former landowners" living in Miami who had lost farms to phase 1 of the agrarian reform and who faced further loss of property held by family members should phase 2 be implemented.[32] Ironically, as William Stanley notes, "It took D'Aubuisson, a man who had been deep inside the military's national security state, to form a party for the private sector elite."[33]

By 1983, the FMLN had become a viable military threat to the Armed Forces, and the government depended increasingly on U.S. aid. The conditions set on that aid became more effective restraints on the violence. Carrying a list of implicated officers, Vice-President George Bush visited El Salvador in December 1983 to deliver a blunt message: if the death squads were not reined in, no more aid.[34] Human rights violations decreased substantially after his visit.

The second "front" in the right's two-pronged strategy in the aftermath of the 1979 coup was to develop a new vehicle to represent elite interests after the military proved no longer reliable in protecting their core interests. After his arrest for plotting a coup, D'Aubuisson managed FAN and death squad operations from Guatemala. Counseled by Guatemalan rightist Mario Sandoval Alarcón on the utility of political parties, D'Aubuisson and his group in September 1981 announced the founding of the ARENA Party to compete in the upcoming elections for delegates to the Constitutional Assembly.[35]

Electoral competition has its own rhythms, and the U.S.-PDC promotion of political liberalization had an unintended effect: the formation and strong showing of the rightist party that represented precisely those elements that the counterinsurgency package was supposed to undermine.[36] When the PDC won only a plurality, ARENA, together with its ally the PCN, had a majority and the power to name D'Aubuisson interim president. The Reagan administration intervened through the military to

---

[32] The origins and current operations of the deaths squads were investigated by the Joint Group for the Investigation of Illegal Armed Groups with Political Motivation in El Salvador, a group of Salvadorans mandated by the Commission on the Truth to investigate the death squads, as well as the Commission on the Truth itself. The quotation is from U.S. Embassy cable, January 6, 1981; see also CIA, March 4, 1981, as summarized in Joint Group 1994: 12, 65.

[33] Stanley 1996: 232. [34] State Department cable, December 14, 1983.

[35] Norton 1991. [36] Karl 1986a.

prevent disastrous consequences for congressional approval of further aid. On a visit to El Salvador, General Vernon Walters made clear to the High Command that the United States was opposed to D'Aubuisson's nomination. As a result, a set of compromises was reached that effectively ended implementation of agrarian reform. Moderate Arturo Magaña was named president and ARENA took control of the Ministry of Agriculture and the agrarian reform institutions. Moreover, the new constitution that emerged from the bargaining protected elite coffee interests by introducing a higher ceiling for landholding (245 hectares) than that allowed under the agrarian reform legislation (100 hectares), reducing the potential distribution of land under phase 2 from 343,000 hectares (less the retention of "reserve-right" land to expropriated owners) to 17,000 hectares.[37]

Despite the rollback in reform that these measures represented, the constitution institutionalized a new party system, reflecting some commitment of the right to electoral competition. New features of the electoral laws included multiparty competition and participation in the electoral commission, secret and voluntary voting, a new electoral register, and an institutionalized balance of power.[38] But after ARENA candidate D'Aubuisson lost the 1984 presidential election to Christian Democrat José Napoleón Duarte and the Christian Democrats won a clear majority in the 1985 legislature elections, disappointed party members and financiers began to consider alternatives.

The Consolidation of ARENA as the Dominant Political Party

> Let it be very clear to all ARENA members that as a party we will follow and we are going to support without question the policy that our President Cristiani is pursuing.
>
> – Roberto D'Aubuisson on the Tenth Anniversary of the founding of ARENA, September 28, 1991

In little more than a decade, ARENA evolved from an extreme right-wing party without a broad political base to become the dominant political party in the country, sweeping the 1994 "elections of the century." Of the right's two responses to the crisis of the early 1980s – it financed and organized the violent repression of activists and founded a political party to represent its interests directly – by the end of the decade the latter strategy was

---

[37] Diskin 1989: 444; Pelupessey 1991.   [38] Acevedo 1991.

dominant as its success became increasingly evident. In the 1982 Constituent Assembly election and the 1984 presidential election, the party won less than 30 percent of valid votes cast. In every election from 1988 through 1994, the party won more than 40 percent of the votes. The party almost won a majority of votes cast in the 1994 presidential race, and won the second round handily. In the course of those few years, the party consolidated a range of support much broader than its founding group and projected a new ideology.

ARENA's candidate, D'Aubuisson, lost the 1984 presidential election in a second round of voting to the PDC's Duarte, who enjoyed considerable U.S. financing for his electoral campaign. In the 1985 legislative election, the military backed the PDC in its broad victory, despite ARENA's accusation of electoral fraud. These defeats despite influxes of campaign money from Miami sparked a major debate within ARENA concerning the party's choice of D'Aubuisson as its presidential candidate.[39] D'Aubuisson began to court wider circles of business interests, building support around their opposition to the PDC's interventionist economic policies and, later after the October 1986 earthquake, around allegations of governmental corruption in the handling of international aid. An additional reason for the attempt to broaden the party's base was the revelation that a ring of kidnappers preying on the elite included military officers associated with D'Aubuisson.[40] In September 1985, Alfredo Cristiani replaced D'Aubuisson as party president, and party rhetoric began to shift from opposition to "the communists" to "a change for the better."[41] Cristiani was a wealthy coffee grower and processor with a wide range of economic interests; an exemplar of the agrarian-financial-industrial group, he commuted by helicopter from his pharmaceutical company in San Salvador to his San Vicente coffee estate.[42]

With the nomination of Cristiani, the internal dynamics of the party began to shift away from the recalcitrant right of the Miami group to those business circles still in the country that were weathering the reforms and

---

[39] Acevedo 1991: 30; Miles and Ostertag 1989: 16.
[40] On the kidnapping ring and its consequences for elite-military relations, see Stanley 1996: 238–40.
[41] Norton 1991: 201.
[42] Miles and Ostertag 1989: 37; Paige 1997: 321. Cristiani's ascension was a source of considerable confusion at the time: some analysts considered Cristiani just a front for D'Aubuisson until Cristiani appointed many FUSADES technocrats to head key ministries (interview with UN official, September 1995).

the war in one fashion or another.[43] In part the shift represented a broadening of the party's constituency as elites with diverse interests took over business organizations and the party now appealed to the urban middle class, particularly the owners of small and medium businesses in the service sector. D'Aubuisson himself pushed forward the transition, backing Cristiani repeatedly in the following years, as indicated by the quotation at the beginning of this section. The political potential of this wider spectrum of interests was demonstrated in January 1987 by a successful business strike against an economic austerity policy proposed by the Duarte government. As a result of accusations of corruption and ongoing factional infighting during Duarte's administration, middle-class and small business support for the PDC eroded steadily during the late 1980s and helped ARENA gradually consolidate those sectors.

Party tactics also shifted, from the confrontational stance of those with only assets to lose to the bargaining strategies of those with fluid interests (including, for some, holdings in other Central American countries, Mexico, and the United States).[44] Generational changes contributed too, as did the waning of the influence of those who had left the country. According to one report, the reconstruction of the party saw a shift in ARENA's financing: some 80–90 percent of campaign financing for the 1989 presidential election was from domestic sources (and not from Miami or Guatemala).[45]

ARENA's ideology also shifted. The party's founding ideology combined strident anticommunism with an exclusivist vision of *la nación*. In contrast, after Cristiani became president, party leaders and documents increasingly focused on neoliberal philosophies and policies. Two factors may explain the party's embrace of neoliberalism.

First, the private sector think tank Fundación Salvadoreña para el Desarrollo Económico y Social (FUSADES) was instrumental in this transformation. With generous support from the United States – almost $25 million over eight years – FUSADES came to be the institutional basis for the emerging leaders of the business organizations, performing the essential service of articulating the neoliberal program as an agenda around which a broad spectrum of elite and middle-class business interests could

---

[43] For a discussion of the evolution of ARENA's core constituency in the 1980s, see Miles and Ostertag 1989, Johnson 1993, and Paige 1997.

[44] See Wolf 1992; Johnson 1993; Overseas Development Council 1994: 70; and Stanley 1996: 234.

[45] Miles and Ostertag 1989: 20.

unite.[46] Only 11 of the 248 founding members of the foundation had export agriculture as their principal economic interest, one indication of the shifting political economy.[47] The technical skills of the staff also assured the business sector of a policy voice whether or not the right won elections. Indeed, after ARENA won the 1989 presidential elections, a large number of FUSADES technocrats became ministers and other high-level government officials. FUSADES developed a set of policies based on the "Chilean model," which focused on export promotion, trade liberalization, exchange rate liberalization, and privatization of state institutions.

Second, neoliberal philosophy and policy promised to circumscribe future economic policy in such a way that key elite interests would be protected. On the one hand, neoliberalism was clearly acceptable to the United States, given that USAID had promoted neoliberalist development policies since the mid-1980s. More important, the elite would benefit from neoliberalism's minimal state. Even if another party won elections in the future, a minimal state would not be capable of posing a significant threat to elite interests. Moreover, the privatization of the financial and export sectors might restore key economic sectors to the elite. Liberal monetary and financial policies would mean that the threat of capital flight would constrain social spending and other redistributive policies. Decentralization of public administration to the municipalities would be to the party's advantage as well, given the financial and organizational strength of ARENA in much of the countryside.

The first ARENA government (1989–94) succeeded in carrying out a range of neoliberal policy initiatives: most notably, it reduced import tariffs and export taxes, privatized the financial sector, dissolved the coffee marketing board, and liberalized exchange markets.[48] By the end of the war, elites (that is, those who no longer relied narrowly on agriculture) were doing extremely well economically. The commercial and service sectors continued to grow most strongly, thanks to the ongoing influx of remittances rather than strong growth in the manufacturing and export of products. Many of ARENA's measures designed to promote nontraditional exports (and exports in general) were undermined by the continuing

---

[46] U.S. GAO 1993: 27; Johnson 1993. The channeling of U.S. economic assistance to FUSADES reflected in part the increasing impatience of the United States with Duarte's reluctance to impose austerity measures and in part a more general policy shift from "aid to trade" under the Caribbean Basin Initiative (U.S. GAO 1993: 20).
[47] Johnson 1993: 226.   [48] Segovia 1996a.

overvaluation of the currency due to the ongoing massive influx of remittances.

Reflecting surging investor confidence in ARENA's governance as well as increased remittances, the economy grew strongly after 1989 (averaging 4.6 percent real growth in GDP from 1990 to 1994).[49] The renovated economic elites captured a remarkable share of national income: profit rates for nonagricultural enterprises increased from less than 10 percent in 1980 to well over 20 percent by 1991.[50] In contrast, labor's share in national income declined across all sectors, as seen above.

One historical characteristic of the political economy did not change: the tax burden on elites remained low. Foreign assistance permitted this low rate to continue – despite the costs of fighting the war. The average tax ratio (total tax revenues as a fraction of GDP) for the 1980s was 10.7 percent, which was *lower* than the 12.1 percent rate of the 1970s.[51] As the economy began to recover in the late 1980s, the tax ratio actually fell, reaching a low of 7.6 percent in 1989. The tax ratio slowly increased in the early 1990s, in part because of the value added tax introduced in 1991, but the tax ratio was only 9.1 percent at the end of the war.[52] The ARENA government had little success in collecting income taxes (which supposedly replaced the coffee export tax) from coffee interests.

By the end of the 1980s, party rhetoric also expressed an acceptance of democratic procedures and a cautious acceptance of negotiations with the insurgents. As Jeffrey Paige argues in his *Coffee and Power*, elite ideology came to allow a limited procedural notion of democracy and a negotiated resolution to the conflict.[53] The "modernizing" faction around Cristiani displayed more expansive notions of democracy than did those members of the elite focused on coffee cultivation. However, their concept of democracy was predominantly juridical, legalistic, and procedural, empha-

---

[49] Segovia 1996b.   [50] Harberger 1993: Table 6.

[51] Calculated from Segovia 1996a: 114, Table 6.3. Pressured by both the United States and multilateral donors, the government has made some effort since the mid-1980s to increase the tax ratio, a task made more difficult by the trade liberalization policies. David Kaimowitz points to the Salvadorans' successful resistance to pressure for tax increases as an example of policy makers' ability to play off the counterinsurgency agenda against the structural adjustment agenda (Kaimowitz 1990: 646).

[52] Of the Latin American countries in the "lower-middle-income" category, only one had a lower ratio of tax revenue to GNP in 1992 than El Salvador: Paraguay (9.07 percent), compared with El Salvador (9.10 percent). Calculated from World Bank 1994b: Table 11, 182–3.

[53] This paragraph relies on Paige 1997: Chapter 6; and FLACSO 1995: 97.

sizing law, state institutions, and adherence to electoral rules in contests for political power. For the elite, democratization did not imply any need for political reforms that might come to entail distributional measures: poverty was said to be rooted in overpopulation; hence reform such as the legalization of rural labor unions was not seen as necessary.

In the 1980s, the ARENA Party integrated – in a remarkably short time – a wide range of political resources into an effective party organization with a broad political base.[54] In addition to gaining control of business organizations and access to major media, the party built a capacity to mobilize tens of thousands of people at massive rallies in San Salvador and elsewhere. Although the internal structure of the party at the end of the war was not well documented, two constituencies appeared to be particularly well organized: rural residents and urban middle-class "youth."

ARENA persuaded many members of the rural paramilitary networks to transfer their loyalties from the military to the party, thereby creating a base from which to mobilize turnout for rural and urban rallies alike. Key to this capture were two related factors. First, D'Aubuisson commanded strong personal loyalty in the networks; his leadership of ARENA tended to lend the party a popular appeal despite being dominated by big business. Second, though their core interests may have resided elsewhere in the boom of the late 1980s and early 1990s, those landowners who retained their properties retained a capacity for intimidation and social control through enduring patron-client relationships.

The presence of large numbers of disciplined young men and women at ARENA rallies led two authors to refer to ARENA as the "Reebok Right." Many young party leaders were educated in the United States and returned to El Salvador in large numbers after Cristiani's presidential victory. ARENA's young supporters appeared to be one of the party's fastest-growing groups in the early 1990s.

Conclusion

We landlords weren't represented at the [negotiating] table in Mexico. No one now represents our interests!

– Tenancingo landlord, December 1992

---

[54] This section draws heavily on Miles and Ostertag 1989; Spence and Vickers 1994; Spence, Dye, and Vickers 1994; and Spence, Vickers, and Dye 1995.

The transformation of elite economic interests and political representation in El Salvador was largely the result of related processes of insurgency and measures taken to counter it. With the eclipse of labor-repressive agriculture as the core interest of economic elites, neither the political nor the economic compromises made in the peace agreement – the FMLN's participation in elections, the disbanding of the security forces, the reduction in the size and prerogatives of the army, or the transfer of land to former combatants and FMLN civilian supporters – would pose a significant threat to postwar elite interests.

Of course, those landowning families who had failed to make the transition away from an exclusive reliance on agriculture would be threatened – indeed, they felt abandoned by the party, as the quotation at the start of this concluding section suggests – but with the decline of the agricultural sector, they had dropped out of "the elite" and were no longer important players.

Although it is difficult to determine the relative importance of the various factors that made ARENA the sole vehicle of elite representation, a few observations are relevant. Early in the war, the unprecedented political and economic exclusion of elites from national power had immediate and dramatic consequences, the most important of which were the founding of ARENA, massive flight of capital, and the move to Miami and Europe of the largest oligarchic families. By the end of the 1980s, the pull of the new opportunities created by the influx of remittances rather than the push of expropriation had become more important. Finally, the accumulating success under the new rules of the game – the constitutional reform of 1983 that effectively ended further agrarian reform, ARENA's 1989 presidential victory, the subsequent reprivatization of key economic interests of the elite, and the high economic returns in the booming sectors – all underscored the benefits of direct representation of elite interests over the prewar arrangement.

The rise of ARENA parallels similar developments that have taken place for similar reasons elsewhere in Latin America. Business elites elsewhere also supported the transition to democratic rule after varying degrees of exclusion by authoritarian regimes, as in Brazil, where business elites feared that the public sector would expand at the expense of the private sector and that they would be excluded from policy decisions.[55] Business associations similarly seized political opportunities for unprece-

---

[55] Cardoso 1986; Payne 1995.

dented activism as transitions from authoritarian rule got under way, and early success under the new rules of the game consolidated business sector support. Some analysts go so far as to interpret these developments as the end of the weak business–strong state paradigm in Latin America.[56] Arguably, neoliberalism's endorsement of a minimal state also explains why business elites in exporting, import-substituting, and import-dependent sectors alike embraced this new outlook despite its divergent implications for these different sectors.

However, the contrasts are also instructive. Most important, El Salvador is not a case of re-democratization; there was no legacy of democratic institutions to draw on. Nor is it a case of a previously economically weak liberal business elite emerging newly confident from an authoritarian interlude. Rather, with the exception of the commercial families that had immigrated from the Middle East, elites formed a conservative oligarchy dependent on coercive agriculture before the war and emerged from the conflict with their core interests redirected toward the remittance-fed boom in commerce, financial services, construction, and real estate. Thus a key part of the stage for the peace negotiations was set: the dominant element of the elite was no longer tied to labor-repressive agriculture, and it controlled not only a new vehicle for elite representation but also the government of El Salvador.

[56] Payne and Bartell 1995.

4

Negotiating a Democratic Transition to End Civil War

For the consolidation of Peace in a State of Law
— President Alfredo Cristiani, handwritten above
his signature on the January 16, 1992,
peace agreement

On September 25, 1991, representatives of the Salvadoran government and the FMLN signed a preliminary accord in New York outlining the terms of the peace agreement to come. The New York Accord stated that existing occupancy in the conflicted areas of the country would be respected in the short run and that land would be redistributed in those areas as part of the settlement. But the accord did not specify who would get what land; and in the uncertain aftermath of its signing, peasant organizations such as the Cooperativa California (described in Chapter 1) raced to consolidate their claims to de facto tenure before the war's end. Further land invasions took place as peasant organizations attempted to increase the occupied area in the rich coastal plain, particularly in the departments of Usulután and the neighboring department of San Vicente. Hundreds of peasant families migrated from the northern departments of Morazán and Chalatenango to the plain to claim abandoned land in anticipation of the peace agreement. The new and consolidation land claims inaugurated a wave of confrontations and violence as displaced landlords attempted to reclaim their property.

Nor did tension over land diminish after the signing of the final peace agreement in Mexico City on January 16, 1992. From that point until the final demobilization of the FMLN on December 15, 1992, two issues – agrarian property rights and military reform – threatened to derail the peace process. Their role in the implementation of the peace was not surprising, of course: land hunger and the repressive practices of the state lay at the heart of the civil war.

The negotiation of the peace agreement, its implications, and its implementation are the subject of this chapter. The political bargaining did not end with the signing of the agreement as the various domestic actors faced new challenges, constraints, and opportunities while attempting to maintain their own organizational cohesion and to extend their political power over the new postagreement political terrain.

For the governing party ARENA, the principal challenge was to negotiate and implement the peace agreement while minimizing the damage to the interests of its core adherents, without compromising its position as the dominant right-of-center party or weakening its neoliberal economic agenda. A stable transition would depend in part on its ability to deliver on the terms of the agreement lest renewed unrest, armed or not, undermine its ability to raise reconstruction funds from international donors and to portray itself in the 1994 election campaign as the deliverer of the peace.

For the FMLN, a transition to a democratic political regime was a necessary but not sufficient condition for its own transition from insurgent movement to political party. The organization also needed to construct a postwar organizational and economic base, a task that would depend in part on delivering an acceptable set of resources to its former combatants and civilian supporters. The transfer of land and the delivery of training, credit, and other agricultural programs to its supporters and potential constituents was therefore a key concern of FMLN negotiators. However, the FMLN's bargaining power depended in important measure on its threat to slow or halt the demobilization of its guerrilla forces. Once the guns were turned in, the FMLN would lose its special stature as an armed force of the civil war and signatory to the peace agreement and would become another out-of-power political party, although one having special relations with international actors.

For the Armed Forces, the principal challenge was to retain as much institutional autonomy as possible given the commitment of a broad spectrum of domestic and international actors to civilian rule. The agreement initiated an extraordinary process of civilian and international intervention in matters hitherto strictly internal: whether the officer corps would in fact acquiesce to that process was uncertain at the beginning of the cease-fire in February 1992.

For peasants in conflicted areas, both the September 1991 agreement and the peace agreement provided a clear incentive to establish a claim to de facto tenancy as soon as possible. This sense of an unprecedented historical opportunity was reinforced by the highly visible presence of United Nations human rights monitors patrolling the countryside even before the peace agreement was signed. Peasant organizations sought to expand their membership by offering advice, coordination, and political as well as armed protection to prospective land invaders.

For landlords throughout El Salvador, particularly for those owning properties within or near conflicted zones, the agreement occasioned a great deal of uncertainty. Many landlords of properties in these areas, including Tenancingo and Usulután, doubted whether they could farm successfully given the new assertiveness of their erstwhile labor force and the eclipse of the close relations with various security forces that had ensured a quiescent labor force before the war. Although a clause in the peace agreement had reasserted their property rights, many landlords, burdened by debts accumulated during the war as a result of sabotage of infrastructure and harvests and intimidated by the FMLN and the prospect of an organized workforce, decided to sell.

In this chapter I first analyze the Salvadoran peace process and the resulting agreement, focusing on the principal trade-offs and tensions underlying the negotiations. I then discuss the implementation of the agreement. Since local factions opposed to negotiations or particular terms of agreements sometimes emerge as "spoilers" of civil war settlements, I show how conditions in the province of Usulután – highly contested during the war – supported the national process of reconciliation.[1]

Negotiating the Terms of Peace

By the end of the 1980s, the Salvadoran civil war was at a stalemate as neither side had achieved – nor, in the judgment of many observers, *could* achieve – a military victory under the prevailing political conditions. The situation in the late 1980s was by no means static, however: the quickly changing geopolitical context created both problems and opportunities for the contending Salvadoran parties as their social, political, and economic worlds were also being reshaped by the civil war. By the end of 1989, four

---

[1] On "spoilers," see Stedman 1997.

elements essential to the negotiation process that eventually led to the peace agreement were in place.[2]

First, the FMLN made an unprecedented peace proposal in early 1989 that indicated its acceptance in principle of elections and its willingness to participate in the upcoming elections if they were postponed for six months. The initiative followed an internal political debate that redefined the stated goal of the insurgency from socialist revolution to the construction of a pluralist democracy. According to the FMLN, although the new objective implied some structural reforms (including further agrarian reform), it did not entail a single-party political system or the abolition of private property.[3] The offer was clearly serious, for the FMLN no longer insisted on an interim power-sharing arrangement and later stopped pressing for the integration of the two armed forces as well. Despite some degree of internal dissension, subsequent negotiating positions signaled that for the FMLN, military, police, electoral, and judicial reform would take precedence over socioeconomic issues.[4] While asserting the FMLN's readiness to launch a major offensive, guerrilla spokespersons reiterated their preference for a negotiated resolution of the war.[5] However, the proposal was rejected and the election was held as scheduled.

Second, the election of Alfredo Cristiani as president put ARENA in the seat of political power. Although tensions remained between modernizers who favored negotiations and hardliners who opposed them, the party now found itself more vulnerable to political pressure for negotiations and more accountable for their failure; indeed, Cristiani had run for office on a platform that included a commitment to some kind of negotiations.[6] In the judgment of the FMLN, ARENA as the representative of the political interests of economic elites was more likely to support a negotiated resolution if its members participated directly in negotiating its terms.[7]

Third, the Bush administration, in response to the FMLN's initiative, signaled its tentative interest in a negotiated settlement of the war. This meant that the new government could no longer assume the United States would continue the same degree of military and economic support as under the Reagan administration.[8]

---

[2] On the 1992 peace agreement, see Karl 1992; Vickers 1992; and Munck 1993.
[3] FMLN 1989.
[4] Overseas Development Council 1994; Gibb and Smyth 1990; FMLN 1990; Murray, Coletti, and Spence 1994.
[5] Beretta 1989; Karl 1989.   [6] Gibb and Smyth 1990.   [7] Beretta 1989.
[8] Karl 1989; Gibb and Smyth 1990.

Fourth, after a few initial meetings between the FMLN and government representatives in mid-1989, the process ground to a halt, and, in a context of increasing political violence, the FMLN launched a major offensive in November 1989.[9] Their initial success erased any lingering illusion that the socialist reverses in Eastern Europe and Nicaragua had reduced the insurgents' military capability. Although the guerrillas did not hold any city for more than three weeks, they now brought the war home to the wealthy neighborhoods of San Salvador, underscoring the inability of the Armed Forces to contain the war. But the populace did not join in the insurrection, which strengthened the position of those within the FMLN who saw negotiations as the only hope for an end to the conflict. The assassination of six Jesuits and their two women employees by the Atlacatl Battalion, an elite unit of the Salvadoran Armed Forces, during the rebel offensive made untenable further U.S. congressional support not conditioned on negotiations.[10] The offensive thus dramatically illustrated the inability of either side to prevail militarily as well as the ongoing costs of continuing the war.[11]

In the aftermath of these events, the five Central American presidents approached the United Nations for assistance in reaching a negotiated resolution to the civil war.[12] The FMLN made a separate approach to the UN. For both ARENA and the FMLN, a negotiated resolution would not only renew their legitimacy in the eyes of international actors (badly tarnished as a result of the assassination of the Jesuits and the offensive) but would also garner internal political support.[13] A series of subsequent agreements, hammered out over a period of more than two years, laid the procedural, constitutional, and institutional groundwork for the final agreement. The FMLN's decision to pursue political and military reform rather than extensive economic reform as a clear priority was consistently signaled throughout the process, despite ongoing internal tension over the issue. For example, at the May 1990 meeting in Caracas, Venezuela, the

---

[9] See Gibb and Smyth 1990 and Byrne 1996: 170–7.

[10] See Whitfield (1994) for a definitive account of the Jesuit case and its consequences for U.S. relations with El Salvador. U.S. support was further undermined by subsequent detailed allegations of human rights violations and corruption on the part of high-level military and government officials (Hatfield, Leach and Miller 1990).

[11] Gibb and Smyth 1990; Byrne 1994.

[12] Regional support for the resolution of the Central American civil conflicts dated from the Esquipulas II agreement of August 1987 in which all five countries agreed to end support for irregular forces operating on their territory.

[13] Stanley and Holiday 1997: 42–3.

FMLN proposed that both armies be disbanded, a civilian police force be established, and a range of political crimes be investigated and prosecuted. The *only* socioeconomic proposal put forth addressed the needs of demobilized combatants.[14]

The first accord of more than procedural significance was signed in San Jose, Costa Rica in July 1990, when both parties agreed to the establishment of the United Nations Observer Mission in El Salvador (ONUSAL) to verify compliance with the accord's human rights provisions. This role for the UN was unprecedented: not only was the organization to enter into the internal affairs of a member nation, but it would do so on terms that extended far beyond its traditional peacekeeping role of monitoring military compliance between states. The parties subsequently agreed that ONUSAL would begin monitoring human rights even before the signing of the peace agreement.

In April 1991, the two parties agreed on a set of changes to the 1983 Constitution, signaling that they were converging on a regime framework acceptable to both. The most important changes concerned the institutional mandate of the Armed Forces: the military's mission was explicitly limited to external defense, and policing was to be under civilian control. The constitutional agreement also provided for a truth commission under UN auspices to investigate past human rights violations. For its part, the FMLN accepted the existing constitutional ceiling on landholding (245 hectares). Despite some opposition by hardline members of ARENA, the agreements were subsequently ratified by the ARENA-controlled National Assembly, an indication of Cristiani's ability to deliver party compliance on at least some of the reforms despite opposition from party hardliners.

Despite this progress, negotiations subsequently became tied up in what UN officials called the "Gordian knot": what would be the future of the two armed parties to the war? In part the issue was one of guarantees: what ensured the security of former guerrillas and the implementation of reforms once FMLN insurgents turned in their arms? When negotiations reached a stalemate in mid-1991, fighting intensified as both sides attempted to expand their putative claims to control of geographical areas.

By mid-September 1991, both the United States and the Soviet Union had expressed their support for the negotiations, which contributed pressure to reach an agreement. The New York Accord, signed on September

[14] FMLN 1990.

25, 1991, cut the Gordian knot: some FMLN members would join a new civilian police force, the National Civilian Police (PNC); the Armed Forces would be reduced in size and the Treasury Police and National Guard eliminated; and the military officer corps world be purged by the Ad Hoc Commission.[15] In addition, the National Commission for the Consolidation of Peace (COPAZ) – a group composed of representatives of the political parties, the FMLN, and the government – would supervise the implementation of the agreements, verify compliance, and draft necessary legislation. The support of international actors (particularly the verification role of the UN) and the supervisory role of COPAZ, which was given the right to access all sites of implementation, assured the FMLN that the agreements would be implemented once its forces were demobilized. Together, the April and September agreements signaled ARENA's willingness to sacrifice the institutional interests of the military to what would once have been a surprising degree.

The New York Accord also included the first outline of the socioeconomic agreement to come. According to a senior UN official close to the negotiations, the government insisted throughout the negotiations that it would not consider changes in its economic policies, a position accepted implicitly by the FMLN through its acceptance of only limited constitutional reform.[16] Within that constraint, the FMLN put forward a list of minimum conditions for a final agreement, including resources for the reintegration of former combatants and civilian supporters, a forum for the discussion of socioeconomic issues important to the opposition, and a commitment to existing agrarian reform laws. Thus the New York Accord reiterated the constitutional ceiling on landholding and also stated that the existing ceiling would be effectively implemented.

The New York Accord also outlined the "definitive" agenda of still-outstanding issues for negotiation. The most difficult issues were the terms of the cease-fire, the terms of the reincorporation of the FMLN, and the various socioeconomic measures, including steps to alleviate the social costs of structural adjustment programs, channels for direct external funding to community development, and the creation of the socioeconomic forum. In addition, the New York Accord stated that the existing state of tenancy in the *zonas conflictivas* would be respected as an interim measure. But it did not specify who would get what land; nor was it clear

---

[15] "Acuerdo de New York" 1991.
[16] Interview with senior UN official, November 1994.

84

what areas would count as *conflictivas* in the urgent sense that tenure claims based on current occupancy would be respected. As a result, conflict over agrarian property rights deepened.

In late 1991, it became clear that Javier Perez de Cuellar would not accept another term of office as UN secretary general beyond the end of the year, and pressure on the negotiating parties to reach an agreement mounted. As the deadline approached in late December, the contested definition of "conflicted zones," a stumbling block throughout the negotiations, resurfaced. In relation to the cease-fire negotiations, the question was one of geography: which forces would be concentrated where? Given the language of the New York Accord, the definition also had consequences for the scope of transfer of land to the FMLN and its supporters. Although negotiators never reached agreement on a set of boundaries – an ambiguity that would complicate significantly the implementation of the peace agreement – the parties felt confident enough not to delay signing the agreement for that reason.

According to a senior UN official, it was clear to UN officials four days before the year's end that the only remaining obstacle to an agreement was the issue of land; only then did the negotiators in New York return to the agenda of socioeconomic issues.[17] A few minutes before midnight on December 31, 1991, agreement was reached, with President Cristiani accepting what became the final draft of the socioeconomic chapter.

The Terms of the Peace Agreement

The peace agreement was in essence a political compromise in which the Left agreed to a democratic political regime and a capitalist economy with only limited socioeconomic reform, and the Right agreed to the Left's participation in a democratic political regime along with some socioeconomic reform. The peace agreement enshrined a democratic bargain: the two sides agreed to resolve their future differences through democratic political processes. The peace process would culminate in the general elections of March 1994, in which the FMLN would compete for executive, legislative, and municipal seats alongside other political parties. In short, the Left accepted political inclusion at the price of economic moderation. The agreement's principal achievement was thus an agenda of reforms that would institutionalize the new – and democratic – rules of the political

---

[17] Interview, senior UN official, December 1994.

game. The main provisions, many of them carried over from the New York Accord, called for reform of the Armed Forces, accountability for past human rights violations, the founding of a civilian police force, and restrictions on the arbitrary exercise of state power.[18]

The core of the peace agreement – around which its democratic promise revolved – was the agenda of extensive reforms of the coercive apparatus of the state, including changes in the structure, size, ideology, and personnel of the Armed Forces. In addition to the assertion of civilian control and the narrowing of the military's mandate achieved in the earlier constitutional reforms, the agreement dissolved the civil defense patrols, called for the regulation of private security forces and the institutional separation of intelligence services from the Ministry of Defense, suspended forced conscription, restructured the reserve service, and absorbed the counterinsurgency battalions into the regular army.

To address the issue of past human rights violations, the peace agreement established an Ad Hoc Commission comprised of three Salvadoran civilians empowered to investigate the human rights record of the officer corps of the Armed Forces and to make binding recommendations that could include dismissal. The agreement also reiterated the commitment of both the FMLN and the government to the Commission on the Truth established earlier. This second commission, comprised of three non-Salvadoran experts in international law supported by a staff of UN personnel, was to investigate past abuses by both sides, issue a public report, and recommend measures to prevent future abuses.[19] The commission had no authority of prosecution; however, some cases of egregious human rights violations were specifically exempted from the amnesties declared as the cease-fire began, and its recommendations were treated by the UN as binding on the parties to the negotiations.

The agreement reiterated the civilian nature of the new police force, which would be completely separate from the Armed Forces chain of command, and also established a new National Academy of Public Security (ANSP) for the training of its officers. In a secret but widely circulated annex to the New York Accord, the parties had agreed that a fifth of the new force would consist of former guerrillas and another fifth of former National Policemen (in the latter case, after an evaluation of their record); both had to go through the ANSP course. The provisions included a special "transitory regime" during which the former police

---

[18] Gobierno de El Salvador 1992.   [19] Buergenthal 1994.

force would gradually relinquish control of successive geographical areas to the PNC until it was fully deployed.

Thus ARENA sacrificed key interests of the Salvadoran military, the chief loser under the terms of the peace agreement.[20] Given the military's long-standing impunity for human rights violations, the promised review of the military records of military officers by civilians of the Ad Hoc and truth commissions was an unprecedented breach in its institutional autonomy. The dissolution of the National Guard, Treasury Police, and the counterinsurgency battalions would drastically reduce the military's role in rural areas (although the army reserve was largely left in place), as did the transfer of policing to civilian authority.

The final agreement also reaffirmed earlier accords on judicial and electoral reforms announced in April 1991. Most important of these was the founding of a new investigative and prosecutorial body, the National Counsel for the Defense of Human Rights (Procuraduría de Derechos Humanos). Constitutional reform also transformed the selection of Supreme Court magistrates as a step toward breaking the traditional dominance of the judicial system by the ruling political party.[21] The agreement included provisions to strengthen the independence of the National Judicial Council in order to promote judicial reform, including the founding of an institution for the training of judges and other judicial personnel. A new Supreme Electoral Tribunal with broad political party representation was established to supervise voter registration and elections. The agreement also mandated the legalization of the FMLN as a political party, recognizing its right to meet, to mobilize, to publish, and to hold licenses for communication (necessary for the legalization of the FMLN's two hitherto clandestine radio stations). In addition, it proclaimed the right of return for exiles and promised special security measures for FMLN leaders.

In contrast to the detailed sections concerning the political reforms, the socioeconomic section left many questions unanswered, both because it was negotiated late in the process and because the parties agreed that negotiations were necessary on political reform, but not on reform that would fundamentally reshape the country's economy. Although the government refused to negotiate the "philosophy and general orientation" of

---

[20] Stanley and Holiday 1997: 27.

[21] Magistrates are now selected by a two-thirds majority of the National Assembly and serve staggered nine-year terms (Popkin 1994).

an economic policy, it recognized that stability in the postwar period depended on the transfer of some resources to former guerrillas and their supporters, perhaps reflecting the awareness of Salvadoran elites (evident in many interviews) of the difficulties in neighboring Nicaragua posed by disgruntled former-combatants on both sides. The limited agenda of socioeconomic reform included (1) land transfer to former-combatants and civilian supporters of the FMLN, (2) the extension of credit for agriculture and for small business, (3) measures to alleviate the costs of structural adjustment, (4) "modalities" for external aid to communities, (5) the founding of a forum of labor, business, and government for further negotiation, and (6) a National Reconstruction Plan (PRN), which was to target the conflicted zones and include programs to help members of the FMLN reenter civilian life.

In view of the social and economic inequality that contributed to the civil conflict, the sustained fall in real wages during the war, and the FMLN's long-standing commitment to egalitarian redistribution, it was notable that the peace agreement did not include a general redistributive agenda but was limited to measures targeting combatants and organized supporters of the FMLN in the conflicted zones.[22] Urban conditions and the right of unions to organize were ignored. The agreement did not authorize new agrarian reform via the usual means of expropriation of properties and compensation of owners by government bonds; instead, the agreement indirectly affirmed the existing constitutional ceiling on land-holding (245 hectares). Nor was poverty directly addressed outside the areas targeted by the PRN except in vague terms.[23] Redistribution was limited to the transfer – more precisely, the purchase – of land to former combatants of both sides and to supporters of the FMLN for two principal reasons: First, the ARENA government's economic policy emphasized diversification away from a narrow dependence on agricultural production and integration into regional and international markets – a policy that would be more threatened by wage and labor policies favorable to urban workers than by the limited transfer of land. That is, for the modernizers in the ARENA Party, the price for peace paid in land did not look steep – *if* it could be limited to the conflicted zones and did not threaten the political and economic base of the party in the western coffee areas and in

[22] For analysis of the socioeconomic section of the peace agreement, see del Castillo 1997 and Wood 1996.
[23] Vickers 1992.

business circles. Second, the FMLN and most observers argued that land transfer was critical to the FMLN's internal political cohesion: given the peasant origins of most of its combatants, the group would have suffered severe internal difficulties in negotiating an end to the war without some transfer of land. Throughout the cease-fire, the FMLN repeatedly conditioned its further demobilization on progress in the transfer of land (and frequently on progress in the restructuring of the military as well).

Given the importance of land both in the civil war and in the political dynamics of the immediate postwar period, its treatment in the agreement merits close attention. The agreement identified various categories of properties for potential distribution: properties exceeding the 1983 constitutional limit of 245 hectares, properties belonging to the state, land offered voluntarily for sale to the state, and properties occupied in the conflicted zones by residents and workers. This last category was one of the most politically sensitive parts of the entire agreement. In a particularly controversial passage, the agreement stated that "in conformity with the New York Accord, the present state of tenancy within the conflicted zones will be respected until a satisfactory legal solution of definitive tenancy is found," thus stating explicitly that those occupying land, referred to as *tenedores* (literally, holders), would not be evicted.[24] The reference to the New York Accord created intense debate as to the relevant date of the "present state of tenancy." Was it September 25, 1991 (when the New York Accord was signed), or January 16, 1992 (when the final agreement was signed)? The difference was significant given the additional claims made in the interval between the two agreements. According to the peace agreement, within thirty days of the signing the FMLN was to present an inventory of properties claimed in the conflicted zones; the government was to legalize tenure definitively within six months.

The agreement did little more than sketch the terms of transfer for each category. Nor did it estimate how much land fell within the various categories, and initial estimates varied widely. In general, credit for purchase was to be extended at the (highly subsidized) terms of the 1980 agrarian reform. In the conflicted zones, the transfer of private property would depend on the voluntary selling of the property by the titleholder; if the landlord chose not to sell, the government was to relocate the occupying *tenedores* on unoccupied land within the same area whose owners did want to sell. Landlords were to be paid market prices, but what that would mean

---

[24] Gobierno de El Salvador 1992: 28.

in areas where the civil war had raged was not spelled out. Nor did the agreement adequately define the process by which these issues would be resolved and the transfer implemented. COPAZ was to be the "guarantor" of the land agreements but was not given any specific authority.[25] COPAZ was to appoint a special agrarian commission (hereafter, CEA-COPAZ) to supervise the land-transfer issue and, in particular, to "verify" the status of properties and *tenedores* in the conflicted zones, but the extent of its authority was unclear.

The agreement also stated that the government would present a draft of the PRN to the FMLN within a month of the signing of the agreement. While the FMLN's recommendations and requests would be "taken into account," its role was clearly secondary: there was no provision for its participation or for that of program beneficiaries in the development of the PRN (except in the case of credit policy). The principal goals of the plan were the integrated development of "areas affected by the war" (there was no reference to "conflicted zones" in this section, a legacy of the debate over the issue), attention to the basic needs of the population most affected by the war and of the former-combatants of both sides, and the reconstruction of damaged infrastructure. Policies facilitating the reincorporation of demobilizing combatants were to include programs such as scholarships, jobs and pensions, housing projects, and business promotion. Appealing to international donors for financial and other support, the agreement assigned to the United Nations Development Programme (UNDP) the role of consultant in fund-raising, project design, and coordination with nongovernmental organizations.

The peace agreement also provided a set of guarantees for the transition period. A detailed calendar defined a schedule of steps for the dissolution of the security forces and counterinsurgency battalions as well as the gradual demobilization of the FMLN by October 1992 in which key actions by the two parties were staggered. For example, the National Guard and Treasury Police were to be abolished before the first 20 percent of the FMLN guerrillas were to demobilize. This linkage thus provided some degree of security to both sides: each was required to take a sequence of significant and costly steps that, if implemented, would signal continu-

---

[25] The agreement mentioned specifically two government agencies, the Land Bank and the Salvadoran Institute for Agrarian Transformation (ISTA), but did not clarify their role in its implementation; nor did it define the overall line of authority among the various governmental organizations.

ing compliance with the terms of the peace agreement. The calendar did not require definitive and irreversible steps early in the cease-fire period, which would have necessitated an unreasonable degree of early confidence in the other party's compliance. The implicit conditionality of the calendar also pertained to programs of economic reintegration: land transfer and training programs were to be under way as combatants were demobilized. COPAZ, the interparty commission that was to verify compliance with the peace agreement, was to designate a commission with wide representation by political parties to follow up on the legal issues involved in the mandated reforms.

As agreed in the New York Accord, other issues – including, implicitly, negotiations over wages and working conditions – were consigned to the *foro para la concertación económica y social* (forum for economic and social negotiation). The agenda for further negotiation ranged from redressing the social costs of structural adjustment to "economic and social problems that will arise due to the end of the conflict." The government also agreed to recommend changes in labor law and regulations in order to promote a "climate of harmony in labor relations." However, the resources that the forum would command were limited.

The Implementation of the Peace Agreement

As the two armies separated to their agreed-on "concentration points" after the signing of the agreement, both domestic and international actors became increasingly aware of the difficult challenges of peace building after more than a decade of civil war. Beyond the immediate issue of the effectiveness of the UN's monitoring of the cease-fire loomed two key issues. First, would the calendar of staggered implementation of the agreement together with the attention of international actors provide sufficient mutual confidence to engender ongoing compliance? Second, who would pay the costs of peace, given the significant resources required for the implementation of the peace agreement? These two issues were inextricably related: the level and channeling of reintegration and reconstruction funding could either reinforce or undermine the political will and capacity of one or both parties to carry out the terms of the peace agreement.

The fundamental challenge was to translate the political commitments of the agreement into adequately funded programs and policies that would institutionalize its underlying democratic bargain. Contributing to the prospects for successful implementation was the commitment of international actors to the peaceful resolution of the war, particularly the United Nations (to which I return later).[26] ONUSAL staff documented and analyzed the demobilization of both armies, negotiations over the transfer of land and the reintegration programs for combatants, the founding of the new civilian police force and academy, the implementation of the recommendations of the Ad Hoc and truth commissions, and a host of other political events central to the peace process. In frequent reports to the Security Council, the UN verified successful steps in the peace process and publicized accumulating problems. As the author of much of the agreement, both parties usually accepted UN interpretations of contested passages as authoritative.[27] Since many donor countries conditioned their assistance on compliance with the peace agreement, the reports pressed both parties to comply. ONUSAL's role continually expanded under the usefully vague rubric of "good offices," a process that William Stanley and David Holiday termed "carefully chosen, constructive mission creep."[28] Thus ONUSAL provided the necessary coordination that allowed the two parties to move jointly to a new equilibrium in which continued adherence to peace and democracy by each party was the best response to the other party's ongoing compliance.

Whether the agreement, the apparent commitment of both parties to its terms, and UN involvement would prove sufficient for its successful implementation was an open question as tensions ran ever higher during the first few months of the cease-fire. Some government officials and business organizations mobilized landlords against selling their land in the conflicted zones. The FMLN submitted a first inventory of occupied properties amounting to more than a third of the nation's farmland. Reports of further land invasions and attempted evictions circulated throughout the country. Peasant organizations announced that their "public security commissions" would serve as the local police force and patrol occupied properties. The Ministry of Defense circulated a list of ninety-two properties that had been occupied after the signing of the New York Accord. The Supreme Court instructed judges to act on landlord complaints and, where appropriate, to proceed with evictions.

As the tension over potential eviction attempts mounted, the FMLN halted its movement to the designated cease-fire camps. In light as well of

---

[26] See Holiday and Stanley 1993; Weiss Fagen 1996; and Stanley and Holiday 1997.
[27] Stanley and Holiday 1997: 26.   [28] Stanley and Holiday 1997: 25.

Demobilization of the Atlacatl Battalion, 1992. Note demonstration by FMLN sympathizers in background. Photograph by William Stanley.

the government's apparent reluctance to dissolve the National Guard and the Treasury Police, the UN sent Under-Secretary for Peace Operations Marrack Goulding to El Salvador to resolve this first major crisis of the implementation of the peace agreement.[29] The parties could not agree on a date to define which occupations had to be protected from eviction, but they did accept a two-week freeze on further land invasions and attempted evictions and subsequently permitted a joint investigation of the ninety-two properties. Goulding's visit, one of several *recalendarizaciones* (reschedulings) of the peace agreement's implementation, also led the authorities to resume the staggered demobilization of the FMLN and to dissolve the security forces by mid-1992.

Tensions also eased when a working definition of "conflicted zones" seemed to be in the making and many landlords of occupied properties appeared willing to sell. The FMLN's second version of the inventory of occupied properties comprised 20 percent of farmland, and the third (accepted by CEA-COPAZ and the government) approximately 18

[29] Holiday and Stanley 1993.

percent. As the target areas of successive drafts of what would become the National Reconstruction Plan expanded in response to ongoing pressure from the FMLN, allied organizations, and international actors (particularly the UNDP) from 84 to 115 municipalities, the inventory and those targeted areas showed considerable overlap.[30] Controversy arose over other aspects of the PRN as well, particularly over what the FMLN and its allied organizations saw as inadequate provisions for participation by potential beneficiaries in the design and implementation of the various reconstruction programs.[31] Participation would be modeled on the Municipalities in Action (MEA) program, a model of community development previously financed by USAID through the Commission for the Restoration of Areas (CONARA, an agency founded as part of the government's 1984–89 "hearts and minds" counterinsurgency strategy), which was to be superseded by the Secretariat of National Reconstruction (SRN). The government made some changes in response to opposition criticisms and UNDP recommendations, including the authorization of nongovernmental organizations to apply directly to the SRN for funding without the mayor's approval. However, the principal avenue for local projects continued to be MEA projects, and the mayor and the municipal council remained in charge of local funding.

The prospect of significant international assistance contributed to the tension over the future channeling of resources and also became an incentive to cooperation. Ironically, the long-standing special relationship between the U.S. and Salvadoran governments – combined with the much more recent commitment of the United States to the negotiated resolution of the war – proved an important catalyst to the peace process. According to a senior UN official close to the negotiations, the United States explicitly assured both parties that substantial funding would be forthcoming.[32] A significant degree of European funding was also expected. However, many international donors were reluctant to underwrite the peace agreement until they judged both warring parties were committed to all its provisions – and, in particular, that the government was prepared to finance ongoing costs of reforms once donor funding was exhausted. Substantial funds would be forthcoming only if adequate finan-

---

[30] The eventual target population consisted of 35,400 former soldiers, 11,000 former guerrillas (including war veterans), 60,000 displaced persons, 26,000 repatriates, and 800,000 residents of the PRN municipalities (SRN 1992a).

[31] See Murray, Coletti, and Spence 1994.

[32] Interview, senior UN official, December 1994.

cial procedures were in place, including detailed proposals and budgets and standard accounting procedures. Yet at the time of the signing of the agreement, the overall cost of implementing the agreement had not yet been assessed, and the only estimates for reconstruction at hand were based on a preliminary version of the PRN. According to the senior UN official, no attempt had been made during the negotiations to estimate the agreement's financial implications, a process that would probably have impeded the parties from reaching an agreement by the end of 1991.

At a March 1992 meeting of potential donor nations and agencies (in World Bank parlance, a consultative group meeting), the government argued that it faced serious fiscal constraints, in view of the need to increase social spending in general (not just in PRN areas) and the absence of a peace dividend given the degree of external financing of the war and the only gradual reduction of the Armed Forces.[33] Donors pledged some $600 million ($800 million if previous commitments are included). By June 1992, more than $200 million was on its way – almost all of it from the United States. In addition to other funding, USAID provided the newly founded National Reconstruction Secretariat the 116 million colones needed for the contingency (i.e., immediate) phase of the program.

Despite this significant donor interest, funding for the peace process lagged behind the amounts needed to finance various reforms and programs. The government's inadequate funding of many programs judged essential to the peace process – particularly the new public security institutions and the reintegration programs – troubled some donors and intensified the debate about the relationship between economic and political reform.[34] Moreover, many donors lacked confidence in the National Reconstruction Secretariat, with the result that its programs were funded almost exclusively by USAID, while other donors channeled bilateral assistance through other ministries and through the UNDP.[35]

In particular, the National Civilian Police (PNC) had trouble securing initial funds. According to Stanley (1995), two reasons account for international reluctance to finance an institution so obviously key to the peace process: international donors disliked funding police in general; more par-

---

[33] For analysis of the interaction between the government and international agencies, see Boyce 1996 and Wood 1996.
[34] de Soto and del Castillo 1994; Segovia 1996.
[35] For a detailed breakdown of projected funding needs and commitments by donors, see Boyce 1996: Table 7.2.

ticularly, they did not wish to fund an institution to which the government seemed inadequately committed. A lack of cooperation on the part of the former police force during the transition period also undermined the PNC's initial effectiveness. In the immediate postwar years, despite significant advances, the investigative capacity of the PNC remained inadequate and thus contributed to general insecurity and rising crime. The truth commission made a series of binding recommendations meant to bolster the judicial system's institutional capacity, one being an investigation of armed networks. After a visit by Goulding in November 1993, a "joint group" was convened to carry out the investigation. Despite significant resistance to the recommended reforms, the capacity of the judicial system slowly improved.[36]

In mid-1992, negotiations over the terms of the land transfer – the amount of land to be transferred, the number of beneficiaries, and the applicability of "special conditions" versus "market prices" – collapsed. The promised training and credit programs – the necessary complements to land transfer – were not in place either. The impasse threatened the peace process itself as the FMLN suspended its demobilization process and political tensions increased. In an extraordinary instance of its "good offices" mandate, the UN sent a team of agrarian specialists to evaluate the situation and subsequently offered the two parties a take-it-or-leave-it settlement in October 1992. The settlement made concessions to both sides: the amount of land to be transferred per beneficiary would be less than what the FMLN had argued for, and the government agreed not to press for a ceiling on the amount of credit available to each beneficiary.[37] The proposal, subsequently considered by the UN as an addendum to the peace agreement, defined the scope of the transfer as to the number of beneficiaries (47,500, comprised of 7,500 former FMLN combatants, 15,000 former combatants of the Armed Forces, and 25,000 *tenedores*) and the amount of land per beneficiary (depending on soil quality). If the agreement had been fully implemented (it was subsequently pared down), the transfer of land would have amounted to 12 percent of Salvadoran farmland (slightly more than half the amount distributed under the 1980 agrarian reform).

The FMLN delayed the demobilization of the final group of combatants for two months, in part because of renewed problems with the land transfer. Despite lingering doubts about whether the FMLN

[36] Spence, Vickers, and Dye 1995. [37] del Castillo 1997: 348.

combatants had indeed turned in all their weapons, the UN certified the demobilization of the FMLN as complete. Those doubts proved well founded when a clandestine FPL arms cache exploded in Managua in May 1993. The cache was denounced by the UN as the most serious violation of the agreement to date. Additional arms (including surface-to-air missiles) equivalent to 30 percent of the stated inventory were subsequently turned over to the UN.[38]

Development of programs for reinsertion of the demobilized combatants into civilian life trailed even the lagging negotiations over land. Representatives of the FMLN and the government did not begin discussing the programs until mid-1992, with the UNDP acting as an observer.[39] The FMLN's initial reintegration proposal included training programs for thousands of people ranging in duration from one to five years and employment guarantees for two years, as well as housing for 12,000 households, for a total cost of $258 million. By May 1992, the proposal had been scaled down to slightly more than $200 million, not including funds for land purchase. In September 1992, the government offered a counterproposal that defined two "tracks" available for lower-ranking combatants.[40] The proposal distinguished between short-run and medium-run projects for the two tracks, on the grounds that resources and programs for immediate needs (including documentation, household goods, and living expenses during initial training) should be under way while remaining programs were being designed.[41]

After a series of discussions, facilitated and coordinated by the UNDP, the two parties agreed on three reinsertion tracks (in addition to the PNC track for combatants who joined the new police force). For those pursuing agriculture, training programs by nongovernmental organizations were to begin immediately; once in possession of land through the land-transfer program, they would be eligible for agricultural credit, including a five-year loan to capitalize the farms.[42] Those preferring a nonagricul-

---

[38] This paragraph draws on Stanley and Holiday 1997: 29–32.

[39] The UNDP also coordinated an emergency appeal to international donors to address the pressing needs of the FMLN combatants, ranging from shelter to medical assistance to household goods, and, in the case of those turning to agriculture as their postwar employment, to farming tools as well. See Weiss Fagen 1996.

[40] SRN 1992b.

[41] With the help of hindsight to approximate the missing estimates, a comparison of the two proposals shows that – excluding land – the government's proposal was roughly half that of the FMLN.

[42] UNDP 1993.

FMLN guerrillas turning in their weapons, 1992. Photograph by William Stanley.

tural future would have access to credit for the founding of "microenterprises" after technical-vocational training; university scholarships were also available if appropriate.

The third track emerged as a result of agreements between the FMLN and the government that the UN neither mediated nor approved.[43] In exchange for the government's agreeing to a track of training and credit for the approximately six hundred midlevel FMLN commanders as well as the transfer of some prime parcels of land to higher-ranking leaders, the FMLN agreed to the transfer of two units of the old investigative forces into the PNC (a clear violation of the peace agreement) and to a delay in the resignations of the 103 military officers named by the Ad Hoc Commission.[44] Only after additional delays and extraordinary international pressure did the 103 officers finally leave office at the end of 1993.

Throughout the negotiations, the government maintained that reintegration benefits should be equally available to both sides. Parallel agricultural and technical-vocational training programs were supposedly in place for soldiers, although such programs were not needed for officers, since they either remained in office or retired with substantial benefits. However, former members of the Armed Forces, National Police, and civil defense patrols repeatedly paralyzed the government on a number of occasions from 1993 to 1995, sending thousands of protestors to occupy government buildings demanding land, severance payments, and other benefits.[45] Many demands (particularly by civil defense patrol members, who were never considered eligible for reinsertion benefits) clearly exceeded the provisions of the peace agreement. After UN-assisted negotiations, the government agreed to a compromise set of programs (but not to the extension of benefits to paramilitary groups).

The transfer of land – an essential step in reintegrating former combatants into civilian life – suffered continuous delays, which posed a serious threat to the peace process. The recurrent delays were due principally to two factors. First, the key problem was not a lack of funding for the implementing agency, the Land Bank, but rather a lack of governmental

---

[43] Stanley and Holiday 1997: 29.

[44] Initial academic equivalency courses contributed to the further refining of the track; in their aftermath, the UNDP coordinated the design and implementation of three subtracks: technical-vocational training (33 percent of the participants), business administration (58 percent), and executive training (9 percent). See UNDP 1994.

[45] del Castillo 1997: 355–6; Stanley and Holiday 1997: 32–3.

commitment to its timely transfer.[46] The titling process was remarkably cumbersome, despite repeated agreements to streamline it (which could have been readily enforced by presidential decree).[47] Second, the FMLN and its allied peasant organizations found it extremely difficult to construct a list of beneficiaries for each property to be transferred because of widespread mobility in the countryside after the war and the FMLN's inadequate organizational resources. These problems, compounded by delays in titling, led some beneficiaries to view the terms of transfer as too hard a bargain. As a result, representatives of the government and the FMLN agreed in mid-1994 to scale back the number of beneficiaries of the land transfer from 47,500 to just over 40,000. By the end of 1997, nearly all titles had been formally transferred.

The land reform and the land-transfer program saddled beneficiaries with significant burdens of debt that limited their access to credit and thus led them to resist government efforts to force payments for such land.[48] In 1996, the government offered to forgive significant portions of debt (in many cases nearly 70 percent) in exchange for immediate payment of the remainder and the division of cooperative holdings into individual farms. In response, peasant organizations mobilized their members to influence the specific terms of the potential relaxation of debt. As a result, cooperatives received significant debt relief and were not forced to break up their collectively held land into smallholdings (athough the terms of the arrangement provided significant incentives to do so). Whether the other reinsertion programs provided a successful transition to civilian life was doubtful as many microenterprises failed within a year, leaving many program participants ineligible for loans.

Forging Peace in Usulután

Surprisingly, the contested, uneven, and delayed implementation of the peace agreement did not lead to renewed conflict in Usulután, despite its conflicted history and rich resources. Whether the national guarantees

---

[46] The Land Bank had adequate interim funding from USAID; the bottleneck from month to month in the transfer of land has not been a shortage of cash (interview with Ken Ellis, senior USAID official, December 1994).

[47] The government took a very bureaucratic approach to the process, originally insisting that only those on initial lists would receive land and refusing to extend credit until legal title was transferred.

[48] Foley, Vickers, and Thale 1997.

included in the agreement would suffice locally was at first extremely uncertain. Would militant peasants leave occupied properties if FMLN negotiators committed them to do so? Would regional guerrilla commanders follow demobilization orders from the national command? Would landlords reoccupy properties by force, and would individual retribution threaten the peace? Interviews and personal observation suggest that the process of national bargaining was not unraveled by local "spoilers" because of the evolving relationship in Usulután between the demobilizing FMLN, the downsizing of security forces, landlords, *campesino* organizations, and the ONUSAL regional office. Three developments helped resolve a series of crises "on the ground": the initial unity of the Left despite widespread resentment of the redistributive terms of the peace agreement and a later political split within the FMLN; a shift in elite economic interests in parallel with that at the national level, together with the erosion of landlord-military ties at the local level; and the skillful management of incipient crises by the departmental office of ONUSAL.

Peace-Building in Usulután: Unity on the Left

Throughout the cease-fire there was little conflict between the guerrillas of the Revolutionary Popular Army (ERP), the group dominant in the case-study municipalities, and the *campesino* organizations. In the initial months after the signing of the agreement, the organizations had a direct incentive to work with the ERP: beneficiaries had to be on the FMLN inventory to qualify for the transfer of land. Moreover, because key leaders of some *campesino* organizations were also political officers of the ERP, it had a direct role in the decisions taken by those organizations. As seen in Chapter 2, many *campesino* organizations collaborated deeply with the ERP, and a fairly high degree of trust developed between the two groups. The ERP defended occupied properties by refusing to comply with the agreement until arrested *compesinos* were released. Indeed, ERP field commanders in Usulután – many of them of peasant origins – at times halted the regional demobilization without authorization from their central command in order to protest the inadequate progress on land issues.[49] The armed presence of the ERP (both in the two formal demobilization camps and frequently in other areas as well, in violation

---

[49] Interviews with peasant cooperatives and ERP commanders, San Francisco Javier, Usulután, early 1992.

of the agreement) was seen as interim protection of local land claims. Thus some ERP actions that violated the agreement nonetheless reinforced *campesino* confidence in its provisions. Furthermore, soon after the beginning of the cease-fire, the ERP informally demobilized many officers well before scheduled to carry out a wide variety of political tasks ranging from participating in various negotiating forums to opening offices of the new political party.[50] Finally, the ERP retained a coercive capacity throughout most of the cease-fire, which, though little exercised, was far from irrelevant.

For these reasons, the ERP had the authority to negotiate and insist on the implementation of unpopular decisions. For example, after the FMLN agreed in early 1992 that further occupations would not occur, the decision was adhered to despite grumbling by cooperative leaders who had their eye on further properties. The terms of the land transfer were also eventually accepted, although the land transferred per person was seen as inadequate and the price too high.[51] More difficult for the *campesino* organizations to accept was the reduction in the total land transferred to former combatants and cooperatives compared with that occupied in 1992, which caused significant resentment, particularly among cooperatives that had to abandon hard-won land.

At times, however, relations between the ERP and *campesino* organizations grew tense, especially when several ERP officers moved directly into the leadership of some organizations, displacing existing leaders (in a few cases, from paid positions). In the case of an officer who had worked closely with the organizations before, the resentment was not as strong. But in other cases, *campesino* leaders felt the (already limited) autonomy of their organizations was eroding. For example, the national leadership of the ERP repeatedly interfered in the affairs of CODECOSTA, insisting on appointing persons with little local experience to leadership positions. This intervention was motivated in part by the ERP's financial needs, as wartime funding sources had dried up, and in part by competition between the ERP and other insurgent groups for control of *campesino* organizations and their

---

[50] ONUSAL was aware of most of these issues and pushed informally without publicity for their resolution. One exception was the informal early demobilization of officers to begin political work: it appears that in the judgment of ONUSAL the overall benefits for the peace process outweighed the formal costs.

[51] The payment terms were not in fact market prices (the loans were to be paid at 6 percent interest, significantly less than the market interest rate, and over thirty years) but the nominal transfer price was nonetheless extremely intimidating for many peasants.

(usually shaky) financial resources. In the case of CODECOSTA, the potential for major development projects was significant (indeed, a major project was subsequently implemented in the area by the European Union). The ERP also provoked significant resentment in Jiquilisco by its high-handed selection of candidates to compete in municipal elections; as a result, many activists supported other candidates, and the FMLN candidate lost, resoundingly.

These tensions were discussed and debated in the weekly meetings of *campesino* organizations (of which I observed dozens). Decision-making procedures were rarely democratic, as leaders retained significant prerogatives. Nonetheless, freewheeling discussions took place on occasion, and dissent was frequently overt. Moreover, leaders were well aware that their organizations rested largely on *campesino* participation. FMLN policy was to a degree constrained by this need to retain local militancy and loyalty; most leaders sought to channel and manage participation in accordance with decisions taken by the party. Those organizations that became vibrant postwar associations of cooperatives capable of initiating and managing robust development projects (COMUS and the Land Defense Committee of Las Marías) were those that began seeking an increasing degree of autonomy from the party soon after the cease-fire. Those organizations in which the party intervened directly and repeatedly (CODECOSTA and FENACOA) went into decline.

The transition to peace proved difficult at a personal level for several midlevel leaders of the ERP, which lessened the coherence of the Left to some degree. For example, a former commander of the San Francisco Javier base in western Usulután drank excessively after demobilization and died in a violent bar fight. Others found civilian life boring after the challenges of leadership and combat or found the various reinsertion programs developed by the UNDP of little assistance. However, some did move into new work and new households, settling into peacetime with what appeared sustainable if modest livelihoods.

Despite these tensions, the ERP and its allied organizations in the study areas of Usulután remained a coherent political actor throughout the area during the cease-fire. The dominant reason appeared to be the historical ties forged between the ERP and the organizations during the war itself.

When the ERP withdrew from the FMLN after the 1994 elections, however, the peasant organizations in Usulután suffered a deep crisis. While some leaders (most of CONFRAS and some of CODECOSTA) followed the ERP's national leadership into the vaguely social democratic Democratic Party, most local activists and former combatants did not. Under the leadership of one of the former regional commanders, they remained within the FMLN as the *tendencia democrática*, but a significant fraction of the party's former rural base felt demoralized. Because the split occurred after the elections, it did not threaten the implementation of the agreement.

Supporting Peace: The Shift in Elite Economic Interests in Usulután

The apparent acquiescence of right-wing forces in Usulután in the peace process reflected their fragmentation. The war had so transformed traditional rural relationships that many of their long-standing constituencies were displaced entirely from the department.[52] Many of the contributing factors paralleled those involved in the evolution of elite interests nationally. Most remarkable was what did not happen in Usulután: landlords did not form a coalition to regain their properties forcibly. Such a coalition had been active in Usulután before the war, defeating the attempt at agrarian reform in 1976. The successful defense by the Cooperativa California against the landlord's attempted return (described in Chapter 1) deeply dismayed the landlords of Usulután.

Furthermore, local elite interests had changed, in parallel with those at the national level. For example, when rumors began circulating that a group of some sixty landlords of small and medium coffee estates in northeastern Usulután had formed an association and were meeting regularly, *campesino* organizations and ERP officers feared that an organized attempt to seize occupied properties might occur. However, leaders of the association soon approached the ERP to ask that joint meetings be held.[53] Subsequently, the association, the FMLN, and the peasant cooperatives joined to press CEA-COPAZ and the government to quickly transfer to the occupants the land owned by the sixty landlords. The Left joined the landlords in asking the government to forgive accruing interest on their debt and to pay cash for the land.

Assistance from the United States and European Union financed the land-transfer program in Usulután and made it possible to buy out the

---

[52] However, in San Miguel (the department to the east of Usulután) a vigilante group called the Black Shadow killed several gang members and suspected criminals. The group apparently included a remnant of death squads that had operated during the war.

[53] Interviews with Usulután landlords and ERP commanders, November–December 1992.

landlords. Many observers argued that the amount available was inflating land prices even as the high prices persuaded more landlords to sell. Owing to the unusual combination of circumstances, the FMLN on occasion agreed to prices *higher* than those that government representatives were willing to endorse.

Those landlords who intended to retain their properties in contested areas of Usulután ran into significant obstacles. The war severed the close local ties between landlords and the military (particularly the National Guard) as deployment became more centralized and more oriented toward the war. This undermined the confidence of many landlords, few of whom felt it was safe to visit their occupied properties after the cease-fire without an ONUSAL escort. Any attempt to forcibly reoccupy properties might also prompt an ONUSAL investigation. Although they were unlikely to suffer legal consequences, elites still had to face up to an unprecedented degree of accountability.

Whereas the military and landlords had a significant number of *campesinos* collaborating with them before and in the early days of the war, there was no significant rightwing *campesino* presence in Usulután after the war. Some residents who had been forced from the area by the FMLN returned at war's end, but their position was precarious given the absence of landlord or military presence. As a result, they kept a low profile. Though voting patterns showed a strong rightist electoral block, they showed little capacity to act collectively to derail the peace agreement.

What ARENA did develop in Usulután was a strong party organization that delivered many candidates to office in the 1994 election (but fewer in the 1996 elections). The party drew support in the towns and hamlets alike, reflecting the continuing individual conservatism of many *campesinos*, particularly smallholders and dependents of landlords, as well as a general perception in 1994 that a vote for ARENA was a vote to ensure the peace.

The Role of the UN in Usulután

ONUSAL's regional offices provided a broad accountability – and the credible threat of accountability – throughout the countryside: violations of the peace agreement would be known at the national level and potentially publicly as well. The initial high level of staffing made possible a quick investigation of reported incidents; serious problems were soon resolved by UN mediation, locally or nationally. For example, the UN pressed the ERP to pull back to the designated concentration points those members who were assisting *campesino* organizations in patrols of occupied territories.

Nor should the importance of the constant visible presence of ONUSAL vehicles throughout the contested areas be underestimated, for it reflected the UN's commitment and capacity. Many residents saw the UN as an interim local authority (given the absence of police, mayors, and, as the ERP pulled back to the concentration areas, of guerrillas), a belief that served the peace process well, even though the UN had no such mandate. ONUSAL police officers investigated reports of violence and crime throughout the area, usually accompanying Salvadoran police officers, but frequently with no Salvadoran representatives given the difficult transition in policing under way.[54] For example, when landlords near San Francisco Javier reported receiving threats of violence should they attempt to visit their properties, ONUSAL staff visited COMUS offices to urge the organization to restrain cooperative members from such activities. During the first extremely tense months of the cease-fire, ONUSAL staff accompanied mayors and other officials on visits to contested areas.

Thus ONUSAL's presence throughout the country made up for the varying balance of military and political strength between the two armies from region to region and contributed greatly to the peace process. Without this broad accountability, one side or the other might have tried to take advantage of their strength in a region where the other was weak, perhaps to the extent that the other would need to retaliate in some way (a dynamic underlying cycles of ethnic "cleansing," for example), perhaps leading to a vicious circle that could undermine the peace agreement. ONUSAL's presence arguably deterred such steps. Since national-level elites of both sides were clearly committed to implementing the agreement, given the general discipline of the military forces of the government and the FMLN, if ONUSAL presented a credible case that local party adherents were violating the agreement, that party had both the incentive and the capacity to restrain local actors even without a local countervailing presence by the other side.

Conclusion

Despite the delays and problems, the peace agreement brought remarkable changes to El Salvador. The FMLN participated in the general elec-

---

[54] See Stanley 1995 for analysis of the transition in policing.

tions of March 1994, making a respectable showing at the presidential and legislative levels; indeed, the FMLN became the second party in the national legislature in the 1996 elections. The military was restructured, with more than a hundred officers forced into retirement by the work of the Ad Hoc Commission, and reduced in size; the long-standing close relationship between landlords and local military and police authorities was ended, and a new civilian police force was deployed throughout the country. The programs for fomer combatants proved more effective as economic assistance in the short run than as foundations for adequate livelihoods in the long run, but combatants returned to civilian life, and political violence declined.[55]

Together, the emergence of an insurgent counter-elite to represent the long-excluded interests of peasants, workers, and other poor people; the sustained insurgency that made some accommodation necessary if the war was to be resolved; and the transformation of elite economic interests and representation made possible the negotiated resolution of the Salvadoran civil war as well as the democratization of the political regime. South Africa followed a substantially similar insurgent path to democracy, as the next three chapters demonstrate.

[55] del Castillo 1997: 362–3.

PART TWO

From Racial Oligarchy to Pluralist
Democracy in South Africa

5

Apartheid, Conservative Modernization,
and Mobilization

For most of the twentieth century, South Africa's political regime maintained racial boundaries through political exclusion, repression, and economic marginalization. These aspects of the nation's oligarchic rule reinforced labor-repressive institutions supporting a class structure nearly as segregated as its urban neighborhoods. Suffrage was restricted on the basis of race, and despite limited competition among white political parties, the National Party governed without interruption from 1948 until the first inclusive elections in 1994. Together, these policies maintained one of the world's most unequal distributions of income and the most enduring oligarchic political regime of this century. By the 1950s and 1960s, a wide range of labor-repressive institutions constituted the institutional environment for investment, profit making and sheltered living that defined the interests of the economic elite. The fact that few of these labor-repressive institutions would have been politically sustainable in a nonracial democratic polity provides a key to the antidemocratic recalcitrance of the South African elite for many years. The challenge of conservative modernization was to find a formula for satisfying the democratic aspiration of nonwhites without compromising the labor-repressive institutions and fiscal priorities of the apartheid economy that secured the economic and political interests of South African elites. The extension of at least minimal citizenship in distinct nonwhite polities became the main response to this challenge. Its failure paved the way for the emergence of the African National Congress (ANC) as an insurgent counter-elite.

All states regulate labor organization and working conditions to some degree. What was particularly labor repressive about apartheid South Africa was the combination of what Merle Lipton called the horizontal controls (such as pass laws and other controls on the mobility of labor) and the vertical controls (the color bar that reserved particular job cate-gories for whites) on labor.[1] In addition, the regulation of labor varied by racial category whereby white workers were integrated in a corporatist labor regime while African trade unions could not register as official unions, and strikes by African workers under contract were criminal acts.

Over the two decades preceding the first inclusive elections in 1994, workers, unemployed people, and other marginalized township dwellers sustained escalating levels of political mobilization under leadership com-mitted to significant – indeed, revolutionary by most measures – social and economic reform. During the 1980s, the broad insurgent move-ment encompassing the African National Congress, the Congress of South African Trade Unions (COSATU) and its predecessor union organizations, and township groups (under the umbrella organization the United Demo-cratic Front, UDF) began to encroach on elite interests, while the National Party failed repeatedly in its attempts to create a moderate black opposi-tion with which to negotiate some more limited "political dispensation."

The massive mobilizations of the mid-1980s constituted the ANC as an insurgent counter-elite with which negotiations would have to occur if unrest was to subside. The ongoing unrest eventually convinced economic elites of South Africa that the increasing costs of maintaining apartheid could not be sustained. Beginning in 1990 with the release of Nelson Mandela and the unbanning of the ANC, representatives of the ruling National Party and the ANC (as well as other party leaders) nego-tiated a transition to democracy.

South Africa, like El Salvador, is an instance of democratization from below in an oligarchic society. Yet South Africa is often treated as a unique case because of its peculiar combination of democracy and racial exclu-sion.[2] South Africa differs from El Salvador in other respects, too: the rel-atively long tradition of democratic governance among whites in South Africa, the role of the United States in financing the Salvadoran regime's military, the British colonial heritage in South Africa, and the sharp ethnic divisions among South African whites. Despite these striking differences, the transition to democracy in South Africa was similar in critical respects to that in El Salvador.

Like El Salvador, South Africa was an oligarchic society whose hori-

---

[1] Lipton 1985: 18–20.
[2] The principal exceptions are Trapido 1971; Greenberg 1980; Seidman 1994; and Marx 1998.

zontal cleavages were policed by a state with a labor-repressive history. As in El Salvador, subordinate actors forged democracy from below. South Africa's economic elites were threatened by labor and township unrest and by financial sanctions imposed in response to the repression of unrest; like El Salvador's economic elites, they eventually pressed state elites to compromise. South Africa's regime elites came to recognize the accumulating costs of refusing to negotiate. Together these factors brought once recalcitrant elites and the emergent counter-elite to the negotiating table. As in El Salvador, the negotiated transition to political democracy in South Africa was essentially a liberal revolution in which the insurgents won political inclusion (effective suffrage and political representation) and abandoned their challenge to the status quo distribution of private property rights.

In this chapter I trace the failure of conservative modernization and the emergence of the leadership of the ANC as an insurgent counter-elite, leaving to subsequent chapters the discussion of why economic and National Party elites came to recognize that compromise with the ANC was unavoidable. This chapter analyzes the labor-repressive foundations of South Africa's oligarchic society, the deepening institutionalization of residential and labor-market segregation under the National Party beginning in 1948, the success of apartheid policies in reshaping Afrikaner economic interests, and the evolution of opposition to apartheid. In the conclusion, I discuss why the ANC rather than some other organization emerged as the anti-apartheid movement's counter-elite, even though its leaders spent almost three decades in exile and prison.

The Foundations of an Oligarchic Society

The dominant and peculiar feature of South Africa before 1994 was of course apartheid ("separateness" in Afrikaans), both an ideology advocating racial separation and a set of policies ensuring white supremacy. As an ideology, apartheid was developed early in the twentieth century by Afrikaner intellectuals drawing on elements of Afrikaner culture, particularly its Calvinistic religious traditions, as well as Afrikaners' resentment of their inferior economic position and political status in relation to the British. Under the National Party from 1948 until 1994, the political regime developed a peculiarly legalistic, antiliberal, and antidemocratic form of rule. Apartheid ideology culminated in "grand apartheid," the notion that Africans should exercise their citizenship in the independent bantustans (homelands) and work in South Africa only as temporary migrants.

However, the origins of the racial order in South Africa long predate the coming to power of the National Party. Beginning in the colonial period, the challenge for farmers, and for mining interests as well after the discovery of diamonds in Kimberly and then gold on the Witwatersrand in the late nineteenth century, was how to secure a sufficiently large, cheap, and docile labor force. A low population-to-resource ratio contributed to the inadequate labor supply. Given the tenuous profitability of farms and the fixed price of gold (which meant that profits depended on the containment of costs, particularly labor costs), farmers and mine owners relied increasingly on labor-repressive institutions.[3] These institutions – various tied-labor arrangements on farms, the reliance on migrant labor, the congregation of African labor in controlled compounds on the mines – gave rise to the pass laws and the allocation of skill certificates by race that would control African labor mobility for decades.

Throughout the nineteenth century, tensions intensified between British colonial authorities and descendants of earlier settlers whose principal origins were Dutch (with some French Huguenot and German influence), who referred to themselves as "Afrikaners." Beginning in the late 1830s, many Afrikaners left the Cape Colony in the Great Trek and founded two Afrikaner republics in the interior highlands of southern Africa. After the gold and diamond discoveries in and near those republics, however, Britain sought to strengthen its rule over all of southern Africa, annexing the Kimberly diamond fields and defeating the armies of the Zulu kingdom in 1879. Conflict between the Afrikaners and the British culminated in the South African (or Boer) War of 1899–1902, the defeat of the Afrikaner forces, the annexation of the republics, and, after a period of negotiation, the founding of the Union of South Africa in 1910.

The compromises between English and Afrikaner interests in the immediate aftermath of the war became the constitutional buttresses of the new state, sacrificing the aspirations of those Africans who had fought on the side of the British.[4] The postwar expansion of the diamond and gold mines rapidly increased the demand for labor, a demand met not

---

[3] For further discussion of labor-repressive institutions in South Africa, see Trapido 1971; Greenberg 1980; and Lipton 1985.
[4] Thompson 1995: 144–6. See also Thompson 1960 and 1971; Marx 1998: 14–15.

through increased wages to attract labor from African households but from the organization and rapid expansion of the Witwatersrand Native Labour Association (WNLA) to recruit mine labor from rural households throughout southern Africa and from the forced displacement of African farmers from the land they worked.

To be sure, labor-repressive institutions and politically exclusive policies were propelled by white racism as well as economic interest: many Afrikaners and British believed in white supremacy as the natural and just superiority of the "civilized" over the "uncivilized" peoples and so generally perceived Africans as destined for manual labor. The emergence of South Africa's racially ordered oligarchy – its separation of black from white in the workplace and in living quarters (always excepting domestic labor) and the coincidence of class and race cleavages – was the outcome of the interplay of this history of labor repression, white racism, and compromise between the two white groups.

The consolidation of labor-repressive institutions by subsequent governments institutionalized a legal structure that separated whites from blacks along both race and class lines, as the state systematically curtailed opportunities for the economic advancement for blacks and systematically enhanced those for whites. Economic policy institutionalized protection for the key interests of the "alliance of gold and maize," based on the shared perception of the necessity of breaking down peasant autonomy in order to "free" labor for white farms and mines.[5] Legislation institutionalized the migrant labor system, gradually formalized the color bar that excluded black workers from certain jobs, and made striking by black workers under contract a criminal offense.[6] White mine workers fought against any attempt to relax the color bar or to increase the proportion of black to white workers from its agreed level of eight to one. For example, when the Chamber of Mines announced in 1921 that it would increase the proportion, white unions initiated a strike under the unforgettable slogan, "Workers of the World Unite and Fight for a White South Africa."[7] The strike became a general uprising on the Witwatersrand known as the Rand Rebellion, in which 230 to 250 people were killed.[8] In its aftermath, a corporatist labor regulatory regime for white but not black labor was institutionalized, entrenching the color bar for several decades. To maintain a

[5] Trapido 1971; Bundy 1979: 115.   [6] Wilson 1972; Yudelman 1983.
[7] Thompson 1995: 160.
[8] This paragraph and the next draw on Wilson 1972 and Yudelman 1983.

labor supply adequate for the expansion of the mines without increased wages, the state granted the WNLA exclusive rights to recruit labor from neighboring territories. This policy was highly successful: the wages of black labor remained constant in real terms from 1911 to at least 1969.[9] Thus, the state both supported higher wages for white labor than what would have obtained in the absence of such regulation and actively helped the mines keep African labor costs down through political controls.[10]

In order to limit competition for labor between the mines and farms, the government prohibited mines from recruiting labor over much of rural South Africa, facilitated its recruitment from other areas, and reinforced labor-repressive measures in agriculture. Despite the extension of credit to white farmers on favorable terms after the war, African farmers continued to produce grain at lower prices than white farmers. This independent production provided an alternative to wage labor, and its survival undergirded the bargaining power of agrarian labor and undermined labor supply.

The Natives Land Act of 1913 was in essence an act of collusion by agricultural employers to address this problem and generate an adequate supply of labor at low wages.[11] The act prohibited Africans from purchasing or renting land from non-Africans outside the "reserves": African landholdings were to be confined to the 7 percent (later increased to 13 percent) of land scattered through the eastern half of the country.[12] The measure sought to reduce independent African farmers to employees on white farms. According to Colin Bundy, the transformation of African "squatter-peasants of substance" to farm laborers was "one of the clearest illustrations of the role of extra-economic coercion in the accumulation and control of capital by white interests in the country."[13]

The act was not entirely effective: hundreds of "black spots" endured in white South Africa until the forced evictions of the 1960s. Various illegal tenancy arrangements continued on farms well into the 1950s.[14] On Afrikaner farms, brutality, coercion, and paternalism were combined along

---

[9] Wilson 1972.
[10] On extra-economic coercion in the South African context, see Legassick 1974 and Southall 1983: 23.
[11] Wilson 1971: 127–9.
[12] The analysis of the Land Act draws on Bundy 1979 and Thompson 1995: 163–5.
[13] Bundy 1979: 215.
[14] On twentieth-century agrarian social relations, see Morris 1976; Trapido 1978; Bundy 1979; and van Onselen 1996.

classical patron-client lines.[15] The isolation of such farms arguably intensified the peculiar combination of intimacy and violence of such relations,
augmenting the arbitrary authority of Afrikaner patriarchs. Because of
controls on the mobility of labor and the prohibition of property ownership by Africans, labor repression continued in agriculture despite the
gradual weakening of patron-client bonds.

Even as South Africa's economy developed, the market for black labor
remained highly regulated through the refinement of these institutions.
The 1911 Native Labour Regulation Act prohibited African mineworkers
from changing their place of residence or employment without obtaining
a pass that listed "a host of personal details."[16] The Native (Urban Areas)
Act of 1924 stipulated that workers could remain in urban areas only as
employed workers and authorized urban authorities to establish separate
African "locations" and to expel Africans without contracts or permits,
specifically "surplus females" according to the 1930 amendment to the
act.[17] This ongoing attempt at "influx control" failed to deter the rapid
urbanization of Africans – in 1946, some 24 percent were in towns – but
provided intimidating threats that deterred troublemakers.

In order to address the "poor white problem" during the Great Depression, the color bar was extended from the mines into industry and public
employment. The government's "civilised labour" policy sought to ensure
that white unskilled workers were not "denied entry into unskilled occupations by reason of the fact that the lower standard of living" of Africans
would not allow whites to live "in accordance with the standard generally
observed by civilised persons."[18] Fledgling manufacturing concerns were
granted protective tariffs if they maintained an appropriate ratio of
"uncivilised" to "civilised" labor. As in the mines, the wages of white
workers soon greatly exceeded those of black workers.[19]

From Segregation to Apartheid: South Africa under the National Party

The distinctive political economy of twentieth-century South Africa
was constructed through a combination of labor-repressive institutions in
mining and agriculture, the exclusion of Africans from the franchise, the
cleavage between English and Afrikaners, and the development of state

---

[15] van Onselen 1997.   [16] Southall 1983: 25.   [17] Thompson 1995: 170.
[18] Cited in Wilson 1972: 11.   [19] Thompson 1995: 159–69.

policies that promoted white, especially Afrikaner, interests. The key to the combination was the increasing capacity of the state to reconcile the sometimes conflicting priorities of the electorate and business interests and, in particular, to reduce competition for labor between the mines and farms while protecting white labor interests.[20] By the end of World War II, a set of uniquely illiberal institutions was in place that would underwrite high profit rates and robust investment until the 1970s.

This institutional structure was extended and given a more explicitly racist justification under National Party rule beginning in 1948.[21] Exclusion of nonwhites from the electoral franchise was deepened with the expulsion of mixed-race "coloured" voters in the Western Cape and policies of geographical separation were elaborated. While industrial relations between white workers and employers generally developed along the corporatist route laid out in the 1924 Industrial Conciliation Act, the mobility and residence of nonwhite workers remained subject to intensifying regulation. These policies enabled the National Party to achieve two principal objectives: to continue white supremacy and to support the economic advancement of Afrikaners. The party oversaw decades of increasing living standards for whites, faltering only in the last decade of its rule.[22]

The National Party defeated Jan Smuts's United Party in 1948 in an extremely close race in part owing to an electoral system that gave rural voters significantly more weight than urban voters.[23] A key issue in the elections was what policy should address the increasing African population on the Witwatersrand. The economy had continued to grow strongly through World War II as a result of purchases by the many Allied ships traveling new routes that avoided Axis control of the Mediterranean. As African employment and wages in industry increased, large numbers of Africans (including women) migrated from the reserves to the cities, founding vast shanty towns such as those that would become Johannesburg's South Western Townships, or "Soweto." A National Party com-

---

[20] For an elaboration of this argument in terms of the twin state imperatives of legitimation and accumulation, see Yudelman 1983.

[21] Wilson 1972: 12–13.

[22] This discussion of the National Party draws heavily on O'Meara 1983 and 1996. Unless otherwise noted, his writings are the source.

[23] In 1948, the party was the Herenigde National Party. It became the National Party when it absorbed the Afrikaner Party in 1951. After governing in alliance with the Labour Party beginning in 1924, the party split in 1934, with some members aligning with Smuts's United Party, which governed until their defeat by the alliance of the HNP and AP in 1948 (O'Meara 1996: 40).

mission headed by Paul Sauer prepared an "overall statement of the objectives of apartheid," a term previously more a slogan than a specific policy.[24] The 1948 report elaborated a "Christian principle of right and justice" that would protect the pure white race, allowing other separate national communities to develop in their own areas.[25] Thus apartheid was presented as an ethical policy of equal ethnic privilege.[26] Indeed, the Dutch Reformed Church argued that the moral foundation of apartheid lay in the promise of total segregation.[27] At the core of the program was the control of labor: while separation of the races was endorsed as a long-term goal, as an interim measure visiting labor would be strictly controlled and efficiently distributed and returned to their families in the reserves once their stay was over. The commission's program contrasted sharply with the United Party's Fagan Commission, which advocated that African urbanization be recognized as a permanent phenomenon. The Sauer report reflected the unresolved conflict between the pure apartheid of total segregation and the "practical" apartheid advocated by employers, which recognized that dependence on African labor would continue indefinitely.[28]

Foremost on the party's agenda was the economic advancement of Afrikaners through a rapid consolidation of the party's control of the state. Through a variety of parliamentary and constitutional strategies, the party replaced senior civil service bureaucrats (nearly all English) with Afrikaners (nearly all members of the secret Broederbond or "brotherhood" society), removed coloured voters from the common electoral role in the Western Cape, and increased their parliamentary seats by granting representation to whites of Namibia.[29] Although the party did not follow through on campaign promises to nationalize the banks and the mines, government policies directly advanced Afrikaner economic interests in several ways. The government developed state corporations that preferentially hired Afrikaner managers, professionals, and labor. Its policies favored Afrikaner businesses in contracts with the private sector, advancing private interests through the scope and prerogatives of the public sector. Afrikaners rapidly filled the civil service as public employment burgeoned. Labor policies protected white labor from competition from African labor through influx control policies and the color bar. Government policies subsidized white (generally Afrikaner) agriculture. Finally, the extension of highly subsidized credit to white manufacturers and

[24] O'Meara 1996: 64.   [25] de Villiers 1971: 406–7; Posel 1991: 58–61.
[26] O'Meara 1996: 65.   [27] Posel 1991: 62.   [28] Posel 1991: 58.   [29] O'Meara 1996: 60–2.

farmers benefited owners directly and also favored the adoption of capital-intensive technologies with high levels of labor productivity, thus attenuating the scarcity of labor and generating a limited number of high-wage jobs for white (for the most part Afrikaner) labor.

Both the implementation of apartheid ideology and the advancement of Afrikaner economic interests depended on maintaining an adequate supply of appropriately disciplined labor in urban and rural areas without compromising racial segregation. The National Party moved to consolidate its control of state agencies, including the Department of Native Affairs (DNA), the police, and the military. Particularly important for National Party objectives was the DNA. From 1950, under the strong leadership of Hendrik Verwoerd, the DNA became a "super-ministry," a source of extraordinary political and ideological power. Verwoerd identified four pillars on which "grand apartheid" would be built and developed legislation to implement each.[30] Residential segregation was extended through the Group Areas Act of 1950, laws passed in 1952 and 1955 restricting the right to be in urban areas, and the Prevention of Illegal Squatting Act of 1951, all of which gave the state additional instruments with which to control space. The 1951 Bantu Authorities Act imposed government-chosen and controlled "chiefs" on the reserve populations, deepening the state's administrative control of Africans. The various pass requirements were consolidated in a single pass without which urban Africans risked criminal prosecution. Together with the earlier 1950 Population Registration Act, which assigned every South African to one of four race categories (White, Coloured, Indian, and African), the legislation laid the foundation for an elaborate bureaucracy to oversee the control and distribution of labor. Under the 1959 Promotion of Bantu Self-Governing Act, African areas were to become independent and pursue their own, separate development. Verwoerd resisted the Tomlinson Commission's recommendation that millions be spent on developing the reserves in order to prevent increasing racial integration, but he continued to argue that the eventual economic independence of the bantustans was feasible.

To reconcile the dependence on African labor with its commitment to

---

[30] O'Meara 1996: 68–9. However, Deborah Posel (1991) argues that there was no grand initial plan that was gradually carried out by the DNA, contrary to Verwoerd's presentation of the evolution of these various policies. Rather, the development of the policies that institutionalized the department's "rough plan" was shaped by resistance to proposed policies on the part of workers, by employer organizations, and by struggles within the state.

limited residence for workers, the state introduced regulations that would force employers to hire from existing urban labor pools before turning to the bantustans or other countries.[31] Employers generally preferred migrant laborers who tended to accept less pay for more demanding work and who were thought to be less resistant to discipline than the increasingly proletarian culture of urban labor. Business organizations opposed the regulations, arguing that the DNA's insistence that employers preferentially hire already urbanized labor would tighten urban labor markets, force wages to rise, and encourage militancy.

"Detribalised" Africans, a category defined in Section 10 of the Urban Areas Act, were granted residential rights, while various regulations strictly limited further urbanization by requiring others to obtain permission from the authorities both in the reserve and in the urban area. The regulations sought to control the migration of African women in particular, which was seen as both contributing to the permanence of workers and undermining traditional African patriarchy in the reserves.[32] These policies required an elaborate bureaucracy to issue permits, prosecute pass-law violations, assign African workers, and regulate the tension between legal rights and economic incentives for Africans leaving impoverished reserves to seek work in urban areas.[33]

For several decades, the National Party succeeded in pursuing its principal agenda: white supremacy endured, albeit at the cost of a burgeoning state, and Afrikaner economic interests were advanced. National Party policies after 1948 were particularly successful in increasing Afrikaner ownership of the private sector and in promoting the upward mobility of Afrikaner workers. The percentage of the mining sector owned by Afrikaners rose from 1 percent in 1938–9 to 18 percent in 1975; over the same period, Afrikaner ownership of the manufacturing sector increased from 3 to 15 percent, of the financial sector from 5 to 25 percent, and of trade and commerce from 8 to 16 percent.[34] This advancement was not limited to the new Afrikaner capitalist class. The class positions of most Afrikaners were also significantly transformed: between 1946 and 1977, the proportion of Afrikaners engaged in agriculture fell from 30 percent to 8

---

[31] See Posel 1991.   [32] Posel 1991: 77.

[33] According to Ivan Evans, the development of a *civilian* administrative apparatus, the labor bureaus, to implement these regulations contributed to a routinization of coercion via the bureaucracy's "everyday work" that underpinned racial domination under apartheid (1997: 17).

[34] O'Meara 1996: 139.

percent, those in blue-collar jobs and manufacturing labor fell from 41 to 27 percent, and those in white-collar occupations increased from 29 to 65 percent.[35] Moreover, white wages rose steadily until the 1970s, a pattern to which I return later in the chapter.

The largest Afrikaner-controlled companies, Sanlam and Rembrandt, rapidly diversified their operations into manufacturing and even mining (in part thanks to a politically astute move on the part of Harry Oppenheimer, who facilitated the move of Sanlam into the gold sector).[36] They and other large businesses were well placed to take advantage of fire-sale prices when foreign capital left the country after the Sharpeville shooting in 1960, the Soweto uprising of 1976, and the widespread protests of the mid-1980s.

While successful in raising Afrikaner incomes, these various measures resulted in increasing stratification and differentiation among Afrikaners, making it difficult to identify the "common, collective interest of this highly differentiated Afrikaner *volk*."[37] They also heightened internal tension in the National Party as the interests of the new class of Afrikaner businessmen became more aligned with those of English businessmen than with their Afrikaner workers and their powerful unions.[38] Those tensions revolved around the two poles – *verligte* (roughly, reformist) and *verkrampte* (conservative) – of Afrikaner nationalism. The conservative camp sought to maintain the traditional values and alliances (including racial separation) despite the party's changing social base, whereas the reformists sought to transform Afrikaner politics to match evolving Afrikaner economic interests.

These tensions were exacerbated by other cracks in the apartheid edifice. While effectively controlling wages and sustaining high levels of profit and investment, apartheid failed to wean the economy from its dependence on African labor or to devise a formula that could wed that dependence with a set of political institutions acceptable to all and thereby provide political stability. In particular, the bureaucracy and regulations that proliferated to control the influx of labor failed to halt African urbanization: the urban African population increased from 2.3 million in 1951 to 3.4 million in 1960, while the fraction of the African population in cities increased from 27.2 to 31.8 percent.[39] As a result of this failure and the escalating African resistance to pass laws, the government initiated stiffer

---

[35] O'Meara 1996: 138. [36] O'Meara 1983: 250. [37] O'Meara 1996: 144.
[38] Lipton 1985: 306–12; O'Meara 1996: 197–203, 294–303. [39] Posel 1991: 141.

measures to stem the flow of labor, imposing labor quotas on geographical areas, diminishing Section 10 residential rights, accelerating the forced removal of "surplus population" from "white" areas to resettlement villages in the reserves, and embracing a "multinational" policy that would turn the reserves into self-governing homelands in which urban and reserve Africans alike would exercise their citizenship.[40] In the mid-1970s, the government eliminated dual citizenship, defining all Africans as citizens of one of the homelands, not of South Africa, and setting more stringent limits on leasehold tenure in South Africa.[41]

As the cumulative result of these policies, white and black South Africans, though economically interdependent, constituted two nations when it came to life opportunites: white South Africans lived in first-world communities while black South Africans endured third-world deprivation. Even among male employees living in urban areas, the white and African distributions of earnings in 1980 were virtually nonoverlapping, as seen in Figure 5.1. The figure understates group differences: many whites and virtually no Africans had substantial additional income from property, while many Africans and few whites eked out a precarious existence without formal sector employment (either as unemployed urban residents or in rural areas).

Deteriorating economic conditions contradicted the willfully blinkered perception that the reserves offered workers a "holiday at home" and a place to foster black democratic aspirations and citizenship. Though it decried the more abusive practices of apartheid, the liberal opposition shrank from embracing political inclusion as the counterpart of economic integration.[42] Sustained mobilization from below, not liberal conscience, would eventually drive home the reality that it was impossible to reconcile white dependence on black labor with the political exclusion of black workers.

The Emergence of an Insurgent Counter-Elite

The intensifying influx controls, residential segregation, and ethnic separation were contested by organizations and individuals on shop floors, in city and township streets, and in rural areas. The forms of collective action

---

[40] Posel 1991: 228–35.   [41] Karis and Gerhart 1997: 165.
[42] de Villiers 1971: 417–21. The one exception was the tiny Liberal Party, but it was dissolved in 1968 under the Prohibition of Political Interference Act, which prohibited racially mixed parties (Gerhart 1978: 255).

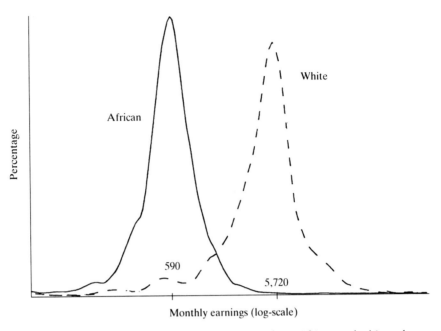

Figure 5.1 Distributions of earnings in South Africa: African and white urban men, 1980 (in 1993 rands). *Source*: Adapted from Moll (1995: 25).

evolved from petitions and meetings to civil disobedience and mass demonstrations, illegal and legal strikes and political "stayaways," military attacks and sabotage, and, finally, campaigns of "ungovernability" and insurrection. At the core of the unrest was the struggle against the institutions of labor repression (influx control, workplace and residential segregation, racially defined labor relations), the definition of citizenship and voting rights on racial grounds, and, more generally, the apartheid project of separate development. By the early 1960s, the ANC was the largest anti-apartheid organization, but its leadership was then imprisoned or forced into exile. For the next twenty years, the ANC only occasionally mounted successful activities within South Africa and thus might have dwindled into irrelevancy. Indeed, in the atmosphere of growing African nationalism within South Africa, the ANC, with its liberal underpinnings of non-racialism, might have been eclipsed by more racially defined groups such as the Pan-Africanist Congress (PAC).[43] Nonetheless, the state's efforts to

---

[43] For a contemporary statement of this expected outcome, see Gerhart (1978: 16).

prevent the ANC from organizing openly and the Umkonto we Sizwe (MK, "Spear of the Nation," the armed force of the ANC Alliance) from provoking insurrection within South Africa in the end proved futile: by the mid-1980s the leadership of the ANC emerged as the insurgent counter-elite necessary to any settlement.

The Radicalization of a Liberal Democratic Movement

From the ANC's founding in 1912 until the coming to power of the National Party in 1948, the Congress's central concern was the small African middle class. Initially the ANC sought to gain the attention of Union governments by petitions and appeals, occasionally petitioning the British government as well. As a liberal modernizing group, the ANC rejected particular ethnic identities. Members saw themselves as Africans and sought integration in South Africa as citizens on liberal democratic terms, which meant equal rights, equal representation, and representative democracy. As African legal status and property became circumscribed, the Congress began to address issues of concern to workers as well. The Communist Party of South Africa (later renamed the South African Communist Party, the SACP), founded in 1921, sought to work with and through the ANC after deciding in 1928 that a nationalist democratic revolution to found an "independent native republic" would be the necessary first phase of the transition from colonialism to socialism.[44] The relationship between the Communist Party and the ANC was a recurring source of tension, which led to the decline of the ANC in the 1930s after an SACP member was elected president of the ANC.[45]

With the rapid growth in the demand for labor in the 1940s, collective action by Africans seeking better living conditions took a new turn. From 1940 to 1943, a series of boycotts of bus services from the township of Alexandra to Johannesburg delayed for years the raising of fares. These activities culminated in a massive boycott in 1944 that had 20,000 workers walking to their jobs. Beginning in 1942, a wave of approximately sixty strikes against mines, commercial enterprises, and manufacturing establishments crested in the August 1946 strike over wages against the gold mines by 60,000 mineworkers. The strike was brutally repressed, leaving

[44] Lodge 1983: 8–9.
[45] In 1928, according to a party publication, some 1,600 of the party's 1,750 membership were natives (cited in Kuper 1971: 448).

more than a thousand wounded, a dozen dead, and the fledgling African Mineworkers Union decimated.[46]

Soon after taking power, the National Party ended the middle-class exemptions to the racial segregation laws by eliminating freehold property rights and subjecting black erstwhile property holders to the pass laws, and transferred nonwhite issues from Parliament to administrative agencies.[47] As a result, an emergent agenda within the ANC that appealed to workers as well as the African middle class gained strength as their interests converged.[48] The repression of strikes and the decline in legal status led the ANC to move toward militant political action and to recognize a new national leadership, which included Nelson Mandela, Oliver Tambo, and Walter Sisulu. This new leadership had founded the ANC Youth League in 1944 and sought to develop African nationalism as a means of overcoming the psychology of racial oppression.

An ongoing issue was the role of whites in the ANC (including some SACP members), organized as the allied Congress of Democrats. A related issue was the role of communists. The Suppression of Communism Act of 1950 defined "statutory communism" as a criminal offense "constituted by doctrines or schemes for bringing about political, industrial, social, or economic changes through disorder or unlawful acts or omissions."[49] The state's repression of communists and non-communists alike under the act had an unintended consequence: it promoted solidarity across races within the ANC, bolstering the position of those advocating a nonracial identity for the ANC. Many of the members of the Youth League who initially supported the Africanist agenda later came to support the ANC's nonracialism, in part because of their experience with whites in the ANC.[50] According to Nelson Mandela in a statement at his trial, "For many decades the Communist Party was the only political group in South Africa who were prepared to eat with us, talk with us, live with and work with us."[51] Nonetheless, the role of whites remained a controversial issue.

The Youth League's Programme of Action, subsequently adopted by the ANC, rejected segregation, apartheid, and trusteeship and called for direct representation and an end to "differential institutions."[52] In order to achieve these goals, the Youth League laid out an agenda of boycotts, work stoppages, noncooperation, and union action to force the National

---

[46] Lodge 1983: 19–20.   [47] Gerhart 1978: 110.
[48] Kuper 1971: 459–60.   [49] Kuper 1971: 460.
[50] Gerhart 1978: 112.   [51] Mandela 1964: 789.   [52] ANC 1949: 337–8.

Party toward reform. The subsequent 1952 Defiance Campaign, a non-violent campaign of civil disobedience against segregation laws, called for full participation regardless of race. Rejecting a permanent distinction between races, the ANC, in announcing the campaign, stated that the issue was not biological difference but citizen rights and systematic exploitation.[53] The campaign peaked in September with some 2,500 arrests in twenty-four locations. The government, however, continued to enforce racial segregation with forced removals of entire communities from freehold property to townships, as in Sophiatown in 1955. There, it deployed massive force (80 trucks and some 2,000 armed police) and destroyed the town of some 54,000 people.[54]

Subsequent legal measures made civil disobedience difficult. Hence a group of opposition organizations – the ANC, the South African Indian Congress, the Committee of Democrats, the South African Coloured Peoples Organization, and the South African Congress of Trade Unions (SACTU) – organized widespread consultations with communities that culminated in the endorsement of the Freedom Charter by 3,000 delegates in 1955. The charter called for universal suffrage, equality before the law, the right to work, an end to migrant labor, a national minimum wage, the end of both compound housings and payment in wine to vineyard workers, the right to join unions in all sectors, and the nationalization of banks, mines, and land as part of a mixed capitalist economy (seen as necessary measures to undergird democracy and nonracialism). Despite the calls for nationalization, the charter outlined a mainly liberal democratic agenda rather than a socialist one; it would remain the central document for the nonracial opposition.[55]

In the aftermath of the Freedom Charter campaign, the National Party increased its harassment of the charterist groups. Forty-two leaders were banned from participation in public meetings in 1955, and the government prosecuted 156 leaders in a trial that dragged on for years, absorbing precious resources, until the defendants were found not guilty of treason in March 1961.[56]

---

[53] ANC 1952: 481. [54] Lodge 1983: 91–5.

[55] Mandela was later to argue as part of his trial defense that the nationalization measures were crucial if racial domination was not to be perpetuated, but that the ANC never condemned capitalist society. He reminded the judge that the National Party had originally argued that it would nationalize the gold mines upon coming to power (Mandela 1964: 787).

[56] Lodge 1983: 76.

At the same time, tensions mounted within the ANC because its Africanists resented the role of the Committee of Democrats in writing the charter. Africanists argued that collaboration with whites would destroy the nation-building agenda of the 1949 Youth League's Programme of Action. White leftists, they claimed, could never free themselves from the privileges they enjoyed, and their participation was at best an unconscious attempt to control the nationalist movement.[57] Moreover, the Africanists held, reliance on white leadership and initiative perpetuated dependency and deference and suppressed the "natural predisposition" to ethnic nationalism that could lead to a spontaneous uprising given the right (ethnic) leadership.[58] Africanists looked to the success of anti-colonial movements in other African countries and blamed the ANC's nonracialism for its failure to achieve similar success.[59] The debate led to a split within the ANC as the Africanists left to found the PAC.

The split led to competition for leadership of the campaigns against pass laws. Opposition to the pass laws intensified in the late 1950s when the state extended the pass laws to women. This move was fiercely contested as women feared the limits on their mobility, the threat of removal to reserves, and their increased visibility and vulnerability to state officials. Sometimes under the leadership of the Federation of South African Women and sometimes under the leadership of local groups, women marched on government offices (some 20,000 marched to present a petition to the prime minister in 1956), refused to take out the required document, and some later burned passes that had been taken out.[60] Pass law grievances also precipitated a series of rural revolts in the late 1950s.

The PAC planned to launch its anti-pass campaign on March 21, 1960 (just before the ANC was to start its protest), during which participating Africans were to go to police stations without their passes for arrest. PAC leaders hoped the mass disobedience campaign would overwhelm the state, paralyze the economy, and lead to a spontaneous uprising.[61] The turnout in Durban, Port Elizabeth, East London, and Johannesburg was small,

---

[57] Gerhart 1978: 154–7. [58] Lodge 1983: 84. [59] Gerhart 1978: 209–10.
[60] Lodge 1983: 144–50. There was an additional grievance that women protested. In resistance to raids against illegal brewing on both commercial and household scales – a valued source of income for many women – women attacked beer halls in Cato Manor, Durban, and across rural areas of Natal. Although the government was forced to delay enforcement of the laws, eventually the women were defeated: from 1963, women were required to carry the pass.
[61] Lodge 1983: 86.

with a few hundred protestors arriving at police stations at various times.[62] However, at Sharpeville, a township near Vereeniging, some 5,000 protestors arrived at the local police station. Policemen fired into the crowd, killing 69 and wounding 180. News of the killing spread, leading to widespread demonstrations, riots, and further violence: by April 9, according to official sources, 83 nonwhite civilians had been killed and 365 injured (including the Sharpeville casualties).[63]

The unrest lasted for almost a year in Mpondo (also called Pondoland) in the Transkei. In an effort to resist "Bantu authorities" and a series of government agricultural rationalization measures, peasant groups attacked constables and tribal councillors and burned down the residences of chiefs and headmen. Before the revolt was suppressed in February 1961, there were several deaths and more than 5,000 arrests.[64] Despite this and other instances of rural unrest, the ANC never developed a strong rural organization because it valued its cordial relationship with traditional tribal authorities and because many rural areas were tightly controlled by white farmers.

In response to the demonstrations and riots that followed the Sharpeville shooting, the government declared a state of emergency and detained many leaders of opposition organizations. The government also announced that beginning December 1, the carrying of passes would be compulsory at all times. Parliament soon passed the Unlawful Organizations Act, under which the ANC and PAC were both banned. After amendments requiring yearly reports to Parliament for renewal of the bans, the United Party supported the act. Sixty-four banning orders were issued in 1961.[65] The protest against the proclamation of the Republic in May 1961 was met with a massive show of strength by the government, with approximately 10,000 arrests; many were detained for twelve days without charges, a practice recently legalized. In 1962, the government was given expanded banning powers: bans on organizations could exceed the previous twelve-month limit, there was no need for investigations, and the minister could ban other organizations without further authorization from Parliament.[66]

In addition to increasing the legal repressive powers of the state, the government intensified the implementation of grand apartheid by seeking

---

[62] SAIRR 1959–60: 68.   [63] Gerhart 1978: 236.
[64] SAIRR 1959–60: 39–47; Lodge 1983: 279–83.
[65] SAIRR 1963: 23.   [66] SAIRR 1963: 31–5.

to bolster the authority of traditional African rulers. In the aftermath of the rural revolt in Pondoland, to refuse to obey "lawful orders" of a chief or headman, or "to treat them with disrespect" was declared subversive.[67] Throughout the 1960s, forced removals accelerated despite increasing publicity about the lack of infrastructure and employment in the "resettlement" villages in the reserves. The government also strengthened its commitment to separate development, announcing incentives for development of industry in "border areas" within thirty miles of reserves.

The anti-pass campaign was the ANC's last attempt at solely nonviolent civil disobedience to pressure the government for reform. In response to the banning, the ANC and the SACP endorsed armed struggle against the state and founded Umkonto we Sizwe (MK). Given the apparent impotence of the politics of persuasion and the growing support for violence, there was little internal debate.[68] The turn to violence was a fundamental shift for the ANC: to that point, "the ANC's typical response to moments of crisis was to call for days of prayer."[69] From the beginning, the MK was open to all races, with a command structure headed by Mandela that drew on leadership of both the SACP and the ANC. The force embarked on a campaign of sabotage, carrying out some 200 attacks in eighteen months, most of a minor nature and with no substantial effect. In retaliation, the entire high command was arrested. After the subsequent Rivonia trial of 1964, both organizations were decimated as their top leaders, including Mandela, were sent to Robben Island for long sentences.[70] ANC and SACP leaders who escaped arrest fled the country, establishing bases of operations in London, Lusaka, and eventually Mozambique.

In prison and in exile, the ANC, SACP, and PAC slowly began building organizational structures to address their new circumstances.[71] The exile organizations found it extremely difficult to infiltrate armed groups into South Africa from neighboring countries (most still under colonial rule) or to develop adequately secure networks within the country. Though the MK continued to carry out sporadic sabotage actions, the organizations were subject to continuing infiltration and the detention of militants. Competition between the ANC and the PAC for resources and alliances

---

[67] SAIRR 1963: 44. [68] Lodge 1983: 223. [69] Lodge 1983: 198.

[70] The PAC also had a short-lived armed campaign, the Poqo movement of the early 1960s concentrated in the Western Cape and Pondoland (Eastern Cape) with some activity elsewhere.

[71] This and the following paragraph draw heavily on Ellis and Sechaba 1992 and Lodge 1983.

with African states undermined any thoughts of a "united front" in exile. The ANC benefited from its alliance with the SACP, as Soviet-aligned countries provided training and some financial support, while the PAC had to rely on the lesser resources of China. Some communication with Robben Island was occasionally possible, but it was insufficient for tactical command.

Tensions within the ANC concerning the role of the SACP continued, and a group of Africanists opposed to the close relationship withdrew from the ANC. After the Morogoro Conference in 1969, people of all races could join the ANC in exile (but not within South Africa) as individuals, but only Africans (meaning nonwhites) could serve on the national executive council. However, the Revolutionary Council formed to implement the executive council's decisions included several non-Africans, notably the SACP's Joe Slovo, who became the lead strategist for the MK. Council membership was opened up to all of the ANC in 1985, and several non-Africans were elected. After the elections, twenty-two of the thirty members of the council were members of the SACP (most of them African).[72]

A second internal issue concerned conditions in MK training camps, which sparked debate about the allowable degree of internal dissent.[73] After ANC security staff uncovered evidence that some members were agents of the South African government, investigations (which in some cases included mistreatment and torture) ensued, and conditions in the camps worsened. A mutiny by guerrillas in the Angola camps in 1984 was short-lived but led to some organizational reforms.

The ANC and the PAC remained isolated and militarily ineffective aside from the occasional "armed propaganda" that served to remind Africans and whites alike that the exiled organizations were still in existence. After the independence of Angola and Mozambique, training and infiltration sites opened up much closer to South Africa and the ANC was able to carry out a series of high-profile attacks against facilities for the conversion of coal to oil in 1980, against the headquarters of the Defense Forces in 1981, and against Air Force headquarters in 1983. However, the ANC was not able to turn this opportunity to significant advantage as the South African state unleashed successive campaigns of economic pressure

---

[72] Lodge 1983; Ellis and Sechaba 1992: 150–1.
[73] For details, see Ellis and Sechaba 1992 and the report of the Truth and Reconciliation Commission.

on neighboring countries, including financial, logistical, and armed support for armed groups such as the National Union for the Total Independence of Angola (UNITA) and the National Resistance of Mozambique (RENAMO) and direct action against exiled militants within Angola, Lesotho, Mozambique, and Swaziland. Although the sabotage campaigns of the ANC and the MK raised the costs of defense, they never posed a real threat to the security of the state.

Labor Militance and the Challenge to White Economic Interests

Labor militance, not guerrilla actions, would eventually constitute the ANC as an insurgent counter-elite. A few isolated strikes occurred in the late 1960s, but the mobilization of the early 1960s was suppressed and the forced quiescence endured until 1973. In that year, however, factory workers carried out a series of strikes in the greater Durban area. The wave of strikes broke a decades-long pattern of enforced labor calm: the proportion of striking workers as a fraction of total nonagricultural employment increased ten-fold from 0.2 percent in 1960 to 2.3 percent in 1973 (Figure 5.2). The great majority of striking workers were black.[74] Note that the data underlying the series *exclude political stayaways*, which are days during which participating workers do not go to their workplace and some attend marches, funerals of activists, and other protest activities.

The 1973 strike wave appeared to be the cascading consequence of the initial strike as workers in additional factories imitated neighboring ones. By February 7, some 30,000 workers were on strike. Informal ties among Zulu workers may have contributed to the spread of the strikes, as well as the invulnerability of Durban workers to being "endorsed out" to some bantustan: most already lived in nearby KwaZulu.[75] Moreover, initially the Zulu traditional authorities supported the strikers. Probably most salient was the fact that the strikes were not met with immediate police action.[76] Workers made repression and co-optation difficult by refusing to nominate leaders or negotiating teams. Many workers won wage gains, and with

---

[74] The strike data are from various issues of Central Statistical Services, *South African Statistics*. After 1973, except for a few years, the percentage of strikers that were black exceeded 99 percent (calculated from Central Statistical Services 1994: Table 7.64). The exceptions were 1972 (95 percent), 1976 (96 percent), 1977 (98 percent), and 1979 (75 percent).
[75] Friedman 1987: 47–8.   [76] Lewis 1997: 203.

Figure 5.2 Strikers as a fraction of workers in South Africa, 1960–1993

a new sense of efficacy, many flocked to join benefit committees, and unions as well.[77]

However, the next year the government and employers clamped down on a new attempt to mobilize labor in Durban: activists were banned and workers fired. In the aftermath of this defeat, union activists developed three distinct models of union building. The first focused on gaining strength in individual factories by focusing on felt grievances, electing shop stewards, and maintaining secrecy until union strength was sufficient to confront employers.[78] This group concentrated on industries in which skilled and semiskilled workers predominated, principally in the Transvaal and Durban. In 1979, various unions endorsing this model formed the Federation of South African Trade Unions (FOSATU). The second group developed sector-wide union organizations that relied on community boycotts as well as factory organization to protect striking unskilled workers from dismissal. This group, working for the most part with the Western Province General Workers Union (WPGWU), won victories in food processing and among dockworkers. A third group formed the Council of Unions of South Africa (CUSA) with an emphasis on black leadership, rejecting FOSATU's nonracialism. There were also "parallel unions" orga-

---

[77] Friedman 1987: 87; Seidman 1994: 73. [78] Friedman 1987: 93, 98–9.

nized as branches of white unions, but they remained firmly under the control of white labor.

African universities also became a hotbed of opposition. Disillusioned with the failure of the anti-apartheid campaigns of the 1950s and 1960s, a group of intellectuals and clergy began developing what would become the Black Consciousness Movement (BCM). Like the Africanists of the 1950s, the group concentrated on eliminating internalized oppression in the self-images of racially subordinated peoples, drawing inspiration from Franz Fanon, Black Power, and Black Theology. A key leader was Steve Biko, a medical student at the University of Natal. Tired of the liberal politics of national student organizations, the group founded the South African Students Organization (SASO) in 1969. To defy the state's divisive use of racial categories, the group used "black" to mean all nonwhites, not just Africans. They believed changing ideology was the key to resisting hegemony, not mass action.[79] The group resisted collaborating with liberal whites: Biko argued that a true white liberal would work within white society to change it and spurned the "tea parties" with white liberals that, he said, served only to relieve white guilt.[80] Despite these similarities with the PAC, the BCM consistently represented all nonwhite South Africans, not just Africans, and was more cognizant of the divisions within black society.[81] SASO kept its distance from the ANC and PAC alike, both of which Biko regarded as "inconsequential."[82]

As the movement spread through colleges and universities, it sought to expand its reach into black society as well, organizing the Black Peoples Convention of 1972. However, the group remained more focused on education than organization, disseminating papers and pamphlets through branches that had little cohesion. Students were one group that the organization reached effectively.[83] Some thirty college students were dismissed from universities as a result of their BCM activism and took up teaching positions in township schools, where they spread the group's message in their classes. The movement also ran "formation schools," weekend-long training sessions, for high school students. One reason for the movement's appeal was the ready assimilation of its rhetoric as "angry self-assertion" by frustrated high school students.[84]

In late February 1973, Biko was banned from meeting with more than one other person at a time and restricted to his home magisterial district,

---

[79] Marx 1992: 13. [80] Gerhart 1978: 264. [81] Lodge 1983: 323.
[82] Karis and Gerhart 1997: 111. [83] Karis and Gerhart 1997: 112. [84] Marx 1992: 65.

as were a dozen others. Then in mid-1973, BCM activists organized the largest demonstration since Sharpeville to protest policies at the University of the Western Cape. In light of the banning of leaders, the movement's members began asking whether the organization should endorse armed struggle, what relationship it would have with the exiled organizations, what difference the independence of Angola and Mozambique would make, and what status the bantustan leaders should have.[85] Biko himself began exploring the possibility of unifying the BCM, the ANC, and the PAC. These efforts failed, most likely because all three were competing for overall leadership and for the new recruits mobilized by the BCM.[86]

In May 1976, students attending a meeting of a Soweto-based BCM organization decided to join other student groups around the country to protest the imminent imposition of Afrikaans as the language of instruction for social studies and mathematics. During the ensuing protest, on June 16, 1976, police in Soweto shot into a crowd of some 15,000 marching students, killing two and wounding several. Widespread unrest followed, as students abandoned schools to march on government offices, saboteurs burned schools, and urban youth rioted. The disorder eventually spread to more than a hundred urban areas, lasting almost a year and leaving 575 dead in its wake.[87] At the height of the protest, students organized worker stayaways: a combination of sympathy and coercion led to more than 50 percent worker absenteeism.[88] Migrant workers, isolated in hostels and loyal to the bantustan authorities denounced by the students, attacked students in some areas, contributing to the violence.

The Soweto uprising and its brutal repression reshaped South African politics. Thousands of township youth – perhaps as many as 5,000 – fled South Africa to join the ANC in exile.[89] The ANC renewed its emphasis on political mobilization while also intensifying military activity, including the attacks on oil facilities and military bases described earlier. Consternation within the BCM deepened as some members fled and others debated doing so. Given the evident limitation of unarmed mass insurrection and the government's increasing efforts to create a black middle class, BCM intellectuals now argued that class and class analysis were important perspectives, thereby narrowing the gap between the BCM, the

[85] Karis and Gerhart 1997: 128–30.   [86] Karis and Gerhart 1997: 149–50.
[87] Karis and Gerhart 1997: 168.   [88] Lodge 1983: 329.   [89] Karis and Gerhart 1997: 281.

ANC, and the SACP.[90] Biko's efforts to unify the opposition were cut short in 1977 by his arrest and subsequent death in detention – he was the forty-second political detainee to die since habeas corpus was suspended in 1963[91] – and the subsequent banning of a number of BCM organizations, including SASO. Internal differences and the banning split the BCM, with one group emerging as the Azanian People's Organization (AZAPO), which was dedicated to mobilizing on the basis of both class and race.

The state responded to the Soweto uprising with reform as well as repression. First, the government restructured the framework of township governance, replacing the Urban Bantu Councils, a particular target during the unrest, with Community Councils. However, the new councils were considered no more legitimate than the old ones – the elections held in Soweto in 1978 had a turnout of 6 percent[92] – partly because the councils were to be responsible for collecting rents and for allocating licenses and houses. A grassroots group of Soweto notables that attempted to negotiate with the government was detained.

Second, the government appointed the Riekert Commission to review urban policy more generally. The commission recommended steps to create a permanent urban population while excluding illegal migrants by tightening influx control. This limited urban population would be stable, enjoying ninety-nine-year leases on property. Rents and transportation costs would be increased so that the urban unemployed would be forced to take up the less attractive jobs that the illegal migrants had been doing.[93] For the first time, employers would face sanctions for employing illegal labor. These measures were not successful: by 1981, only 2,000 leasehold titles had been registered.[94]

Third, the government appointed the Wiehahn Commission to review labor policy. The intent was to end the emerging pattern of bargaining between employers and unregistered unions and to gain control over the new unions by incorporating them into the official labor relations system. The commission proposed that black workers become employees subject to labor legislation: job reservation would end and unions could be registered and therefore could bargain collectively – under certain conditions. The recommended conditions would severely limit the new unions, however, for they would have to work with the existing white unions through caucuses, the termination of crucial job reservations would

---

[90] Karis and Gerhart 1997: 319–20.   [91] Karis and Gerhart 1997: 315.
[92] Karis and Gerhart 1997: 234–5.   [93] Lodge 1983: 337.   [94] Lipton 1985: 70.

depend on negotiations between white unions and employers, racially mixed unions would be prohibited, migrant and commuter workers would be excluded from unions, and the state would retain the power to deny registration to some unions.[95] As a result, unions refused to register, and the government agreed to a compromise: migrants (except those from foreign countries) and commuters would be allowed to join.

Union response to the implementation of the Wiehahn Commission's proposals varied. Some unionists wondered whether the advantages of registration would exceed the disadvantages embodied in the new controls, and more generally whether cooperation with the apartheid state was appropriate. FOSATU unions decided to register on the condition that nonracial unions be allowed, as they subsequently were. WPGWU and similar unions did not, arguing that to do so would jeopardize their internal democracy and that their refusal would deny ideological legitimacy to an attempt to control the political autonomy of unions.[96]

The new labor relations arrangements quickly proved an unmanageable combination of tolerance for unionization and the failure of institutionalized bargaining. There soon emerged a parallel and unauthorized system of bargaining between employers and nonregistered unions, which was what the measures were intended to prevent.[97] Significantly, the chairman of the largest private employer, Barlow Rand, announced that it would bargain with and even recognize unregistered unions. In view of the growing collaboration between unions and employees, the government made additional compromises, with the result that the unions increasingly bargained within the new framework.

The new unions grew rapidly. Between 1979 and 1983, the membership of FOSATU increased from 30,100 to 106,460 and that of GWU from 4,500 to 12,000.[98] Other union groupings grew as well, including the Africanist CUSA, whose membership increased from 32,050 to 140,592. In 1982, GWU joined FOSATU. After merger discussions between FOSATU and CUSA failed, the National Union of Mineworkers left the latter to join the former, depriving CUSA of its largest affiliate. In November 1985, FOSATU and other unions founded the Congress of South African Trade Unions.

The explosive growth in union membership was paralleled by the movement's increasing militancy. Far from creating an acquiescent labor force,

---

[95] Friedman 1987: 152–63.   [96] Lewis 1997: 214.
[97] Friedman 1987: 225–6.   [98] Maree 1987: 8.

the inclusion of the new unions led to further unrest and disruption. At the peak of union mobilization in 1987, more than 11 percent of non-agricultural workers struck, a figure comparable to the 14–15 percent of workers who participated in the great 1926 general strike in the United Kingdom and the 10 percent who participated in the largest U.S. strike wave, which occurred at the close of World War II when workers attempted to regain ground lost because of the austerity of the war.

A broad movement with ties to community organizations, trade unions pressed for political reforms that far exceeded the usual union mandate. A measure of the political rather than purely economic objectives of the trade unions is the fact that strike activity in South Africa during these years did not bear the usual relationship to the business cycle, namely, rising during expansions when union bargaining power is greatest and declining during recessions.

The unions had initially kept their distance from community organizations (called "civics"), judging the organizations incompatible with their union traditions of shop-floor control and accountability and fearing the effects on the union organizations should the state move to repress the civics.[99] Through the early 1980s, the pressure on FOSATU to take up political issues increased as the civics became more militant and organized actions of larger scope.[100] By the early 1980s, many unionists were themselves heavily involved in community politics and some were cooperating with the underground ANC.[101] After the ratification of the 1983 Constitution, FOSATU joined the call for a boycott of the elections.[102]

The civics were diverse combinations of church groups, elements of the BCM that had not joined AZAPO, and student and youth organizations. The government efforts at reform (particularly after those recommended by the Riekert and Wiehahn Commissions) had expanded the political space for limited protest around concrete local grievances. The formation of a national organization was accelerated by the government's proposal to create a tricameral regime, in which whites, coloureds, and Indians would each have separate parliaments to govern their own affairs, with a white-controlled superstructure for general affairs. Urban blacks would have local representation through black local authorities and would exercise political rights in independent states of the former homelands. In response, various organizations founded the United Democratic Front on

---

[99] Marx 1992: 138.   [100] Marx 1992: 196.   [101] Lewis 1997: 217.   [102] Lewis 1997: 198.

August 20, 1983. The UDF constituent organizations shared the nonracial philosophy and strategic emphasis of the Freedom Charter, and, implicitly, those of the ANC.[103] Generously funded from abroad, by 1987 the UDF had eighty full-time staff and dispensed hundreds of millions of rand.[104]

The growing organizational strength of the civics and the trade unions ensured that the new constitution would be followed by widespread rebellion. The reaffirmation of the exclusion of Africans from power and the continued promulgation of new versions of the separate development formula angered many urban black residents. Mobilization against the new constitution began in the Vaal Triangle in mid-1984 with rent strikes and local stayaways. The unrest soon spread to the Transvaal: with the support of the unions, a two-day stayaway mobilized 600,000 workers and 400,000 students. The government responded by sending the army into the townships.[105] As mobilization spread still further, in January 1985, the ANC called for supporters to make the townships "ungovernable."[106] The ANC fanned the flames of unrest with guerrilla attacks, which increased from 40 in 1984 to 136 in 1985 and 228 in 1986.[107] When Anglo American fired 14,000 striking workers from its Vaal Reef mine, the MK attacked the firm's Johannesburg offices.[108]

In July 1985, the government proclaimed a state of emergency covering 155 townships.[109] Activists, including fifty of the eighty members of the UDF's executive council, were detained, some were tortured, and some simply "disappeared."[110] The Defense Forces attacked ANC headquarters in Maseru and blockaded Lesotho, provoking a coup against its sympathetic president.[111] The uprising continued, and the government widened the state of emergency in July 1986. In response to the mobilization and growing repression, COSATU met with the ANC in March 1986 and formally adopted the Freedom Charter in July 1987.[112] In 1988, the government tried to curb union militancy with a set of amendments to the Labour Relations Act, unleashing a campaign for the withdrawal of the amendments that would ultimately lead to an unprecedented agreement between business and labor to jointly press the government for reform.

---

[103] Marx 1992: 113.   [104] Marx 1992: 141–2.   [105] Saul 1986: 216.
[106] O'Meara 1996: 325.   [107] Marx 1992: 157.   [108] Saul 1986: 231.
[109] Saul 1986: 231.   [110] Coleman and Webster 1986.
[111] Ellis and Sechaba 1992: 166.   [112] Marx 1992: 203–5.

COSATU march opposing changes in Labour Relations Act, 1989. Photograph by William Matlala.

Conclusion

Although conservative modernization under the National Party sought to sustain limited suffrage in racially segregated areas, high levels of profit and investment, and high wage rates for white labor, such policies could not resolve the fundamental tension arising from the dependence of white employers on African workers who resided and worked in South Africa but were officially citizens of the outlying proto-states. Many black people responded to elite recalcitrance with increasing resistance in both workplace and residence.

The rising labor militancy and township unrest had two long-range effects. First, the leadership of the ANC emerged from this period as the dominant opposition organization. Indeed, the government's recurrent inability to develop a legitimate moderate black leadership with whom to negotiate both reflected and reinforced the ANC's position. By the mid-1980s, both principal opposition protagonists, the UDF and COSATU, had endorsed the ANC, and no other organization could seriously contest its leadership. That need not have been the case: throughout most of the period, the ANC was organizationally weak and challenged by Africanist rhetoric with wide popular appeal. Despite the presence of a few underground ANC and SACP members in the leadership of the UDF and COSATU, by most accounts the UDF and COSATU operated autonomously. A second consequence of the rising militancy of the trade unions was that business organizations increasingly saw negotiation with labor rather than repression as their best response to mobilization, as discussed in Chapter 6.

Several factors contributed to the movements' success in constituting the jailed and exiled leadership of the ANC as its counter-elite. The long-standing legitimacy of the ANC as an opposition organization appears to have been part of the "social memory" of opposition. The personal prestige of Nelson Mandela's leadership was unmatched by any other opposition figure. Key to this prestige was Mandela's integrity and his refusal to acquiesce: he declined to renounce violence unconditionally in exchange for his freedom. In a statement read to a rally in Soweto, he explained, "I am in prison as the representative of the people and of your organization, the African National Congress, which was banned. What freedom am I being offered while the organization of the people remains banned?"[113] A second reason was that only the ANC was positioned to absorb the newly militant youth in the aftermath of the Soweto uprising; the PAC was in organizational shambles and did not have the ANC's resources in exile. The ANC's policy of "armed propaganda" during the key formative period of the early 1980s was also probably important. Although it is unclear how many leaders of the UDF and COSATU were members of the ANC or SACP during the early and mid-1980s, the disclosure by some of their affiliations in the early 1990s suggests that at least some may have been so affiliated earlier as well. Finally, an unintended consequence of apartheid's racialism was the forging of an opposition identity that rejected racialism, an identity emphasizing claims to citizenship that was deepened by the experience of insurgency.[114] The universalism of liberal democracy proved a more effective rhetorical weapon against white supremacy than the no less racially defined assertion of African nationalism.

Underpinning the success of the ANC is the paradoxical logic of

---

[113] Cited in Sparks 1995: 50.
[114] On the origins of the ANC and associated organizations' nonracialism, see Price 1991; Seidman 1994; Marx 1998.

apartheid itself. The white supremacist rhetoric of the National Party destroyed the legitimacy of any black leaders collaborating with the government's separate development, tricameral, and bantustan projects, thus giving the ANC few competitors on its right (except for the Inkatha Freedom Party, but its appeal was limited by its Zulu ethnicism). A purely racial populist opposition failed to develop, as the waning of PAC fortunes indicates. Perhaps surprisingly, the ANC's nonracialism contributed to its success, for without it, important links would have been jeopardized: those to the SACP, to international financial and political support, and, most important, to the nonracial COSATU unions.

Moreover, the structure of apartheid itself accounts for much of the power of unions during this period. The highly concentrated structure of the economy through the vertical integration of firms, the high value added per worker as a result of high capital intensity, and the resulting inelastic demand for labor combined to reinforce the bargaining power of trade unions and thus rendered South African firms vulnerable to union pressure. In the end, it would be the ANC's ties to the organizations of those whom the business elite could not do without – namely, the unions – that would convince business – and eventually the governing party as well – that the ANC had to be part of a negotiated solution.

6

The Challenge to Economic Elite Interests

[There was] no legitimate political avenue for political unrest so it had to be channeled into the only vehicle that's available. And the only vehicle that you cannot take away effectively is labor. You may damn the organization, but you can't damn the workers.

– Barlow Rand executive, 1997

South Africa's economy grew strongly through the 1960s and political unrest subsided. Remarkably, the Sharpeville shooting had ushered in a golden age of white supremacy in South Africa: it would be the last. In September 1985, after more than a decade of increasing mobilization by workers and township residents, a group of executives of the largest firms, including Gavin Relly of the Anglo American Corporation, flew to Lusaka for a clandestine meeting with the ANC's executive committee to discuss economics and government after apartheid, thereby inciting the wrath of State President P. W. Botha.[1] This was the first in a series of extraordinary initiatives reflecting the profound concern among leading businessmen about the future of South Africa and their perception that fundamental change was necessary: the institutions that had worked well for several decades were no longer effective.[2] Not only was mobilization recurring, but its evolving pattern posed an ever-growing threat to elite economic interests. Defense of those interests came to require an unprecedented engagement with the fundamental dilemma underlying South Africa's oligarchic society: how to reconcile increasing economic interdependence

[1] Price 1991: 238–40.
[2] For a formulation of the crisis in Gramscian terms as an "organic crisis," see Saul and Gelb 1981.

among races with ongoing political exclusion. Frustrated with the government's vacillation between limited reform and increasing repression, representatives of business interests took autonomous initiatives that were crucial to the accumulating pressure on the state to negotiate with the ANC, as explained in Chapter 7.

Mobilization and repression in South Africa did not result in profound sectoral changes, as had occurred in El Salvador during the civil war. The distribution of GDP by sector in South Africa continued its general trajectory since World War II, reflecting the gradual expansion of finance, services, and government as a percentage of GDP, the steady decline of agriculture's share, and (until 1990) the widely varying but on average steady share of mining. Rather, elite compromise was impelled by a crisis of confidence among investors in the institutions governing the economy of South Africa, and the resulting sustained decline in investment. Eroding confidence was largely the result of sustained mobilization by workers and others in the anti-apartheid movement.

To show how this came about, I first analyze the logic of the apartheid political economy and suggest how mobilization might have affected the realization of profits and the expectation of future profits. Next, I explain how institutions help create favorable conditions for investment and how these conditions might be undermined by sustained political instability. I then document the virtual suspension of investment in South Africa by both domestic and foreign investors. I argue that political mobilization was a principal cause of that decline and that plausible alternative explanations are less consistent with the evidence than the mobilization argument presented here.

The Economic Logic of Apartheid

Many authors stress the distortionary effects of apartheid institutions on labor markets and argue that apartheid transferred income away from black workers to white workers. In some versions, apartheid transferred income away from employers as well. This second claim raises a puzzling question: why did white employers support apartheid over several decades if it depressed profits? The literature on the economic history of South Africa offers two answers to this question, reflecting distinct positions in a long-standing and ideologically charged debate concerning who benefited from apartheid institutions.[3] The first position denies that white employers in fact supported apartheid; rather, apartheid was a National Party policy not in the interest of economic elites; employers merely adjusted to government policy as best they could. Eventually labor market distortions became so great as to undermine business conditions, leading to economic crisis, reform of labor market restrictions, and finally political change. In this view, usually referred to as the "liberal" position, mobilization did little to bring about democracy. The second interpretation is that economic elites, including employers, benefited from apartheid: it secured the political conditions for disciplining a low-wage labor force and helped erect a bulwark against populist or socialist encroachments on the material privileges and status of the economic elite, both in the workplace and in society at large.

These views also differ in the counterfactuals they propose about what kind of society would have existed in the absence of apartheid: the former often contrasts apartheid South Africa with an economy and state embodying liberal principles and structural constraints, while the latter poses a populist and possibly socialist counterfactual. The views also draw on different models of the economy. The former view typically adopts a neo-classical model of labor markets in which complete contracts obviate the need for employer strategies to ensure labor discipline and markets clear. The latter view stresses the paramount importance of control of the labor process and the ability of apartheid to manage the problems of labor supply and worker effort in the interests of employers.

The view developed here combines some of the assumptions of the second approach with an emphasis on the role of mobilization in gradually shifting the attention of key economic elites from the perceived costs and benefits of recalcitrance to those of compromise. I return to the liberal approach in the penultimate section of the chapter.

The following interpretation treats apartheid as an institution for the discipline of nonwhite workers, extending the work of Ronald Wintrobe.[4] Workers prefer not to expend effort on the job, that is, not to work, but will work if the utility of working (which includes the utility

---

[3] For an overview of the debate between "liberals" and "radicals," see Lipton 1985; Saunders 1988; and Nattrass 1991.

[4] Wintrobe 1998: 182–91. Wintrobe's model develops for the case of apartheid the labor-discipline models developed by Stiglitz and Shapiro 1984 and Bowles 1985. My model emphasizes how worker mobilization affects the logic of such models.

of the wage earned as well as a negative term, the disutility of working) exceeds the expected utility of shirking, which depends on the probability of being caught not working and as a result fired, and in that case, the probability of being reemployed and the available income if unemployed. Of course "shirking" is simply shorthand for failure to work, refusal to work, work resistance, and other profit-reducing activities by workers.

To ensure labor discipline, employers will therefore pay a wage such that the utility of working just exceeds the utility of shirking, thus implementing the *no-shirking condition*. The utility of working is simply $w - d$, where w is the wage and d the disutility of labor (where we assume the utility of the wage to be just the wage, i.e., neglecting risk aversion). The utility of shirking is $(1 - \tau)w + \tau[nw + (1 - n)r]$, where τ is the probability of being caught and fired if shirking (assumed constant), n the probability of getting another job if fired, and r the utility of not having a job (the *reservation wage*). The no-shirking condition is thus:

$$w - d \geq (1 - \tau)w + \tau[nw + (1 - n)r].$$

Assuming that employers implement the condition as an equality (otherwise they would be paying workers more than they need), the wage is (after rearranging)

$$w = r + d/\tau(1 - n),$$

the analogue to the labor supply curve in market-clearing models.

Under non-apartheid, competitive conditions, one can take n to be equal to the employment rate, the ratio of employed workers to the workforce. (More empirically grounded assumptions will not alter the essential fact that n *varies with* the employment rate.)

In this model, apartheid markets differ from liberal markets in four ways. First, by declaring some occupations and skills unavailable to non-white workers and by systematically underfunding black schooling compared with white, apartheid restricts the supply of skilled labor. Second, losing a job for shirking does not just mean the worker rejoins the labor pool with a probability of n of being reemployed, as in the liberal model. Rather, the worker loses his or her pass and returns to the bantustans, dropping out of the urban labor pool altogether (what is crucial is that because the chances of reemployment depend on obtaining a new pass, the probability of finding work again is significantly less than the employment rate).[5] Third, the apartheid reservation wage, r_a, is less than in liberal economies owing to apartheid's success in dispossessing Africans of alternative sources of income, such as land, and the lack of government benefits for the unemployed, such as unemployment insurance. Fourth, the highly conflictual labor relations of the apartheid economy – especially during its last decade – both reflect and foster an elevated level of work resistance which is represented here as an enhanced disutility of labor, d_a. Thus, the no-shirking condition under apartheid labor markets is

$$w = r_a + d_a/\tau,$$

where $r_a \ll r_l$. Assuming $d_a = d_l$, apartheid ($_a$) significantly raises the cost of job loss in comparison with liberal ($_l$) arrangements, and hence lowers the cost of hiring labor.

The implications are illustrated in Figure 6.1, which shows the no-shirking condition for hypothetical liberal and apartheid markets. Because $r_a \ll r_l$, the apartheid no-shirking condition gives a lower wage than the liberal condition. And because the fired worker returns to the bantustans, the apartheid no-shirking condition is flat (or, more realistically as there is *some* probability of being employed as n rises, nearly flat).

In this model, employers gain from apartheid institutions: the advantage to the employer of apartheid over liberal institutions is the difference, for any given n, between the two no-shirking conditions. Employers prefer apartheid to liberal labor markets – more so for higher employment rates – because the political control of labor keeps wages lower than they would be under liberal conditions whereby wages necessary for workers not to shirk increase with the employment rate. How much employers gain depends as well on how much of this transferred income is captured by white (i.e., skilled) workers rather than employers.[6]

---

[5] Approximately 1,400 Africans were "endorsed out" from Johannesburg each month from November 1967 to April 1968 (House of Assembly Debates, May 7, 1969, col. 4766, cited in Johnstone 1970: 127).

[6] Note that when applied to a skilled labor market, the effect of apartheid on wages may be of either sign. The restriction in the number of skilled workers available for employment, by the exclusion of black workers, for example, increases the probability that a fired worker will be reemployed as white workers are not banished to a homeland, and thereby works to raise the wage dictated by the NSC. Whether the resulting wage is higher or lower under apartheid than under a liberal labor market cannot be determined in general.

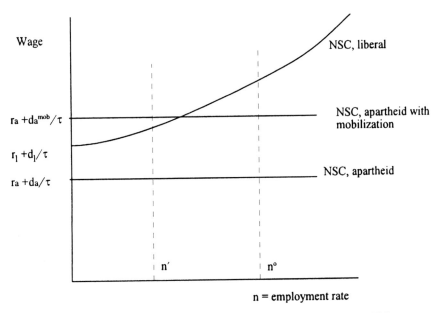

Figure 6.1 Worker discipline in liberal and apartheid economies (NSC = no-shirking condition)

Now consider two effects of mobilization by black workers in this model. First, if mobilization is widespread, worker alienation and discontent with working conditions would increase. The resulting increase in worker resistance and thus the disutility of labor displaces the apartheid no-shirking condition upward (d_a^{mob} is greater than d_a), perhaps even beyond the liberal no-shirking condition for some values of n, with the result that over that range, employers prefer liberal to apartheid policies. Second, mobilization alters investment priorities and choice of technology, leading to increasing capital intensiveness of the economy as employers attempt to minimize their reliance on the restive factor, with the result that n decreases from $n°$ to n'. For smaller n, the advantage of liberal over apartheid institutions decreases, so employers would have less reason to oppose political reform.

These theoretical considerations cannot in themselves make a case that employers benefited from apartheid. Nor was the regulation of the labor market the only apartheid policy relevant to the interest of South African elites. Apartheid restricted suffrage to the richest fifth of the population, tilted policy priorities sharply toward that fifth's interests, and thereby precluded the shifts in government policies – including perhaps a significant redistribution of economic resources as well as political power – that universal suffrage would have occasioned.

Nonetheless, this model of the labor market appears to capture a number of aspects of the working of the apartheid and its unraveling. According to an econometric analysis by the World Bank, unskilled wages do not vary significantly with the rate of unskilled employment (i.e., the regression coefficient has the correct sign but is not even close to significance at conventional levels), a finding consistent with the model's flat no-shirking condition under apartheid.[7] This is in sharp contrast to liberal economies, where the estimated unemployment effect on real wages is both large and highly significant.[8] Moreover, the World Bank authors found that influx control policies did indeed discipline labor: the number of prosecutions of Africans for violations of those policies significantly depressed unskilled wages.[9]

As shown in the next section, sustained mobilization was followed by increasing capital intensiveness. Particularly striking is the decline in the African employment-to-population ratio (n) from 73 percent in 1970 to 63 percent in 1980 to 57 percent in 1985.[10] This decline was partly driven by a sharp increase in the capital intensity of private sector production beginning in the 1970s, largely as a result of the strong labor-replacing bias of the pattern of investment. Hypothetically holding average capital intensity (as well as the sectoral distribution of GDP) of the economy constant between 1976 and 1992, more than 2 million additional formal private sector jobs would have been created by the accumulation of capital that took place over this period. Instead, jobs *declined* by 372,000.[11] The difference, a loss of some 2.4 million jobs, is accounted for by the shift of capital into more capital-intensive sectors of the economy and into more labor-saving technologies within sectors. In addition, the weakening of influx control meant that fired workers could more easily return from the bantustans and reenter the urban labor pool, shifting the apartheid no-shirking condition up. At the same time, this enlargement of the urban pool of unemployed workers shifted the liberal no-shirking condition down. The result of both

[7] Fallon 1992; Fallon and Pereira de Silva 1998: 206–7.
[8] Oswald and Blanchflower 1994.   [9] Fallon and Pereira de Silva 1998: 206–7.
[10] Fallon and Pereira de Silva 1998: 40.   [11] Bowles 1995: Table 1.

processes may have been to reduce the advantage of apartheid over liberal institutions.[12]

Business Confidence and Investment

Mobilization may lead to elite accommodation in another way: it may undermine elite confidence in the ability of a country's political and economic institutions to render an adequately high and certain return on investment. Wealth holders do not invest if the expected after-tax profit rate is not sufficient when compared with competing potential uses of funds. Martin Feldstein summarizes a vast economic literature: the "most fundamental determinant of the extent to which individuals channel resources into nonresidential fixed investment should be the real net-of-tax rate of return on that investment."[13] The expected rate of return is based on the present value of the expected stream of profit that would result if the investment were made. Expected after-tax profit rates depend on the expectation, over uncertain outcomes, of future prices, wages, and tax rates, as well as the level of demand for the goods produced (for which important indicators are the recent rate of growth of the economy and the extent to which the firm is using its existing capacity).

Investors decide whether to invest income in new productive assets or to retire debt (or to loan it out on credit markets), depending on whether the expected profit rate is greater than what economists term the user cost of capital (which depends critically on the current real interest rate, as well as tax rates). If it is, then the investment will be made; if not, then either the funds will be lent out, invested in more attractive foreign opportunities, or some of the investor's own debt will be retired. Investors will not invest if they are unable to make "reasonably determinate" calculations about their expected rate of return under the available options; rather, they will wait in the hope that some of the uncertainty will clear, meanwhile parking their liquid assets in some accessible and reasonably safe holding place, perhaps out of the country.[14] Thus, economists believe that invest-

---

[12] Wintrobe (1998: 195–6) notes that his (more complex) labor-discipline model may better account for two other salient facts than does the liberal job reservation analysis: it predicts that both black resistance and economic sanctions depress black employment, while they increase it in the liberal approach.

[13] Feldstein 1982: 836.   [14] Gordon, Edwards, and Reich 1994: 13.

ment depends on expected after-tax profits, which depend on recent and present tax and profit rates and the general "business climate."[15]

The question is, what determines expected profit rates and borrowing costs, the proximate determinants of investment? Answers from a range of approaches in social science converge on the role of institutions. Institutions governing the workings of markets for labor, credit, foreign exchange, and goods, as well as business-government relations determine present profit rates and borrowing costs and shape expectations regarding the future, thereby determining investment as well as growth. The current literature emphasizes a variety of institutions, ranging from property rights,[16] to transactions costs,[17] to political regimes,[18] to sets of institutions that together create conditions for sustained growth – the "social structure of accumulation,"[19] or in another formulation, the "mode of regulation."[20] Similarly, recent endogenous growth theory stresses the returns to scale of complementary investments in human and physical capital supported by appropriate institutions; the resulting externalities impel growth.[21]

Political mobilization may affect the proximate determinants of investment in any one of three ways. It may depress present profit rates (because of extended strikes or subsequent wage increases, for example), dampen expected profit rates (if mobilization is seen as likely to recur), or render expectations so uncertain that investors suspend investment. If political unrest is driven in part by distributional conflicts, the resulting instability may be of particular concern to investors as the security of property rights and the distribution of surplus between profit and wages go to the heart of their expectations of return to investment. In econometric studies, political instability has generally been found to reduce investment.[22]

---

[15] For reviews of different approaches to investment and growth, see Bhaskar and Glyn 1995; Heye 1995; and Clark 1979.

[16] North 1981; Knight 1992.   [17] Williamson 1985.

[18] Barro 1997: Chapter 2; Przeworski and Limongi 1993.

[19] Gordon 1980; Gordon, Edwards, and Reich 1994.

[20] Aglietta 1979.   [21] Romer 1986 and 1994.

[22] For example, in an econometric study of seventy-one countries for the period 1960–85, Alesina and Perotti (1996) found that sociopolitical instability "by creating uncertainty in the politico-economic environment, reduces investment." See Benabou (1997) for a review of recent literature on inequality, instability, investment, and growth. Of ten studies that tested the relationship between instability and growth or investment, all but three found that instability had a consistent, negative, and generally statistically significant effect on investment (and/or growth, depending on the study). See also Barro 1997; Persson and Tabellini 1992; Alesina and Perotti 1993; Przeworski and Limongi 1993.

Thus, investment and investor confidence are in part politically determined by institutions and their perceived stability: what rates of return they render and whether they undergird stable and favorable expectations of future rates of return. An example of such political determination of investment is the rapid decline of private investment in France after the electoral victory of the socialist François Mitterrand in 1981. From 1981 to 1985, business investment fell 7.8 percent, which was more than double the decline in Europe as a whole in the same period (an indication of the effects of nonpolitical factors as the difference is thus credibly attributed to Mitterrand's election). Between 1981 and 1983, U.S. foreign direct investment in France fell an average of 15.0 percent in real terms (deflated with the capital goods deflator).[23]

The U-Turn in Investment

Beginning in the 1970s, investors had growing reason to doubt the future economic performance of South African domestic institutions. Capital/labor relations had become contentious, mobilization and repression increased throughout the period, and in response, so did international sanctions against South Africa, culminating in the imposition of financial sanctions in 1985. The following figures make it clear that the dramatic decline in investment beginning in the mid-1970s was due principally to the deepening mobilization by workers and township residents.

Time series of investment, production, and capital flows are always difficult to interpret because of the cyclical nature of the relevant values. In South Africa the problem is compounded by a decisive increase in volatility during this period. The figures that follow therefore combine a variety of averaging and normalizing techniques. All variables are real values, deflated by the appropriate deflator, or have been normalized on the most relevant principal value.[24] Some variables have been averaged over a five-

---

[23] U.S. data are from the Department of Commerce; European data from Andrew Glynn, Oxford University, personal communication.

[24] For example, long-term foreign direct investment (net long-term private capital flows) are analyzed as a percentage of capital stock, which is the relevant reference variable (such investment increases the capital stock) and has the further advantage over the alternative variable GDP as the capital stock is less volatile. Real values of variables related to investment are defined as the ratio of nominal values to the price index of investment goods (a different "basket" of goods than that underlying the consumer price index, the usual deflator).

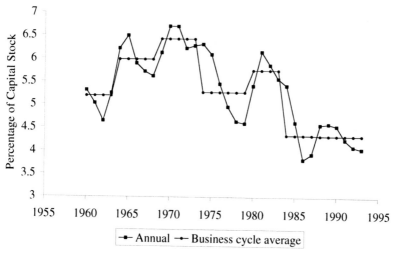

Figure 6.2 Private investment in South Africa, 1960–1993

year period or over the business cycle.[25] The data underlying the figures are taken from publications of the South African Reserve Bank (see the *Note on Statistical Sources*).

From 1960 to the early 1970s, investment rose from business cycle to business cycle (see Figure 6.2, which shows the ratio of private gross domestic investment to capital stock for each year and for each business cycle).[26] From the 1970s until the transition to democracy, investment fell, with the exception of a brief increase from 1979 to 1981 (thanks to a booming world gold price, which was ten times greater in 1980 than in 1970).[27] This sustained rise followed by a sustained decline – the *investment u-turn* – suggests that investor confidence declined as well. The period from the business cycle trough of 1972 to the next trough in 1979 saw the Durban strike wave and the Soweto uprising. The rate of invest-

[25] The business cycles were defined as the period from peak to peak of the growth rate of (real) GDP: 1959–64, 1964–9, 1969–74, 1974–80, 1980–4, 1984–8, 1988–95. Peak values were split between adjoining cycles.

[26] Gross investment (not net investment, which deducts for depreciation of assets) is arguably the best indicator of investor expectations.

[27] The world price for gold rose dramatically essentially because of the failure of the effort from 1968 to 1973 to demonetize gold (Nattrass 1981: 151). With the ending in 1973 of the Bretton Woods system, the resulting instability in international markets increased the demand for gold (and for silver and platinum). As the price was no longer fixed, it soared.

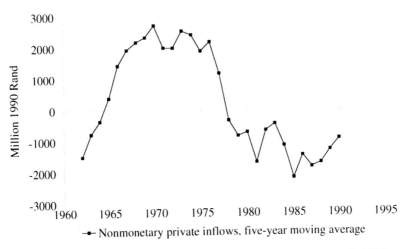

Figure 6.3 Long-term private capital inflows to South Africa, 1962–1990

ment at the trough also declined, from 6.2 percent in 1972 to 4.6 percent in 1979. The rate at the next trough, in 1986 after the uprising of 1984–6, was still lower, at 3.8 percent. Thus, investment fell as the unrest increased.[28] As investment lagged, the economic crisis of which it was a leading symptom deepened: without strong investment, growth in output will subsequently be limited.

Another measure of investor confidence is the flow of long-term capital investment into the South African economy. This indicator is a sensitive measure of investor confidence as foreign investors have many alternative sites for investment. The flow of long-term private capital (excluding that related to reserves, in real terms, averaged over five years; Figure 6.3) rose steeply during the boom of the 1960s and remained high during the early 1970s, before falling steeply.[29] After 1977, the (averaged) flow was an *outflow* of capital.[30]

---

[28] One explanation for declining private investment could be increasing public investment that "crowds out" private investment. However, that was not the case as total investment also declined.

[29] "Boom" is, of course, a relative term: while growth and investment were strong during the 1960s, the profit share has declined since 1948 (Nattrass 1990). Nonetheless, it was significantly higher than that of the advanced capitalist economies.

[30] For more analysis of short-term capital flows, see Padayachee 1988: 326–33.

The Challenge to Economic Elite Interests

South African Reserve Bank analysts – generally wary of extraordinary explanations – attribute the u-turn in investment to explicitly political factors. Among those listed are a "'diffused' lack of confidence," "pervasive" uncertainty about South Africa's future, increased civil unrest, growing negative foreign perceptions of the socioeconomic and political situation, trade sanctions and boycotts (especially financial sanctions), disinvestment by foreign enterprises, and after the early 1980s, the domination of the labor market by "strong and militant labour unions that negotiated successfully for high real wages that were not matched by productivity growth."[31]

Political mobilization also affected flows of short-term capital (see Figure 6.4, which shows both short-term private capital flows and the South African Reserve Bank's index of the user cost of capital for the manufacturing sector).[32] During the boom of the 1960s, capital flowed into South Africa, but beginning in 1975 the flows were outflows, except for a sharp peak of inflows during 1981–3 following the surge in the price of gold. After Soweto, new foreign direct investment by transnationals dried up, and new private investment was portfolio, not subsidiary, investment.[33] In 1985, capital fled the country on a massive scale.

A key determinant of investment, the user cost of capital – seemingly a nonpolitical variable – was also shaped by the contentious politics of the period. According to Reserve Bank analysts, the massive outflows of capital in the mid-1980s precipitated a sharp drop in the real effective exchange rate – which declined by 34 percent from 1983 to 1985 – and caused a sharp increase in the real price of capital goods as a significant portion is imported.[34] Thus by the mid-1980s, the mobilization against apartheid had landed one of its most decisive if unsung blows, removing the long-standing subsidy of investment goods.

Direct evidence that political unrest in South Africa led to rising investor uncertainty comes from an analysis of foreign exchange prices by Michael Melvin and Kok-Hui Tan (1996). They used the spread between

---

[31] Prinsloo and Smith 1996: 36–7. They also list other, nonpolitical factors such as drought and the reduction of investment by some of the parastatal enterprises.

[32] This user cost-of-capital index is the only one readily available; it is based on Prinsloo and Smith 1996.

[33] Much of the foreign loans of the 1970s financed public projects such as SASOL's coal-to-oil conversion project. After Soweto, the government received more difficult terms and shorter repayment terms (Moorsom 1989: 258).

[34] Prinsloo and Smith 1996: 37.

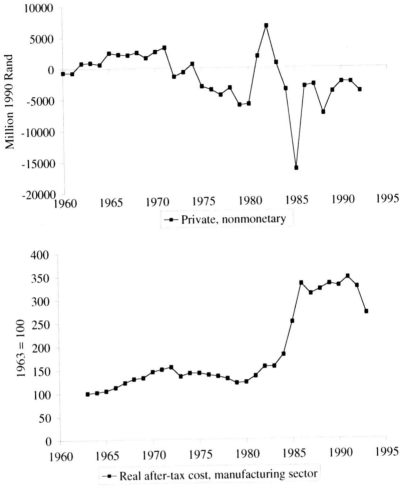

Figure 6.4 Short-term private capital flows (*top*) and user cost of capital (*bottom*), South Africa, 1960–1993

the prices at which international currency traders were willing to buy and sell the South African rand between October 2, 1985, and August 31, 1990, as a measure of the risk premium associated with holding the rand. They found that news of political unrest reported in the *New York Times* and the London *Times* significantly increased the spread: on days following events of political unrest the difference between the bid and ask quotes rose to almost three times the normal spread. Others have also found that political instability (an index of various measures) was a significant determinant of capital movements from 1960 to 1996.[35]

Intensifying international sanctions also contributed to the suspension of investment, the outflow of capital, and the fall in the exchange rate. However, such sanctions were not exogenous to the South African political process but reflected the domestic dynamic of mobilization and repression (as well, of course, as mobilization by foreign activists in their own countries). An econometric study of the timing of a large number of "sanctions episodes" over the entire period concluded that the increasing number and intensity of sanctions reflected the rise in opposition political activity as measured by the number of black workers participating in strikes in South Africa.[36]

The most serious wave of sanctions was triggered by the government's imposition of a partial state of emergency on July 20, 1985. The following week, the market value of shares on the Johannesburg stock exchange plummeted, leading to a three-day closure of the exchange. On July 31, Chase Manhattan announced it would no longer extend credit to South Africa. Though some banks continued to lend to South Africa, the number refusing to roll over debt increased through August. On September 2, the government announced a moratorium on debt payment. South Africa was particularly vulnerable to the banks' refusal to extend new credit or to reschedule existing loans because of a sharp increase in borrowing from banks from 1982 to 1984.[37] As already mentioned, capital flows in the 1980s were mainly in the form of short-term loan finance rather than long-term investment capital.[38] According to Reserve Bank analysts, the informal financial sanctions implemented by banks beginning in mid-1985 imposed a binding balance of payments constraint, limiting investment to domestic savings, and required increasingly restrictive financial policies as a result: real (and expected real) interest rates were high, corporate taxes were increased, and tax rebates were phased out.[39]

One indication that the sanctions reflected declining international confidence in South African institutions *as a result of political mobilization* was

---

[35] See Fedderke, de Kadt, and Luiz (n.d.a) and Fedderke and Liu (n.d.). However, their political stability index does not include strike data, only social unrest.
[36] Kaempfer, Lowenberg, Mocar, and Topyan 1995: 23.   [37] Padayachee 1988: 363.
[38] Davies 1989: 217. Short-run loans increased from 20 to 44 percent from 1981 to 1985 as a percentage of total foreign liabilities, accounting for 72 percent of foreign debt in 1985 (Moorsom 1989: 258).
[39] Prinsloo and Smith 1996: 37.

Figure 6.5 Capital-to-labor ratio in South Africa's private sector, 1960–1993

the foreign banks' requirement that the government abolish pass laws and lift the state of emergency (which was subsequently reimposed throughout the country).[40] The immediate debt crisis was not resolved until some months later when a committee representing creditors agreed to a repayment schedule.

Packages of official sanctions on the part of the United States (the 1986 Comprehensive Anti-Apartheid Act, which banned new investment and prohibited bank loans) and the Commonwealth countries soon followed. South Africa was potentially vulnerable to trade sanctions as the country's overall exposure to trade was significant (the ratio of the sum of exports and imports to GDP averaged about 55 percent from 1980 to 1985).[41] Although some sanctions could be evaded through third parties (as the previous arms and trade embargoes had largely been), via the diversion of trade elsewhere or the rapid development of domestic alternatives (such as the oil from coal projects of South African Synthetic Oil, Limited, SASOL), reimbursing additional middlemen imposed costs on South African exporters and importers and the economy generally.[42]

A final effect of labor mobilization was a remarkable increase in the capital intensity of production (Figure 6.5), which accelerated dramatically after the strike wave of the mid-1980s (despite the simultaneous sharp

[40] Hirsch 1989: 270.   [41] Moorsom 1989: 254–7.   [42] Innes 1989.

158

increase in the cost of capital; Figure 6.4).[43] The effect was to swell the ranks of the unemployed and to significantly reduce the benefits of apartheid as a labor discipline system, along the lines suggested earlier.

Thus, the combined result of mobilization, repression, and sanctions was a prolonged trough in investment, a sustained hemorrhaging of both long-term and short-term capital, and unprecedented costs of capital. By 1986, business organizations themselves attributed much of the crisis to mobilization, as demonstrated in Chapter 7. The mobilization of 1984–7 and the international reactions to its repression intensified the u-turn in investment that had begun more than a decade earlier.

Assessing Alternative Explanations

According to the liberal analysis, which provides the principal alternative explanation of the stagnation of the South African economy, the costs of apartheid rose during the economic modernization after World War II, until they began to undermine sustained growth in the late 1960s.[44] According to this account, costs rose for four reasons. First, labor market regulations, "Bantu" education policies, and influx control created a shortage of skilled labor that increased wages for skilled (white) laborers and unfilled positions, limiting growth and impelling inappropriately capital-intensive development. Second, government decentralization policy limited investment in previously developed areas without providing adequate compensation to investors for their increased costs.[45] Third, protectionist policies, initially a step to reward firms hiring white labor, resulted in inefficient domestic manufacturing, intensifying the economy's reliance on primary exports, particularly gold, and capital inflows. Fourth, under the National Party the state sector absorbed an ever-increasing share of investment, which rose from 35 percent of gross fixed investment in 1950 to 53 percent in 1979.[46] As the economy modernized, key groups

---

[43] The sharp decline in 1967 reflects a break in the employment series underlying Figure 6.5 and should be disregarded.

[44] This argument was developed most carefully by Lipton 1985. For a summary of her argument, see also Lowenberg 1997.

[45] For example, from 1968 to 1978 government regulation forbade the issuing of permits for new jobs in "white" areas. In 1982, the government offered a wage subsidy of 80 percent for new employment creation in outlying areas.

[46] Lipton 1985: 243.

of employers lost interest in labor-repressive institutions; reform to those institutions were now in their interest. According to this "skilled labor argument," the investment u-turn is thus a symptom of the accumulating irrationality of apartheid, particularly the shortage of skilled labor, and its incompatibility with modern capitalist institutions.[47]

Merle Lipton, a prominent exponent of this view, argues that these increasing costs forced economic elites to choose between limiting growth and eroding apartheid.[48] Business elites chose the latter course, according to Lipton, lobbying for the reform of labor market regulations and influx control. As a result of the rapid mechanization of agriculture, agricultural interests no longer lobbied for the continuance of influx controls.[49] By the mid-1970s, capitalists were converging on a reform program to increase the competitiveness of the labor market, to raise living standards, to recognize the rights of labor, and to erode social apartheid.[50] The biggest mining houses, such as Anglo American, Gencor, and Barlow Rand, had diversified interests not only in domestic manufacturing but worldwide.[51]

According to Lipton, their efforts were unsuccessful initially because of the National Party government's commitment to apartheid, reflecting the party's traditional coalition of white agriculture and white labor. Business pressure on the government to reform increased as the accumulating costs of apartheid mounted. But business pressure was not powerful enough to make changes against the power of white labor and the state bureaucracy. Business was weakened by the lack of social cohesion among "the English," comprised of various national origins.[52] Moreover, "social pressures must have deterred liberal (or rationalizing) employers from breaking rank" with other employers not committed to reform.[53] The emergence of Afrikaner manufacturing and financial interests brought new tension within the party's coalition. According to Lipton, class interests eventually trumped ethnic identity, and Afrikaner business interests became allied with English interests in urging fundamental change. Both Afrikaner and English business leaders were optimistic that reform candidate P. W. Botha would address the accumulating irrationality of the apartheid economy.

Mobilization plays a relatively minor role in the transition to democratic rule in this explanation, which states that the interests of economic elites shifted toward reform not because of mobilization, but because

---

[47] For an analysis of the crisis as a crisis of accumulation, see Gelb 1991: 16–22.
[48] Lipton 1985: 249.   [49] Lipton 1985: 92.   [50] Lipton 1985: 227.
[51] Lipton 1985: 133–4.   [52] Lipton 1985: 292.   [53] Lipton 1985: 251.

further modernization of the economy required liberalizing reforms, particularly of the labor market.[54] Although the interest of businessmen in political stability is sometimes advanced as part of the argument, it generally plays a secondary role. For example, according to Anton Lowenberg (1997), the end of apartheid would have come about even without sanctions, given the accumulating costs of the irrationality of the system. The argument relies principally on claims concerning the increasing shortage of skilled labor, and to a lesser extent on public statements by business organizations calling for reform.

How does this view square with the empirical record? For a skills shortage to account for the transition to democracy, all three of the following claims would have to be true. First, a shortage of skilled labor must have arisen in the years *prior* to the elites' decision to compromise; the necessary evidence for such a shortage would be a sustained increase in the price of skilled labor (wages) in relation to other input prices. Second, that shortage must have caused a negative impact on the profit rate and profit share of value added, the mechanism that would occasion pro-reform political activity by business elites. Third, repairing this squeeze on profits must have required a transition to democracy.

Requirement One

An examination of wage patterns belies the claim that there was a sustained shortage of skilled labor during the years leading up to the decision to compromise. Employers, particularly manufacturing employers, had long complained of the high costs of skilled (overwhelmingly white) labor that resulted from the color bar and the reduced competition among unskilled labor due to influx control. Despite evidence of a skills shortage during the 1945–69 period – apartheid's golden age – however, there is little such evidence in subsequent years.[55]

---

[54] Lowenberg (1997) argues that after 1979, South Africa was caught in a vicious circle whereby recession and rising unemployment led to political unrest, which impelled capital flight, which made contractionary economic policies necessary, which further deepened unemployment and unrest (1997: 70). But his emphasis is on the gathering inefficiency of the economy rather than on protest per se. On his argument, improved wages and increased jobs rather than political rights would end black unrest. Gelb emphasizes mobilization more, attributing to labor unrest the unraveling of South Africa's "racially despotic" system of labor regulations (1991: 22).

[55] Even in the "golden age" the color bar was applied with flexibility: up to June 1967, only 74 of 891 applications for exemptions to the color bar had been refused (Johnstone 1970: 129).

Table 6.1. *Growth rates of real wages in manufacturing by race in South Africa, 1945–1984*

Period	African	White
1945–59	0.1%	3.1%
1959–64	5.8	2.7
1964–9	2.6	4.1
1969–74	3.7	2.8
1974–80	4.5	1.0
1980–4	3.4	1.7
1984–8	0.3	–2.4

Source: Calculated from Hofmeyr 1994: Table A2: 177–8.

African wages in manufacturing were essentially stagnant from 1945 to 1959, growing at 0.1 percent per year while those of whites grew at 3.1 percent, the direct consequence of white labor's control of skilled labor positions through white unions and the color bar (see Table 6.1). The growth spurt of the 1960s brought increased wages to Africans, which grew at an unprecedented 5.8 percent during the 1959–64 business cycle, compared with 2.7 percent for white workers. White wage increases were significantly higher than those of Africans in the following business cycle. Beginning with the 1969–74 business cycle, however, African wages rose, whereas those of white workers tended to stagnate. As a result, white wages as a fraction of the total wage bill declined from 61.7 percent in 1970 to 51 percent in 1975, and the ratio of white to black wages in manufacturing fell from 5.6:1 in 1960 to 4.8:1 in 1975.[56]

The relative decline in white wages after 1970 suggests that the shortage of skilled labor was being successfully met by various liberalizing measures. The "skill shortage" was an artificial shortage due to racial regulations in the workplace; once the color bar was relaxed and allowed to "float" up the hierarchy of occupations, and in the wake of the "fragmentation" of particular jobs into skilled and unskilled components and other measures, the demand for labor was met by cheaper African labor. If skills shortages continued to be significant, one would expect rising wages for skilled labor in comparison with unskilled labor in the key period leading up to the call by business for fundamental reform, but that was not the

[56] Calculated from Hofmeyr 1994: Table A2: 177–8. See also Nattrass 1990: 118.

162

case; rather, as a result of mobilization, unskilled wages increased. In a careful analysis of wage movements, Julian Hofmeyr (1994) argues that three distinct phases are evident in recent wage data. The first phase from the mid-1960s until 1975, is characterized by a growing shortage of both skilled and unskilled labor, and hence an increase in wages across all categories and a gradual dismantling of the color bar. During the second phase from 1975 to the early 1980s, supply exceeded demand across nearly all sectors and occupation levels, as evidenced by stagnating wages in all occupations and sectors. Average African wages nonetheless continued to rise during this period, as more African workers were hired at higher grades (and thus higher wages, which raised the average paid to African workers).

A principal reason that wages for unskilled labor increased from the early 1970s was the growing competition for South African labor from the mines. As colonial regimes in Angola and Mozambique faced unprecedented threats from national liberation forces, the future reliability of migrant labor became a concern to South African mining interests. In an unprecedented break with the history of mining, mine owners decided to develop South African labor as a significant source to diversify its labor supply. In order to do so, they had to offer more competitive wages. The project was successful: employment of South Africans in the mines increased from 20 to 58 percent of mine labor between 1974 and 1982, and South African black wages in the gold mines rose from 4 percent of value added in 1973 to 15 percent in 1978.[57] The increase in mine wages pushed up manufacturing wages as well (as wages became competitive for some grades and pay scales) and even agricultural wages.

But the change in wages accounted for by the change in labor policy in the mining sector does not explain the wage movements in the subsequent period. According to Hofmeyr, African wages – particularly unskilled wages – continued to rise despite the slack demand for labor during a third phase that began in the early 1980s. Indeed, while a dramatic shift in the relative prices of inputs took place in the mid-1980s, rather than an increase in skilled labor wages, it was the cost of capital compared with labor costs (either skilled or unskilled) that rose steeply (Figure 6.4).

Hofmeyr shows that the increasing level of unionization, not general

---

[57] Lipton 1985: 122; Nattrass 1981: 159. However, it took much longer for the color bar to be abolished on the mines, thanks to the power of the white Mine Workers Union. It was not until 1988 that it was eliminated, after a costly strike in 1987.

labor market conditions such as the supply of labor in different categories, provides the best explanation for the pattern of this third phase, the crucial phase for the transition to democracy. Thus, whether or not one agrees that the increased wages during the boom primarily reflected shortages of labor, those shortages ended in the mid-1970s, undermining any claim that shortages led to the political transition more than a decade and a half later.

Similarly, the costs of an inappropriately capital-intensive structure of production (stressed in some liberal interpretations) did not arise until late in the period, in response not to skill shortages, which by then had dissipated, but to labor mobilization (see Figure 6.5).

Increases in state spending on domestic and external security and on the proliferating bureaucratic structures under the 1980s attempt to build an ethnically defined consociational formula were another cost of apartheid. Government expenditures as a percentage of GDP increased slowly, from a level of 14.1 percent in 1960 to 18.3 percent in 1970 and 20.7 percent in 1980, then rapidly increased to 29.4 percent in 1985 and 29.5 percent in 1990.[58] However, these rising public expenditures were responses not to apartheid's "irrationality" but to ongoing political mobilization.

Requirement Two

The evolution of the profit share and the profit rate do not readily support the notion that a profit squeeze due to a skills shortage propelled the transition. The liberal view requires that declines in the profit share and profit rate should precede the transition to democracy. The profit share (the ratio of profits to value added) dropped during the first three business cycles beginning in 1960, perhaps reflecting the skills shortage at the time, but after 1970 it generally stagnated (with the exception of an increase resulting from the 1980 spike in the price of gold; Figure 6.6).[59] This pattern not only fails to provide a profit-squeeze explanation of the change in business opinion in the 1980s, it also does not explain the pattern

---

[58] Calculated as the ratio of current expenditure of general government to GDP.

[59] Bhaskar and Glynn (1995) argue that the profit share, not the profit rate, is the relevant determinant of investment (along with prices and demand). The movement of profit share and investment in South Africa is opposite of what they would predict, further suggesting that investor confidence in the institutional structure of apartheid is the explanation.

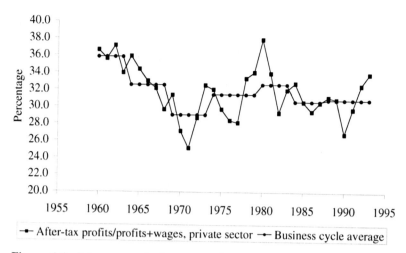

Figure 6.6 Private sector's after-tax profit share in South Africa, 1960–1993

in investment: investment *rose* rapidly in the 1960s (Figure 6.2) despite the steady decline in the profit share and then fell steadily despite the halt in this decline beginning in the mid-1970s.

Nor did the after-tax profit rate, the ratio of after-tax profits to capital stock, decline sharply before the transition. Rather, it declined uniformly from business cycle to business cycle beginning in 1960 (Figure 6.7).[60] Although the windfall profits of the gold price booms brought peaks in the profit rate, as is evident in the annual data, the business cycle average declined steadily (with the exception of a slight increase in the last cycle). Moreover, this movement of the profit rate cannot explain the movement of investment as one would expect the profit rate and investment to move together.[61] This suggests that the emphasis here on investor expectations and the dampening of those expectations resulting from ongoing political mobilization, rather than past profitability per se, is a better explanation for the investment u-turn. Together, the movements of the profit share

[60] The figure shows the trend in the profit rate of the entire economy. That of the private sector (not shown) moves similarly (the correlation coefficient between the two profit rates is 0.98).

[61] According to Nicoli Nattrass (1990: 108), the profit rate declined from 1948 to 1986. Despite the time trend, investment (both of foreign and domestic capital) continued until the u-turn as the profit rate was significantly higher than that of the advanced capitalist countries (until 1975, roughly 12 percent compared with South Africa's 20 percent).

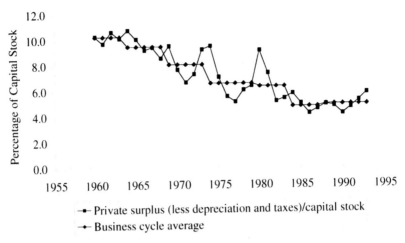

-■- Private surplus (less depreciation and taxes)/capital stock
-■- Business cycle average

Figure 6.7   Corporate after-tax profit rate in South Africa, 1960–1993

and profit rate reflect the decline in capital productivity after the mid-1970s.[62]

Further evidence against a profit-squeeze explanation for the u-turn is given in Figure 6.8, which shows that net private investment fell not only as a fraction of capital stock (as in Figure 6.2) but as a fraction of total private savings (personal and corporate savings combined). Because the curve repeats the u-turn pattern of investment, the crisis could not have been due to a lack of savings – there were abundant savings of both types available for investment during the 1980s, suggesting it was a lack of investor confidence rather than economic irrationality that led to the downturn in investment.

Requirement Three

If the liberal argument is to account for the transition to democracy, it must hold that democratic rule, and not just economic reforms such as the relaxation of the color bar, was needed to address labor shortages, a point

---

[62] The profit rate is the product of the profit share (the ratio of profits to income) times the ratio of income to capital (capital productivity). Thus, the steady decline in the profit rate even as the profit share leveled off reflects the ongoing decline in capital productivity beginning in 1970 as investment strongly favored capital intensive technologies and sectors.

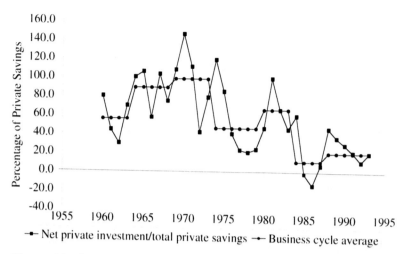

Figure 6.8 Private investment as a fraction of private savings in South Africa, 1960–1993

that is implied but not usually argued explicitly. If mobilization was not a principal factor, liberalizing the labor market to address the skills shortage and other "irrationalities" of apartheid should have been sufficient to restore profitable economic conditions. Thus, investment should have recovered after the reforms recommended by the Wiehahn and Rieckert commissions were implemented.

The liberal view is of course correct in pointing to the potential inconsistency of racially regulated markets and capitalist growth. However, the costs that apartheid imposed did not begin in the 1970s but were long-standing characteristics of South Africa. Although the interests of some economic elites – particularly those of Afrikaner economic elites – did shift away from labor repression as the economy modernized, as Lipton argues, that shift occurred in the 1960s and 1970s – which was too early to be a persuasive cause of the later political transition.

Conclusion

Thus, it appears difficult to account for the transition to democracy in South Africa on the basis of modernizing elite interests and increasing economic irrationality of apartheid alone. Although labor shortages in the 1960s and early 1970s pushed businesses to advocate regulatory reform and to increase African wages, significant labor shortages did not persist past the mid-1970s. Had these been the only causes, South Africa would have undergone a successful process of conservative modernization, stopping far short of the calamitous political events that led to its transition to democracy in 1994.

Rather, it was the rising militancy of the emerging unions and the increasing unrest of the townships in the 1980s that convinced business elites that fundamental political reform – not merely labor market reform – was necessary, and that such reform required negotiation with the ANC. By the mid-1980s, labor mobilization had sharply reduced, perhaps even reversed, the advantages of apartheid labor markets to economic elites. One mechanism by which this took place was growing alienation on the part of black workers, increasing the costs of maintaining shop-floor discipline. Another was that the sharply reduced rate of employment in the formal sector, itself the product of the mobilization-induced economic downturn, strengthened market discipline of labor as an alternative to influx control.

While the advantages of apartheid labor-market regulation had waned, the associated costs were rapidly rising. Political mobilization, particularly that by labor unions, imposed direct costs on firms as strikes and boycotts deepened. Continued labor unrest undermined business confidence in the ongoing ability of South Africa's institutions to render a sufficiently high and certain rate of return. The growth of security forces and racially segregated bureaucracies failed to contain the unrest but contributed to the growing tax burden. Financial sanctions – imposed as a result of the regime's repressive response to mobilization – led to a decline in the value of the rand, prompting a steep increase in the real price of capital goods and the user cost of capital. The decline in investment prompted in the 1970s by the unraveling of business confidence thus deepened in the 1980s. The rising wave of protest initiated by the Durban strikes and its far-flung ramifications had engulfed the apartheid economy and would shortly prompt a profound political transformation.

7

From Recalcitrance to Compromise

> *By the time we reached the 1987 wage negotiations, the NUM [National Union of Mineworkers] was at its peak. The political situation in the country was really dismal and we knew that we were going to have one mother of wage negotiations. And that the issue really wasn't what level of increases we negotiated; the issue really was do we survive or not? Will there, after this negotiation, still be such a thing as managerial prerogative? Who controls the mines, really? That was what it would boil down to.*
>
> – Chamber of Mines executive, February 1997

In response to the growing insurgency and the failure of reforms intended to liberalize but not end apartheid, key members of the South African economic elite eventually turned to negotiations with the ANC in an attempt to resolve the ongoing crisis of investor confidence and political unrest. The defection of some economic elites from the oligarchic alliance that had long been the foundation of South African society was a principal factor that set the process of compromise in motion. Business organizations and individual business executives undertook a series of extraordinary political initiatives that demonstrated their growing recognition that negotiations with the ANC would have to occur.

These initiatives increased the pressure on the National Party to negotiate as it became more isolated from these hitherto centrist interests, threatened on its left by ongoing mobilization and shedding voters to the right as the Conservative Party proved increasingly attractive to voters. From about 1985 to 1989, one obstacle to compromise was the recalcitrance of President P. W. Botha, who could not countenance formal negotiations with the ANC. That obstacle was finally removed when Botha gave up some of his control of the National Party in 1989. A year later, F. W.

169

de Klerk removed the ban on the ANC and the SACP and released Nelson Mandela. Though negotiations were prolonged and violence worsened, the first inclusive elections in South Africa's history were held in April 1994 under the terms of a new nonracial constitution that created a unitary state with universal suffrage. Strikingly absent were the guarantees for the white minority on which the National Party initially insisted. Gone, too, was the nationalization of banks, mines, and land called for by the Freedom Charter. This chapter takes up the negotiation process and its outcome.

From Conservative Modernization to Political Inclusion

From the 1980s the whole thing shifted around and – though it might sound very trivial – it suddenly became important to put something in your firm's annual report each year saying that if we don't have a political settlement the country will never grow, etc. You were dealing with a wide variety of things, but there was certainly a very strong sense that you didn't know whether your workforce was going to come to work in the morning in conflict-ridden areas and very often 20 percent of the workforce did not because there were barricades. People just couldn't get through. Or when they arrived they were exhausted and they'd been terrorized the night before. Essentially it was harming the productivity of the labor force. You didn't have any access to international markets. Financial sanctions were biting. So a variety of factors got together to create a climate of opinion which says the current order is unsustainable.

— South African academic, 1997

Over the apartheid years, business organizations had called occasionally for reform of the myriad regulations governing the hiring of labor. Indeed, industrial and commercial business organizations pressed for such reforms just after World War II. Although the reform agenda broadened over time, before the mid-1980s, business organizations had not called for measures that would have ended residential and school segregation and separate development or ensured inclusive political citizenship. Even when political issues were addressed, white supremacy was assumed: in the 1978 constitutional proposal of the Progressive Federal Party (the party of the liberal intelligentsia and liberal English capital, particularly Anglo American chairman Harry Oppenheimer), minority veto power would be ensured under a consociational power-sharing formula.[1] All major corporations supported the National Party in the 1983 referendum on the new constitution,[2] apparently failing to anticipate the greatly intensified unrest that it would provoke.

[1] Lipton 1985: 329.   [2] O'Meara 1996: 295.

Episodes of political unrest generally prompted business to call for reform.[3] Such statements followed the protests over Sharpeville and Soweto and the Durban strike wave, suggesting that political mobilization rather than labor shortages was the dominant concern of these elites. Sustained mobilization eventually convinced them of the need for a new political dispensation, especially when they saw mobilization occurring *after* limited reforms: the Durban strike wave followed a wage increase for Africans and the uprisings of 1984–6 took place after constitutional reforms widened the race-based franchise to coloureds and Indians. It was only after that uprising – and the imposition of financial sanctions – that business organizations began pressing for wide-ranging political as well as economic reform, particularly for universal suffrage in a single state.

Prior to the uprising, business leaders and organizations had tried persuasion rather than confrontation in urging the government to consider reform on limited issues.[4] In addition, business representatives successfully lobbied the government behind the scenes on issues such as the repeal of the Masters and Servants Act (in this instance, a coal tycoon led the appeal, following a boycott by Atlantic dockworkers), the repeal of the color bar, and the extension of labor rights. The repeal of influx control legislation after a campaign coordinated by the Urban Foundation was "the clearest and most significant example yet of successful business lobbying."[5] Business interests, particularly big capital from England, played a role in the election of the then reform-minded P. W. Botha over Connie Mulder in 1979.[6] Through the Urban Foundation, many business executives also contributed to private efforts in housing and nonracial education to alleviate urban conditions.

After the 1984–6 uprising, business organizations and groups embarked on several unprecedented political interventions. Many business leaders believed that time was running out. According to a high-level Anglo American executive:

Clearly in the business community we were extremely concerned about the long-run ability to do business, the health of the South African economy. Equally we were concerned about preserving international linkages which were related to the ability to do business. Our assessment was that if left too long, the costs would be too high and the ability of the economy

---

[3] Torchia 1988. [4] This paragraph draws on Bernstein and Godsell 1988.
[5] Bernstein and Godsell 1988: 171. [6] O'Meara 1996.

to support democratization would have been removed. And so it was important, to the extent that one could, to try to hasten the process. (Interview, 1997)

Some businessmen articulated dismay at the country's backwardness and fear that the alternative to reform was revolution. According to a Chamber of Mines official,

Obviously the route we were on could have led to absolute ruin, to scorched earth. Increasingly it was difficult for us to do business, increasingly it was difficult for SA businessmen to travel abroad. It just wasn't the way to go. And it was contrary to all the trends in the world, the winning-nation trends. . . . We could actually see a revolution on its way. It was there for everybody to see. Some of us were making a lot of money with apartheid, then there wasn't too much complaint. (Interview, 1997)

For employers, an additional concern was the politicization of labor relations, which reflected the exclusion of workers from politics: employers understood the strikes as struggles over general political issues as well as over wages and working conditions. According to one official of the South African Chamber of Business,

Because [workers] did not have a way to express political freedom, they used the labor situation, the shop floor, to do that. And that was an important pressure point on business. (Interview, 1997)

According to one well-placed executive in the Chamber of Mines reflecting on the 1987 gold mine strike,

Well, I think the most important lesson that both sides learned is that you mustn't underestimate the bargaining power of your opponent and his ability to hurt you. Some very, very hard lessons were learned, especially in the period 1983–4 through to 1987. In 1988 when the social partners met each other to go through another round of negotiations, they had a healthy regard for the abilities of the other party, which made a very, very big difference. Gone was the NUM's "This was the year that we take over the mines" and on our side, gone was the thought if they strike it will be for only four days. And another 50,000 people will lose their jobs and we'll lose $150 million on gold production and everything else. It's not just a question of win or lose. There are possibilities of having integrative bargaining where win-win is the outcome. (Interview, 1997)

These concerns and experiences led business leaders to take unprecedented steps toward compromise.

There were six principal initiatives. First, some business organizations pressed for political reform in public campaigns. In January 1985, all the leading business organizations, including the usually conservative Afrikaner

172

business organization, the Afrikaanse Handelsinstituut (Afrikaner Commercial Institute, AHI), issued a manifesto calling for common and meaningful citizenship, the scrapping of the pass laws, and the ending of forced removals.[7] The Federated Chamber of Industries went further in 1986, announcing a "business charter" of rights to strengthen its commitment to reform and calling for unitary citizenship and universal suffrage:

[South Africa's] society is rifted [riven] by conflict and an escalating pattern of violence and repression. Despite the significant political reforms introduced by the government there is growing black frustration and agitation for political rights as reflected in rising protest and increased determination to secure fundamental change. Domestic unrest, consumer boycotts and external sanctions and pressures have all taken their toll on the economy, and in particular have seriously undermined local and international investment and business confidence.[8]

In justifying its extraordinary action, the Chamber explained:

What is now needed to restore credibility and confidence in South Africa is a realistic and visible programme both of political reform and economic reconstruction as a rallying point to address internal unity as well as the international community . . . The unacceptable alternative is the negative reaction of retreating into growing economic and political isolationism and a drift into a repressive siege society, necessitating greater government intervention and direct control over foreign exchange, imports, prices and wages. . . . Economic prospects have come to be increasingly dominated by the polarisation of political conditions which directly threaten the stability and prosperity of the country as a whole, in consequence the business community has accepted that far-reaching political reforms have to [be] demonstrably introduced to normalise the environment in which they do business.[9]

After affirming the members' willingness "to contribute to the processes of ongoing reform and to create the necessary conditions of peace, stability, and prosperity for all South Africans on the foundations of democracy," the charter endorsed a set of rights and principles, including the right to own property; the right to South African citizenship; universal suffrage and secret ballots; "due regard being given to the protection of the rights of minorities"; freedom from arbitrary arrest, detention, and exile; and the enjoyment of all rights irrespective of race, sex, ethnic origins, and property. The member organizations committed themselves to working for the "termination of turmoil, unrest and conditions of emergency, the release of political prisoners, and to explore and support debate and constitutional negotiations." The government responded with pressure

---

[7] Lipton 1985: 254.   [8] FCI 1986: 71.   [9] FCI 1986: 71.

against liberal elements of the organizations, forcing two officials to resign in 1987.[10]

Second, a group of prominent businessmen traveled to Lusaka in 1985 to meet with the ANC. While other organizations and groups would soon carry out similar encounters, business executives were the ones who initiated the "Lusaka trek," thereby making it easier for subsequent groups to do so. Business representatives also participated in meetings with the ANC in London. According to one participant,

We had the same experience that others had: meeting with these guys and finding that they're really quality leaders. And the stereotype image, you know, just sort of disintegrated. I think the second thing as far as our meetings in Britain were concerned was the discovery of a common sort of patriotism which had nothing to do with ideologies: the country, South Africa together, South Africanship, and the enjoyment which the environment gives us. When it came to the political matters, it was something different. Because there the whole discussion initially focused on the past: from the insider South Africans – because they're also South Africans – about the liberation struggle and why [the outsiders] made use of violence, and from their side how the hell could we try to defend apartheid? (Interview, 1997)

According to participants, such discussions gradually paved the way for the transition.

Third, individual enterprises also took steps to change their internal practices in light of the unrest of the mid-1980s. The Anglo American Corporation developed a set of policies to assist its executives and supervisors in "managing political uncertainty." Managers were encouraged to take on new roles: that of "innovator" within the factory, to address in-house worker grievances; of "facilitator," to mediate between groups outside the factory; and of "campaigner," to advocate change in the interests of the workers when such activity had a likely chance of being effective.[11] In granting all employees a half-day holiday to commemorate the tenth anniversary of the Soweto uprising ("to attend religious services and to commit themselves to peaceful change towards a non-racial democratic South Africa"), Anglo American urged the government "to facilitate the emergence of national political leadership for black South Africans," which would "require the unbanning of certain organisations, as well as the release from prison of key black leaders."[12]

Fourth, Ned-Cor and Old Mutual, two of the largest corporations, developed an "exercise" in imagining the new South Africa. It evolved

[10] O'Meara 1996: 361.   [11] AAC 1986a: 13–19.   [12] AAC 1986b: 2.

174

from an internal planning technique used within Anglo American to stimulate management brainstorming into a public exercise involving presentations to hundreds of groups (mostly business groups) around the country in 1990 and 1991.[13] The exercise consisted of examining two contrasting scenarios of South Africa's future: in one, the economy declines under a one-party regime dedicated to African socialism; in the other, democratic government by a black and white coalition conducts a pragmatic economic policy constrained by a bill of rights. According to one executive involved, the message was clearly that if South Africa was to survive as an economy, political changes would have to be made and negotiations would have to occur.

Fifth, at the end of 1986 a group of executives of major corporations concerned with growing social polarization decided to initiate contact with opposition organizations *within* South Africa to seek a mutual understanding of the crisis and possibilities for change. After several contacts with ANC and UDF leaders both in South Africa and in Dakar, the group and its small staff convened a meeting of two delegations near Broederstroom for a weekend discussion (despite the banning and arrest of many of the opposition participants). The "representatives of the majority" included union and civic leaders from various levels of COSATU and the UDF. The "creative minority" were business leaders and academics. During the weekend discussion was sometimes contentious as the representatives of the majority insisted that the ANC was necessarily part of the solution, that a "measure of nationalisation" would be necessary although its "extent, form and depth" could not be easily determined.[14] Rejecting further conversations with a collection of individuals, the representatives pushed the creative minority to form an organization that would pursue an explicitly anti-apartheid agenda. As a result, the Consultative Business Movement (CBM) was founded to promote the principles of nonracial democracy.[15] In the following years, the CBM's governing body of some two dozen business leaders met with senior members of the civil service, with the cabinet, with business organizations and diplomats, and after the release of Nelson Mandela, with the ANC. The group organized informal meetings between opposition leaders and business representatives, which

---

[13] This description of the scenario project is based on Tucker and Scott 1992; Kentridge 1993; and interviews with business executives in 1997.
[14] Du Preez, Evans, and Grealey 1988: 47–53.
[15] Du Preez, Evans, and Grealey 1988: 78–9.

in the judgment of some observers were more important than formal processes in sustaining a climate of negotiation among business interests. The CBM was later to play an important role both formally and informally after negotiations between the ANC and the National Party began, serving as the secretariat for negotiations between 1991 and 1994.[16]

Sixth, business organizations and labor representatives negotiated wideranging agreements on many aspects of labor relations during the late 1980s. As the reforms suggested by the Wiehahn Commission were slowly implemented, individual firms and various employer organizations engaged with the newly registered trade unions in negotiations over wages and working conditions. After the costly confrontation of the 1987 strike on the gold mines, according to an Anglo American executive,

the key lesson for the trade unions was that there was a line that would be drawn by business. Even the most progressive would not tolerate a degree of damage to their businesses beyond a certain level and would act to defend those. Equally, while we had the capacity to fire 50,000 people, which we did, that was not something one could do more than once. We were moving towards radically changing the model of mining through agreements with the unions from a low-wage, low-skill, highly labor-intensive and rather low-productivity model to a higher-wage, higher-skill, more productive but much less labor-intensive one. And in that model tests of strength on that scale were unbearably costly. One had to get into a far more cooperative mode. (Interview, 1997)

Anglo American and NUM also agreed to a "code of conduct" to govern the behavior of both management and trade unions, which then spread to other mines.

After another costly conflict – over amendments to the Labour Relations Act in 1988 – key leaders of both groups began meeting to devise a more constructive relationship, a process that culminated in the government's withdrawal of the changes to the act. Leaders of these groups, progressive industrial relations executives of the largest corporations in South Africa, and labor negotiators would continue to forge agreements through the transition. These efforts eventually led to the founding of a trilateral corporatist institution with a strong legislated mandate to review not just labor market policy but economic policy more generally. According to one executive who participated,

The whole pattern and culture of democratic elections – accountable representatives, mandating, etc., the whole democratic ethos – got built from the grass roots of the unions. Which

---

[16] This paragraph draws on Du Preez, Evans, and Grealey 1988 and Chapman and Hofmeyr 1994.

would not have been built if you would have had mass democracy through a central system. And the skills of bargaining wouldn't have developed and the leaders would have been different. (Interview, 1997)

This experience would serve the opposition well: key negotiators, particularly NUM leader Cyril Ramaphosa, would later play leading roles in political negotiations across a broad range of issues, including constitutional deliberations.

Thus by the late 1980s, many business executives and nearly all business organizations had come to agree that the country should move toward a liberal nonracial democracy. Moreover, according to two well-placed business leaders, most leading executives agreed as well that the state should play a role in redistributing wealth and addressing poverty from the proceeds of growth without any nationalization, and negotiations with black leadership were necessary.[17] Some took explicit *public* positions that only negotiations with the ANC could resolve the economic and political issues. The publication in mid-1988 of the ANC's "Constitutional Guidelines for a Democratic South Africa" encouraged these individuals, for the document endorsed a mixed economy and a bill of rights.[18]

But significant differences within business lessened the effectiveness of these efforts, and some retreated from politics.[19] While some endorsed negotiations with the ANC, the organization's socialist rhetoric troubled many others. Differences over post-transition economic policy were also important, as Afrikaner businessmen generally favored protectionist policies, whereas Anglo American and other English groups favored export-led growth and an open economy. It would take a change of leadership of the National Party for viable negotiations to emerge.

The National Party: From Reform to Negotiation

With the emergence of mass mobilization, the National Party faced ever-deepening problems. Successive attempts to resolve these issues either failed outright or exacerbated other issues. Although Botha came to power as a reformist candidate with the help of business interests, his administration gradually turned to repression and to militarization of the state to deal with the gathering political crisis.[20] Unable to manage the crises and

---

[17] Bernstein and Godsell 1988: 170–1. See also the interviews with business leaders in *Innes Labour Brief* 1990.
[18] O'Meara 1996: 386. [19] O'Meara 1996: 364.
[20] See Saul and Gelb 1981: 87–9; O'Meara 1996: chaps. 11–13; Price 1991: 86–7.

adamant in his refusal to take the only possible step forward – negotiations with the ANC – he was pushed out of office by a coalition of his own party in 1989.

Tensions within the party had emerged earlier, in the aftermath of the Sharpeville shooting. Members of the Cape National Party called for resumption of the franchise to coloured people and the ending of the pass laws. A group of Afrikaner clergy issued the Cottesloe Declaration in December 1960, a statement that rejected racial separation, detention without fair trial, the scriptural basis of the ban on interracial marriages, and the migrant labor system. The AHI issued a memorandum with other business organizations representing largely English business, calling for steps to ease racial tension and allow more mobility for urbanized Africans.[21] Verwoerd rejected these calls for reform, vowing to build "a wall of granite" in defense of apartheid, echoing the conservative modernization project he referred to as a policy of "separate freedoms."[22] In reaction to the threat of African nationalism, Verwoerd courted English as well as Afrikaner voters, emphasizing the unity "of people who agree on the cardinal principle of colour,"[23] and was rewarded with rapidly increasing support.

The reforms introduced in the late 1970s as a result of the Riekert and Wiehahn commissions recognized the permanence and the importance of the urban black population; however, measures for their implementation failed. The National Party was internally divided between conservatives who insisted that the exercise of political rights in the bantustans was an adequate provision and a more liberal element that insisted that some additional political accommodation had to be made.[24] Botha's election to head the National Party brought the latter group to power, but subsequent measures proved insufficient to quell the unrest. As noted in Chapter 5, the concessions on labor regulation had brought forth a militant rather than a quiescent union movement. Government efforts to create or attract black moderates to new constitutional discussions failed.[25] Despite the fact that by 1985 some members of Botha's government were carrying on conversations with Nelson Mandela, the meeting of Botha and Mandela in 1989 did not lead to any further conversations.[26]

A second problem facing the National Party was the collapse of its long-standing coalition of constituents. The split of the National Party over

---

[21] Posel 1991: 234–5.   [22] O'Meara 1996: 107.
[23] de Villiers 1971: 375.   [24] O'Meara 1996: 201.
[25] Giliomee 1997: 9.   [26] Sparks 1995: 55–6.

reform led to the founding of the Conservative Party and the departure of many white voters, particularly white labor, from the National Party.[27] By 1982, a quarter of National Party voters were English and only 42 percent of Afrikaners supported it.[28] The civil service was the remaining remnant of the party's coalition, but this posed problems because it limited the party's options for responding to the fiscal crisis, now deepened by the imposition of financial sanctions. More Afrikaner businessmen began calling for reform, working with English capital to press the government for concessions. In 1989, some Afrikaner intellectuals and businessmen supported the founding of the new political party, the Democratic Party, which was committed to nonracial democracy, civil liberties, and private enterprise.

After the repression of the 1984–6 uprising, the party faced growing dissent among Afrikaner intellectuals and clerics. The Dutch Reformed Church announced that there was no biblical basis for apartheid, throwing religious circles into upheaval.[29] In 1986, following a decision by the Broederbond that the abolition of statutory discrimination was necessary for Afrikaner survival, the organization's chair, Pieter de Lange, met with Thabo Mbeki in New York, signaling a sea change within the Afrikaner organization.[30] In 1987, approximately fifty Afrikaner intellectuals went to Senegal for discussions with the ANC. This meeting was followed by twelve secret meetings from November 1987 to 1990 between Afrikaners – mostly members of the Broederbond – and ANC officials in London, where topics ranging from group rights to economic policy were discussed.[31]

A third problem confronting the party was the growing militarization of the government. When Botha's reforms failed, he reinforced the role of the security establishment in the government. The State Security Council gradually displaced Parliament, the National Party caucus, and even the cabinet as the site of debate and policy definition.[32] Party regulars chafed under the growing role of the "securocrats."

The fourth problem was national security. The defeat of South African forces at Cuito Cuanavale in Angola was the direct result of sanctions, as the underequipped South African forces proved vulnerable to the Cuban MIGs. This led to the withdrawal of South Africa from Namibia (in return for the withdrawal of Cuba from Angola) and the negotiated independence of Namibia.[33]

---

[27] O'Meara 1996: 312–15.   [28] O'Meara 1996: 308.   [29] O'Meara 1996: 336.
[30] Giliomee 1997: 14; Sparks 1995: 73–5.   [31] Sparks 1995: 82–3.
[32] O'Meara 1996: 280.   [33] O'Meara 1996: 377–8.

Despite increasing repression, the uprising of 1984–6 deepened, which led Botha to announce in January 1986 that he accepted the principle of universal citizenship in a single nation and the formation of a National Council that would include the bantustan leaders, elected township representatives, representatives of the three houses of Parliament, and ten presidential appointees.[34] He also announced procedures for the writing of a new constitution. Botha subsequently agreed to meet with a group of "eminent persons" sent by the Commonwealth to mediate the crisis. Because Botha had frequently said that he would agree to negotiate if the ANC renounced violence and suspended armed struggle, the group explored the issue with the ANC in prison and in exile. Both Mandela and Tambo agreed, but hours before the group was to meet with the Constitutional Committee, the South African Defense Forces attacked ANC sites in neighboring countries. Botha told the group that he was "not interested in negotiations about transfer of power."[35] As a result, the Commonwealth group recommended strengthening sanctions as the only way forward, given the government's refusal to surrender white control despite an avowed commitment to power sharing. The government subsequently renewed and broadened the state of emergency, arresting some 26,000 people between June 1996 and June 1997 and marginalizing civilian politicians. Moreover, Botha's proposed political arrangement was rejected by Inkatha Freedom Party (IFP) leader Mangosuthu Buthelezi who made release of Mandela a condition for participation. In February 1988, Botha banned the UDF. Despite these measures, the three-day stayaway in June 1988 was the biggest ever.[36]

The failed reforms created accumulating layers of racially segregated bureaucracies. By the late 1980s, there were five "presidents," 1,500 members of Parliament and other legislative bodies, tens of thousands of local councillors, a central bureaucracy for general affairs, three bureaucracies for "own affairs," and ten parallel national bureaucracies, as well as local and regional bodies.[37] In this context of unresolved crisis, accumulating failed reforms, and paralysis, P. W. Botha resigned as leader of the National Party (although not initially as state president) after a stroke. In a closely contested election for party leader in February 1989, the more conservative candidate F. W. de Klerk won by a narrow margin. De Klerk won the national presidential elections in September 1989, drawing more

---

[34] Price 1991: 141.   [35] Cited in O'Meara 1996: 341.
[36] O'Meara 1996: 380.   [37] O'Meara 1986: 351.

support from English voters than from Afrikaners in an election that saw four times as many people on strike that day than those who voted.[38] The *Weekly Mail* headline reporting election results read "Nat: 93, Con: 39, Dem: 33, Hurt: 100, Dead: 23."[39] In a context of gathering expectations as well as impending debt negotiations, the ANC signaled its willingness to negotiate, and Margaret Thatcher warned that she could not hold off further sanctions forever.[40]

On February 2, 1990, F. W. de Klerk crossed the Rubicon, announcing the unbanning of the ANC and the SACP and the freeing of Nelson Mandela, thereby taking the step that Botha had long resisted and implicitly acknowledging the ANC as the insurgent counter-elite necessary for negotiations to resolve the crisis confronting the country. (While Botha was aware of the contact between Afrikaner intellectuals and the ANC and knew that contacts had widened to include Niels Barnard, the head of the National Intelligence Service, the discussions had been held in secret, with no public commitment.)[41]

The end of the cold war gave de Klerk an important window of opportunity: it made such a step more acceptable to the party's constituency. According to a politically influential Afrikaner academic,

The moment that the Berlin wall collapsed in November, you saw that he was now in a position to sell the unbanning to his constituency. And so I think the wall was quite significant in that in September of 1989 he was still very tough on the ANC but by November he had moved. And I think it was a psychological change, it's not as if the wall caused the whole kind of events, but he simply saw that now he can get the albatross off his neck. You know, where they had spoken about the ANC as being dominated by the Soviet Union, dominated by communists and all, now they could say, "well the ANC is also nationalist." Without the Soviet Union they are a much more manageable proposition than otherwise. (Interview, 1997)

While the end of the cold war contributed to the timing of the release of Mandela and the unbanning of the ANC, it was domestic political processes – sustained political mobilization, the ongoing crisis in investment, and the failure of various efforts to construct a moderate black opposition – that made negotiations with the ANC necessary. On the anniversary of de Klerk's unbanning speech, the National Party scrapped remaining apartheid institutions, including the Group Areas Act and Land Acts.

---

[38] O'Meara 1986: 400. [39] O'Meara 1986: 401.
[40] O'Meara 1986: 399. [41] Sparks 1995: 80–1.

The Liberal Democratic Pact

Thus by 1990, the government and ANC were prepared to negotiate with the support of business, the principal labor unions, and a wide range of civic and religious organizations. The parties faced a formidable agenda of issues with a bitter history of violence, repression, and contempt. Three issues in particular had to be resolved if a new and enduring "constitutional dispensation" was to be devised.

First, the parties had to agree on an electoral formula and institutional structure. The National Party was committed to power sharing among a nation of minorities, not simple majority rule, and sought to construct a consociational regime that would ensure veto power on the part of the white minority over policies concerning its core interests. According to the party's constitutional strategy, each ethnic group would govern its own affairs, with general affairs decided by consensus among the majority parties of each group: group rights and minority vetoes were the party's bottom line.[42] Indeed, in a September 1991 proposal, the party argued for a rotating presidency, equal representation in the cabinet of political parties garnering a share above some threshold of the legislative vote, a decision-making rule within the cabinet based on consensus, similar power sharing at the regional level, and the entrenching of particular clauses in the constitution.[43] The party's commitment to a power-sharing formula reflected its expectation that there would be a permanent black majority: it did not have a realistic hope of governing again soon.[44] Ensuring the autonomy of Afrikaner schools and other cultural institutions and the future of the Afrikaans language were also key concerns of the party as it embarked on negotiations with the ANC.

The ANC was long committed to majoritarian rule through a one-person, one-vote electoral system in a unitary state structure. The ANC's initial position on constitutional issues was taken in the April 1991 "Constitutional Principles and Structures for a Democratic South Africa," which called for a strong central government and majoritarian rule based on proportional representation and rejected group rights. It was presumed that the ANC would argue for a continuation of South Africa's first-past-the-post rules as it would further entrench the power of the majority.[45]

[42] O'Meara 1996: 404–5. [43] Hamill 1994: 16.
[44] Friedman 1993b: 59. [45] Sisk 1995: 188.

182

Given its long-standing opposition to apartheid-era constitutioneering on the basis of ethnicity, the party would be reluctant to compromise on the issue. Moreover, there was disagreement as to the order of progress on constitutional issues: would new elections be held before constitutional negotiations to ensure broad representation of the newly enfranchised populations, or would some other group negotiate the constitution before elections were held?

The second challenging issue was the degree to which the constitution would circumscribe future economic policy: whether the constitution would enable nationalization; whether the rights to private property, to strike, and to lock out striking workers would be explicitly protected; and if so, whether special supra-majorities would be required for their amendment.

The third issue had to do with the legacy of violence and the prospects for prosecution, retribution, or amnesty. This concerned all parties to the negotiations: the National Party, given the violence by state forces against the opposition (some but not all of which was legal at the time); the ANC, given the trouble in the guerrilla camps and the deaths of civilians from guerrilla attacks; and the IFP, given the violence of its members against ANC militants during and after the 1984–6 uprising.

Negotiating the Transition to Democracy

Initial negotiations between the ANC and the government led to interim agreements (the Groote Shuur, Pretoria, and D. F. Malan Minutes) that provided a transitional security framework for the ANC as it returned to the country. The armed struggle would be suspended while further negotiations took place, although the combatants would not be demobilized. There were various contentious issues: the timing of the demobilization of the insurgent armed forces, the definition of "political prisoners" and the pace of their release, and the government's failure to halt the rising violence between supporters of the IFP and the ANC. Despite an apparently cordial meeting between Mandela and Buthelezi in January 1991, violence between the rival forces deepened throughout the year, spreading from KwaZulu-Natal to the greater Johannesburg area and leaving hundreds dead in a series of clashes. Allegations grew – proven later in the Inkathagate scandal of July 1991 to be true – that elements of the security forces were funding the IFP in a joint effort to undermine the growing understanding between the ANC and the National Party.[46]

As the violence intensified, the ANC withdrew from negotiations in April 1991, issuing an ultimatum that if political prisoners were not released, violence were not controlled, some security forces not suspended, and two ministers not dismissed by May 9, the ANC would call for a two-day general strike, mass protests in commemoration of the Soweto uprising, and a consumer boycott.[47] While some demands were met, most were not, and the violence continued.

Mediation by church and business leaders, including the CBM and businessmen involved in negotiations with COSATU, led to the signing of the National Peace Accord on September 14, 1991, and cleared the way for constitutional negotiations. Using their contacts and experience from previous negotiations with COSATU and the UDF, the group built a coalition to support the initiative despite the tension between the ANC and the National Party.[48] The document affirmed that the common goal of the signatories was the founding of a multiparty democracy and included a "code of conduct" for political parties and police forces, a national peace committee to develop and supervise a variety of conflict-resolution forums, and a commission of inquiry to investigate the violence, later known as the Goldstone Commission.[49] The leaders of the National Party, the ANC, and the IFP signed, as did a host of other organizations.

Following the agreement that multiparty negotiations would begin addressing some issues, the Convention for a Democratic South Africa (CODESA) was convened on December 20, 1991, with the CBM serving as its administration and secretariat. The ANC had agreed in January 1991 that some sort of initial negotiation would have to precede a constitutional assembly, but it remained committed to the ratification of the final constitution after inclusive elections.[50] All major parties sent representatives, but Buthelezi refused to attend because the IFP had been denied two delegations (one for the party and the other for the homeland government).[51] However, the process soon foundered on the fundamental issue of process:

---

[46] Sisk 1995: 95.   [47] Sisk 1995: 103–4.

[48] Some businesses made extraordinary commitments to the National Peace Agreement process. For example, Barlow Rand seconded two of its executives as well as some secretaries to the process, and provided offices, conference halls, and meals for several months (Charney 1994: 9).

[49] National Peace Convention 1991.

[50] Sisk 1995: 99, 192.   [51] Sparks 1995: 130.

184

whether the constitution would be negotiated by representatives of existing political parties or by representatives elected in fresh inclusive elections. Separate working groups were established to address subsets of
issues. After an all-white referendum in which voters overwhelmingly supported de Klerk and his program of negotiated reform, the National
Party became intransigent, arguing that power sharing had to be a binding
principle on the final constitution and that constitutional amendments
should be approved by 75 percent of Parliament, which would ensure a
white veto over the final constitution. As a result, the ANC withdrew from
Working Group II in May 1992, and later from the convention itself.

In the face of the negotiation impasse, the ANC and COSATU
unleashed campaigns of political mobilization to press the National Party
for concessions. Widespread strikes and demonstrations in June 1992 –
"Mandela's referendum" – demonstrated the continued capacity of the Left
to mobilize massive support and to threaten the economy.[52] This period
of mass action partly reflected tensions within the ANC alliance, between
those who saw mobilization as a tactical accompaniment to negotiations,
those who believed mass actors remained the key to a settlement, and those
who thought a "Leipzig option" was possible.[53] After an ill-judged march
on Bisho, the capital of Ciskei, from the nearest South African town, two
dozen ANC supporters were killed. This incident apparently sobered the
Leipzig advocates.

The period of mass action, despite the human costs, ultimately fur-
thered the negotiations.[54] First, it reminded all parties that a return to
mobilization and repression was too costly, underscoring the advantages
of compromise.[55] Second, the militance of the campaign suggested to ANC
leadership that it should make concessions with caution. Third, the degree
of support demonstrated once again to the government that the ANC had
an unparalleled following.

Violence between the ANC and IFP also deepened in this period. For
example, IFP supporters attacked a hostel in Boipatong, a township south
of Johannesburg, leaving almost fifty residents dead. Policemen killed a
number of township residents in a subsequent demonstration. Where
political violence had left 5,500 dead between 1984 and 1989, it left 13,500
dead between 1990 and 1993.[56] The Goldstone Commission subsequently
uncovered detailed evidence of a "third force": military intelligence and

---

[52] O'Meara 1996: 411.   [53] Hamill 1994: 27–8.   [54] Hamill 1994: 39–41.
[55] Hamill 1994: 31.   [56] Charney 1994: 3.

other security forces had carried out dirty tricks against the ANC and were heavily involved with the IFP.[57]

Key concessions were made by both parties in response to the growing violence and the breakdown of the negotiation process. In the Minute of Understanding, a bilateral agreement signed in September 1992, the ANC and the government addressed several outstanding issues and resolved to renew multiparty negotiations. Most important, the National Party scrapped its insistence that an upper house with veto power be mandated by the constitution.[58] This meant that a key procedural question was settled: an interim constitution would be negotiated before elections; representatives elected in that framework would then serve both as an interim legislature and the assembly that would negotiate and approve the final constitution.[59] One compromise offered by the ANC (on the initiative of Joe Slovo of the SACP) eased the way toward the final agreement: a "sunset clause" ensuring continued employment and pensions for the white civil service. Soon after, Slovo also argued publicly that some form of power sharing should be acceptable as it would contribute to the transition. Details were still to be worked out, but together these concessions met key National Party concerns. Although they also sparked fierce dissent within the ANC, party policy did not change.

The Multiparty Negotiating Process (MPNP) was convened on April 1, 1993. The new commitment of both the ANC and the National Party to reaching an agreement was soon evident in the speed with which troublesome issues were resolved. Under the MPNP's nested structure, final policy decisions were to be made by a large plenary that would meet occasionally, as needed. Two representatives of each party would form the Negotiating Council, which would discuss emerging agreements several times a week. A planning council of ten members was also to meet continuously and secretly, advised by a technical subcommittee.[60] Decisions were to be made by "sufficient consensus," which meant the process could continue despite some disagreement.[61] On several occasions, difficult issues were settled in side conversations between the ANC's Cyril Ramaphosa and the National Party's Roelf Meyer. In addition, a series of encounters at game parks by subsets of participants provided less formal settings for discussions. The process survived the April 1993 assassination of Chris Hani, a top-level MK commander and high-ranking member of

---

[57] Sparks 1995: 153.　[58] Hamill 1994: 33.　[59] Friedman 1993: 63.
[60] Atkinson 1994: 24.　[61] Atkinson 1994: 29.

the SACP, by a white conservative. By July, negotiators had agreed on an April 27, 1994, date for elections. In September, Parliament passed legislation creating the transitional executive council to govern South Africa until the elections.[62]

The Concerned South Africans Group (COSAG), an alliance of the IFP, some bantustan leaders, and white conservatives, withdrew from the MPNP when the election date was announced, but trilateral negotiations between the National Party, the ANC, and COSAG continued.[63] The members of the alliance had little in common except for their hostility to the idea of the ANC and the National Party dominating discussion and a vague predilection for some form of federalism. In June 1993, three thousand armed whites invaded the negotiating forum.

Despite these events, Meyer and Ramaphosa negotiated a key set of agreements. The National Party accepted that they would not have a veto in the cabinet, and the ANC agreed that the National Party would be part of the government for five years. The National Party won additional if vague assurances such as a commitment that the cabinet would make decisions in the spirit of consensus and national unity. The ANC won a single ballot for both regional and national elections. The ANC conceded that 60 percent, not 50 percent, of the members of Parliament would need to approve the final constitution if the negotiation process deadlocked.[64]

On November 18, 1993, the interim constitution was adopted by the multiparty forum's Negotiating Council. The agreement defined a transitional power-sharing arrangement, the Government of National Unity, which would govern between the 1994 and 1999 elections and ensure cabinet seats to minority parties that won more than 5 percent of the seats (twenty) in the lower house in proportion to their share. Cabinet decisions were to be formulated in a "consensus-making spirit," and deputy presidencies were to be assigned to parties receiving more than 20 percent of the seats (eighty) in the lower house.[65] The constitution also included a Bill of Rights, an independent judiciary, and a new Constitutional Court,

---

[62] This paragraph draws heavily on Sisk 1995, particularly his chronology.
[63] Sisk 1995: 36.   [64] Atkinson 1994: 34.
[65] The constitution mandates a two-chamber legislature (Jung and Shapiro 1995: 276). In the lower house, half of the 400 members are elected from national lists and half from provincial lists. The 90-member senate is nominated by majority parties of the provincial legislatures, themselves elected from provincial lists. If no party earns more than eighty seats in the lower house, then the two largest name the executive deputy presidents.

all supported by the National Party, in the expectation that it would not win the coming election.[66]

In February 1994, further agreements were approved in an attempt to bring COSAG into the negotiations. The revised constitution allowed a double ballot for regional and national elections and enlarged regional powers, changed the name of Natal to KwaZulu-Natal, and provided for a commission to explore the possibility of an Afrikaner *volkstaat* if sufficient support was demonstrated.[67] These measures effectively drew into the electoral process the white right, demoralized by the televised shooting by a Bophuthatswana soldier in early 1994 of a member of an invading force of white militants as he begged for mercy.[68] Ciskei and Bophuthatswana joined the process soon after. But the IFP raised the ante, insisting on international mediation and the recognition of Zululand as a sovereign kingdom.[69] The international mediators came and left, unable to broker an agreement.

A last-minute deal in April 1994 ensured the participation of the IFP in the election. The agreement, mediated by Washington Okumu with the support of the CBM, was that the IFP would participate if the parties agreed to recognize the "constitutional position of the King of the Zulus and the Kingdom of KwaZulu."[70] In a secret agreement, representatives of the ANC, IFP, and National Party agreed to transfer 1.2 million hectares (about 95 percent of the old KwaZulu bantustan) to the king's trust to reassure traditionalists that traditional land allocation would continue.[71] The last act of the KwaZulu legislative assembly was to pass a bill affirming these arrangements, which de Klerk quickly signed into law.[72]

On the one hand, ANC concessions protected National Party interests: the sunset clause protected military, police, and civil service members from replacement once the new government came into power, and the transitional structure meant a continued policy-making role for the National Party if they could win 20 percent of the vote. The constitution founded a regime of limited federalism (the precise degree of provincial autonomy remained unclear). However, the ANC did not agree to the consociational

---

[66] Friedman 1997: 5.   [67] Atkinson 1994: 94.

[68] The white conservatives had joined the electoral process earlier: shortly before the March 1994 deadline, conservative leader Constand Viljoen registered the Freedom Front Party to compete in the election.

[69] Atkinson 1994: 37.   [70] Atkinson 1994: 38; Rothchild 1997: 207–9.

[71] Johnson 1996b: 335. Rothchild puts the transfer at 3 million hectares (1997: 209).

[72] Atkinson 1994: 40.

arrangements promised to white voters by de Klerk before the 1992 referendum: although the National Party would play a role in both the interim and transitional governments, it would do so without the power of veto. Indeed, the role proved so meager that the party later withdrew from the Government of National Unity.[73] The interim constitution also recognized certain cultural and economic rights; most notably, it recognized eleven languages as official languages.

In the view of Hermann Giliomee, an Afrikaner academic with wide contacts in the Afrikaner establishment, several factors contributed to the National Party's failure to achieve its principal goal in the negotiations (namely, to ensure a minority veto). The party lacked an ideology to justify such a veto, given its acknowledgment that apartheid had failed. The ANC's jettisoning of nationalization undercut any argument that the National Party was needed to protect private property and free enterprise. The end of the cold war removed any international ideology or bilateral support to justify racial domination. And finally, according to Giliomee, de Klerk lacked the will to endure the mass action campaign of mid-1992 and thus dropped the party's insistence on formal power sharing.[74] Nor had the party protected the Afrikaans language: Afrikaans would become one of eleven official languages, which "looks like a barely concealed formula for English to become the sole official language."[75] Nor did the party win concessions for "mother-tongue education or single-medium schools" as constitutional rights in the negotiations over the final constitution in May 1996.

Yet the ANC made significant concessions in the negotiations, many of them on economic issues. The interim constitution limited the power of the state to override private property rights: nationalization would be possible only in the public interest, under the rule of law, and with due compensation, generally at market value. The protection of private property thus met a core concern of economic elites. A special section of the constitution on land rights allowed claims for restitution for property seized under racially discriminatory measures after June 19, 1913 (the passing of the Land Act). Restitution could take the form of title to alternative state

---

[73] Friedman, 1997: 4. Courtney Jung and Ian Shapiro (1995) argue that the constitution was a consociational arrangement, despite the lack of an effective veto. This does not seem to have been the case, given the National Party's inability to affect policy and its resulting withdrawal from the government.
[74] Giliomee 1997: 17–19.   [75] Giliomee 1997: 17.

land or the payment of compensation by the state. That it was to be determined on a case-by-case basis made large-scale redistribution unlikely.[76] The right to lock out workers was included in the Bill of Rights (but subsequently deleted from the final May 1996 Constitution), as was the right to strike (which was not). (As recommended by the new Constitutional Court in its review of the May 1996 text, the final constitution required that a supra-majority of 75 percent would be necessary to amend the Bill of Rights.)[77] The ANC also agreed that a Truth and Reconciliation Commision could grant amnesty to petitioners.

Many of the economic compromises were initially worked out in the separate negotiations between labor and business representatives described earlier. This process of corporatist bargaining resolved several issues that might have led to significant conflicts and thereby helped consolidate the new order.[78] The origins of this bargaining process illustrate key aspects of the transition itself. In a 1989 agreement, business and labor organizations had signed an accord that forced the government to withdraw the changes made in the Labour Relations Act of 1988 after the mineworkers strike.[79] In 1991, COSATU led a two-day stayaway (according to one estimate, it involved 90 percent of black workers) in opposition to the government's attempt to impose a value added tax. This campaign represented a general political challenge in that it advocated there should be no taxation where there was no representation. As part of the campaign, the unions insisted that a forum be founded for the discussion of economic policy.

Business representatives agreed to the forum because they thought negotiations in such a chamber would be preferable to labor militant activity. According to a Barlow Rand executive,

We have to acknowledge that we're in this boat together. We row together or we will sink it together. Therefore create a system that will lead up to the political transition but where we can evolve, where we together can actually begin to make the political decision making. Begin to build content and that will lay the groundwork for the political transition itself. This was 1989. It became a formal understanding. Because the groups that were there were mandated to be there. And we were working with one another, it wasn't an agreed vision before, it was an evolved vision that we will reform this, we will channel the political conflict into here. (Interview 1997)

The ANC's move away from the commitments to nationalization in the

---

[76] Simkins 1994: 42. [77] Ebrahim 1998: 229.
[78] Friedman 1993: 560. [79] Klug 1995: 220.

190

Freedom Charter contributed to this corporatist climate.[80] According to an Anglo American executive, business understood as early as 1990 that there would be no significant nationalization efforts. In the judgment of one academic close to the negotiations, the ANC was not itself interested in nationalization but "used the nationalization hammer to kick all those businesses into a new mode of thinking." Under pressure from business and labor organizations, the government reluctantly agreed to participate in the forum as well.

The result was the National Economic Forum (NEF) and a reinvigorated National Manpower Commission (NMC), which together gave labor an unprecedented role in policy formulation, a role institutionalized after the elections as the National Economic Development and Labour Council (NEDLAC). The NEF resulted in diffuse rhetorical commitments to growth, equity, and participation, but few concrete agreements; however, the discussions removed a number of contentious issues from the constitutional process for a significant period. For example, in discussions in the NMC, the labor unions and business organizations agreed that both the right to strike and the right to lock out would be entrenched in the new constitution. The NEF was also the site of initial negotiations over labor relations that would be legislated as the Labour Relations Act of 1998, which institutionalized a range of new forums for worker participation and institutions for conflict management. Some capital-labor efforts failed: an attempt to carry out a joint one-day suspension of business in mid-1992 failed when businesses refused to implement the agreement reached.[81]

Although agreements reached in this trilateral process contributed to stability during the transition, final negotiations over economic clauses of the constitution proved difficult. Business organizations followed the process closely, making almost daily submissions to the relevant commissions, according to a South African Chamber of Business official. After a campaign by COSATU in the final days of negotiations over the final constitution in 1996, the right to lock out striking workers was deleted from the Bill of Rights.

On April 27, 1994, black South Africans endured long lines to vote for the first time. The ANC won 62.65 percent of the vote, short of the two-

---

[80] Kentridge 1993; CBM 1993. The ANC and COSATU initiated two economic policy research projects during this period, the Industrial Strategies Project and the Macro-Economics Research Group, both efforts to define post-apartheid policy.

[81] Kentridge 1993: 46.

thirds necessary to make some constitutional changes unilaterally. Massive mobilization of voters by COSATU contributed to the ANC turnout; indeed, some thirty COSATU leaders stood for election on the ANC's list.[82] The National Party won 20.4 percent of the vote and control of the Western Cape. The IFP won 10.5 percent, the Democratic Party 1.7 percent, and the PAC 1.2 percent. The voting did not fall along sharp ethnic lines: the National Party vote exceeded its 13.1 percent of the population, reflecting significant coloured and Indian support, and only one out of three Zulus voted for the IFP.[83] By one estimate, some 40 percent of lower-class whites in Durban had voted for the IFP.[84] While the proportional representation rubric probably reduced the ANC's share of the seats in the lower house from more than two-thirds to 62 percent, it did so mostly at the expense of the smallest parties, not of the IFP and the National Party.[85] Although there is some evidence that the KwaZulu-Natal outcome was a "negotiated" election result, most observers and all parties concurred that nonetheless the overall result reflected the general pattern of voting. Evidence of a "negotiated" result were the suspension of vote tallying for forty-eight hours, the refusal of the Independent Electoral Commission to release the number of votes invalidated, and its refusal to allow international observers to attend the final discussion of disputed ballots.[86] The most serious problem was the existence of 165 "no-go zones" where other parties feared to campaign.[87] In the end, the parties did not go to court to contest the outcome, although the national ANC had to put pressure on the KwaZulu Natal branch to accept defeat at the provincial level.[88]

Conclusion

Attempts at conservative modernization of the apartheid regime and reforms of the labor regulation system failed to quell unrest in South

---

[82] Adler and Webster 1995: 95.   [83] Jung and Shapiro 1995: 297.

[84] Johnson 1996a: 321.

[85] Friedman 1997: 9–10. The 1996 Constitution replaced the Senate with the National Provincial Council.

[86] Johnson 1996b: 330–4.   [87] Johnson 1996b: 328.

[88] Johnson 1996b: 334. The KwaZulu Natal results were contentious because the reported vote was quite distinct from polls and because the ANC garnered many fewer votes than it expected (Johnson 1996b: 343). Johnson concludes that the polls were erroneous because a substantial fraction of IFP supporters lied to pollsters.

Africa. While the repression succeeded to a degree against the UDF, labor militancy continued. In response, business pursued negotiation rather than confrontation, not only in the workplace but also in politics. National Party leaders reluctantly came to understand that their future was better ensured by engagement with the ANC. Thus, changes in elite interests occur twice in this explanation: the success of the National Party in advancing Afrikaner economic interests beginning in 1948 caused Afrikaner business interests to merge with those of English-speaking elites, and the subsequent threat mobilization by township residents and workers posed to elite interests (both English and Afrikaner) motivated the powerful members of this ethnically diversified economic elite to push regime elites toward compromise. Indeed, the bargaining between business and labor that preceded and then paralleled the political negotiations reinforced mutual confidence that compromise on the terms of the transition was possible.

During the negotiations, the National Party proved unable to defend what it had advertised as its bottom line: a white-minority veto over general government policy. Although the National Party won cabinet seats and deputy presidencies under the provisions for the Government of National Unity, these provisions were not accompanied by any consociational decision rule to effectively limit majoritarian power. The ANC, despite a period of socialist rhetoric, achieved at long last its founding objective: participation as equal citizens in a liberal democratic polity.

Conclusion

8

The Insurgent Path to Democracy in Oligarchic Societies

The [peace] agreement is a ray of light. What we hope for is to be equal before the law. We have lost the fear we had before the war, we have lost the fear.

– Leader, Cooperativa La Maroma,
Usulután, 1992

The most important change for labor is the protection of people out on legal strike. . . . We don't want the government to give things on the table; we want the government to create space for us to be able to organize and be able to fight our own battles.

– National Union of Mineworkers leader,
March 1997

The idea that political freedoms and universal suffrage are the prize won by common people in their struggle for justice is part of the folklore of democracy. Rarely, perhaps never, has democracy come about in so simple a fashion. South Africa and El Salvador are not exceptions to this pattern. Nonetheless, in both South Africa and El Salvador transitions to democracy were forged from below by workers, the urban poor, and by *campesinos* – previously marginalized social actors whose militancy in the face of repression transformed the interests of the well-to-do and eventually forced hitherto recalcitrant elites to the bargaining table. The repressive state and impermeable class boundaries of these oligarchic societies originated in long-standing labor-repressive practices such as forced labor, debt peonage, restrictions on labor mobility, and the repression of labor organization. The emphasis on redistribution and democratic reform in the rhetoric of insurgents proved a powerful mobilizing force. Fueled by the resulting dire material circumstances and by outrage at ongoing political exclusion and poverty enforced by repression, these social movements constituted their leadership as an insurgent counter-elite. Sustained unrest eventually persuaded elites that the costs of repression were too high and that negotiations with the insurgent counter-elite were therefore in their interest.

These two civil conflicts proved amenable to negotiated resolution based on a transition to democracy because their similar oligarchic pasts forged contending forces principally defined by economically interdependent class interests, a structure of conflict different from that of many civil wars. Even in South Africa, where racial and ethnic identities were of course extremely salient, apartheid had succeeded in shaping the racial structure of classes so that by the late twentieth century class and race coincided to a remarkable degree. Structurally linked both by conflicting interests and by mutual economic dependence, the antagonists were not free to simply go their own ways, as the South African case richly illustrates. The insurgents were thus not simply those excluded from privileges enjoyed by dominant groups (as in many civil conflicts); they were the tenants and employees of the economic elites. This economic interdependence meant that the opportunity costs of lost production were added to the direct military and other direct costs of the ongoing conflict. This, along with the fact that a divisible prize – present and future income – loomed large among the stakes of the game, facilitated a solution to the conflict. Regime elites, the other party to the conflicts, were not dependent on the insurgent classes except indirectly as the threat of insurgency historically provided reason for the cohesion of regime and economic elites in their political exclusion of subordinant classes. Not surprisingly, the impetus to compromise with the insurgents came in both cases from those elites who depended on the insurgents for their livelihood.

As a result, the compromises that resolved these class-based civil conflicts were similar. Economic elites surrendered their privileged relationship to the state, exposing their interests to the vagaries of electoral competition. The insurgent counter-elites abandoned their aspirations for a socialist outcome, agreed to the status quo distribution of private property rights (with few exceptions), and accepted stringent constraints on subsequent populist redistribution because, as long-excluded political actors, they valued the right to full citizenship in a democratic polity.

In this chapter, I point out some contrasts between the insurgent path to democracy in South Africa and El Salvador and then compare these two with the cases of Guatemala and Poland. I then discuss the characteristics of the civil conflicts in El Salvador and South Africa that rendered them amenable to negotiated resolution via a democratizing political pact, in contrast to many other civil wars.

The Transitions to Democracy in El Salvador and South Africa

Although El Salvador and South Africa exhibit the general logic of the insurgent path to democracy, the constitution of their leadership as an insurgent counter-elite took distinct paths. The FMLN developed a highly effective military capacity based on superior intelligence networks and on widespread peasant support that defied the state's response. It also had a close relationship with a wide variety of opposition organizations, which ranged from occasional coordination of protest to direct if clandestine incorporation of key leaders into the command structure of the guerrilla forces. The ANC, by contrast, was militarily ineffective and had much less direct contact with or control of insurgent social movements in South Africa. Although some leaders of the UDF and COSATU were members of the ANC or SACP, insurgent organizations in South Africa were more autonomous from the ANC than the Salvadoran organizations were from the FMLN. Ironically, the racism of apartheid policies gave rise to a strong oppositional nonracial ideology that rejected state-defined ethnic categories and claimed a common citizenship in a single nation, which helped constitute the ANC leadership as the insurgent counter-elite over competing candidate organizations such as the Pan Africanist Congress.[1]

Sustained unrest challenged the interests of economic elites in distinct ways in the two cases. In El Salvador, those interests shifted dramatically, away from its traditional reliance on export agriculture and toward commercial and service sectors fueled principally by a huge influx of remittances from Salvadorans in the United States. In South Africa, insurgency transformed elite economic interests not because it reduced the economic importance of sectors in which profits depended on labor-repressive institutions but because it undermined the commitment of economic elites to the society-wide labor-repressive institutions on which they had long relied for their livelihoods.

Elite interests in both countries changed for more subtle reasons as well. The mounting cost of forgoing new opportunities also impelled compromise. In El Salvador, some economic elites feared that if they did not

[1] Marx 1998; Sisk 1995: 264.

resolve their enduring civil war they would miss foreign investment and marketing opportunities promised by expanding regional economic integration. In South Africa, a deepening distaste for the pariah status of the country also contributed to elite accommodation, according to interviews with business leaders. The spread of neoliberal ideology contributed to both transitions, as elites could assume with some confidence that international financial agencies and the global mobility of private capital would discipline any post-transition government that encroached too severely on holders of wealth, professionals, and other globally mobile economic elites.

Why did regime elites agree? Though initially united by pressure from below, the alliance between economic and regime elites characteristic of oligarchic societies eventually unraveled as insurgency forced a wedge between those economic elites who saw a way of retaining their privileges in a liberal environment and hardline regime elites who had more to lose. As a result of sustained insurgency and counterinsurgency measures believed necessary in response, Salvadoran economic elites founded their own party, an unprecedented move toward direct political representation of economic elite interests. Moreover, after the transformation of elite interests shifted the balance of power within the party, leaders moved to support negotiations despite hardliner opposition. In South Africa, important economic elites broke decisively with the oligarchic alliance in the mid-1980s by moving autonomously to talk with the ANC. The decision by the National Party to negotiate with the ANC was the result of pressure from economic elites, but it probably also reflected the direct budgetary pressure insurgency exerted under the mounting costs of elaborate ethnic bureaucracies and growing security forces.

Insurgency contributed in other, less direct ways. In El Salvador, U.S. support for a settlement further undermined military hardliners stalemated by the FMLN. In South Africa, the National Party's coalition dissolved as recalcitrant elements disillusioned by reform efforts and declining incomes joined parties to the right and as Afrikaner economic elites found their core interests converging more with those of other economic elites than with the party agenda. The failure of efforts to modernize apartheid without compromising white supremacy left the party without an agenda around which to unite, particularly after the end of the cold war undermined hardliners' canonical justification for continued resistance to nonracial elections.

Of course, when they entered into negotiations, neither economic elites nor regime elites were unconditionally committed to ending the conflict through compromise and democratic rule. If increased concern about the costs of continuing conflict brought elites to the bargaining table, only a conviction that they would do better – or at least no worse – in peacetime under democratic rule would make an end to hostilities and a transition to democracy possible. Thus whether or not the structural basis of compromise was in fact in place depended on the expected distribution of the returns to compromise. Distributional issues must be settled, or at least the range of uncertainty about distribution restricted, if powerful actors are not to defect from a democratic transition, a requirement that Guillermo O'Donnell and Philippe Schmitter refer to as the "economic moment" and Terry Karl and Tim Sisk call the "social contract."[2] (See the Appendix for a formal model of these issues.)

In both countries, a long process of negotiation hammered out the key trade-offs of the democratizing pact. Economic and state elites secured significant guarantees for the protection of their core interests. Most important, negotiations granted constitutional protection for private property and other institutions of a liberal market-based economy with only limited exceptions. In return for suspending militant political mobilization, insurgents of both countries achieved full citizenship, political inclusion of their organizations, and a varied degree of institutional reform that, if fully implemented, would in each country mark a transition to political democracy. Insurgent parties were legalized, electoral reform made fair elections more likely, and domestic policing became normalized. In both countries, efforts to end the long-standing judicial impunity of regime elites included judicial reforms as well as a process of limited accountability for human rights abuses through truth commissions and partial or conditional amnesties. The pacts also contained additional concessions to the most mobilized insurgent constituents: land was distributed to former-combatants of both sides and to militant FMLN supporters in El Salvador, and labor unions were given an institutionalized role in policy setting in South Africa.

The National Party failed to realize key elements of its agenda in the negotiations. Its racially and ethnically based consociational proposals

---

[2] O'Donnell and Schmitter 1986: 45–7; Karl 1990; Sisk 1995. While Burton, Gunther, and Higley argue that social contracts need not be part of a pact, they do so only by making an unsustainable distinction between institutional and substantive pacts (1992: 34–5). To agree on institutions (such as private property rights) is to agree on substantive issues (such as their distribution).

were adamantly opposed by the ANC, largely because they were understood as continuing apartheid privileges under a more generic and internationally palatable guise. Concessions were made by the ANC, but the constitutional settlement did not include a racially defined minority veto or any explicit recognition of group rights. It only provided for sharing of cabinet seats and deputy presidencies between the lead party and minority parties above certain thresholds.[3]

In both cases, international forces helped coordinate the move to peace by enhancing the power of moderates over hardliners, holding out potential economic rewards for peace and thereby reinforcing the structural basis of compromise and threatening reprisal should negotiations not prove successful. In South Africa, sanctions were an important element of the structural conditions supporting negotiation but in important measure were a consequence of the domestic dynamic of mobilization and repression (as well as the pressure of activists in other countries). The role of international actors was significantly greater in El Salvador, where military stalemate and U.S. support of the negotiations undercut the autonomy of military hardliners and the United Nations provided the coordination and guarantees that moved the two parties to compromise, particularly in demobilizing armed combatants. In South Africa, many of these mediating and coordinating roles were played by domestic actors. Poland and Guatemala offer interesting contrasts to these cases.

Although the transition in Poland was made possible by the liberalization of Soviet foreign policy in the 1980s, popular mobilization played a crucial role in both its path and its timing. Labor mobilization by the insurgent trade union Solidarity in the 1980s eventually led the government to recognize that it must negotiate with the organization in order to end labor unrest and to begin to resolve an ongoing economic crisis.[4] After Solidarity's unexpected and overwhelming victory in a fight for contested seats under a compromise electoral formula in which not all legislature seats were contested, the governing party's minor coalition partners supported Solidarity, and in short order fully contested elections were held for all government offices. The role of Solidarity as an insurgent counterelite parallels that of the FMLN and ANC. However, it does not seem

---

[3] On different aspects of the debate concerning the degree to which the interim government arrangements were consociational, see Jung and Shapiro 1995 and Friedman 1997.

[4] On the transition to democracy in Poland, see Goodwyn 1991; Bernhard 1993; Stokes 1993; Zielinski 1995; and Poznanski 1996.

that ongoing mobilization led to a negotiated transition via the same mechanism as in El Salvador and South Africa (via a shift in elite economic interests). Perhaps the defection of party members to the nascent private sector throughout the 1980s, which can be thought of as a change in elite economic interests, contributed to the transition, but it was probably not the dominant factor.[5] Although party control of labor was a form of extra-economic coercion and the intermingling of economic and regime elites in the party had oligarchic aspects, some elites may not have perceived democratization to be a threat to their economic interests (once the Soviet Union was out of the picture). Party elites did not think they would lose the election, given its restricted formula. Perhaps of more enduring importance, managers had every reason to expect higher, not lower, incomes in a liberal market society.

The transition in Guatemala, on the other hand, appears to be quite similar to that in El Salvador: negotiations between a guerrilla insurgency and a government led by a party representing a modernizing faction of economic elites ended a long-standing civil war on terms similar to the Salvadoran peace agreement.[6] But there are three important differences. First, the Guatemalan guerrillas were much weaker; as a result, the military made fewer concessions on its prerogatives. Nonetheless, pressure from international actors as well as from domestic groups led elites to agree to a number of democratizing provisions, including the recognition of indigenous languages and rights, a limited degree of land transfer, and a narrowing of the military's mandate. Not all of the provisions were implemented, however. Second, because the guerrillas were weak, the civil war, though long-enduring, did not transform elite interests. Although some members of the economic elite thought it was important to end the war if they were to pursue new opportunities under spreading free trade agreements, opposition from conservative elites prevented implementation in key areas. Third, the party that negotiated the end of the war was not a hegemonic party of the center-right like ARENA. As a result, Guatemala's democracy after the transition appeared more fragile than that of El Salvador. Significant military prerogatives endured, and the political party system was more fragmented.

---

[5] Poznanski 1996: 140.
[6] See Trudeau 1993; McCleary 1996 and 1997; Holiday 1997; Spence et al. 1998; Azpuru 1999; Stanley and Holiday 1999; and Whitfield 1999.

Resolving Civil Wars with Democratizing Pacts

I began with two puzzles: why did the elites of these two societies abandon their long-standing opposition to democratic rule, and why did these protracted civil conflicts prove amenable to resolution by negotiation? My answer to both is that after insurgency transformed elite economic interests away from coercive institutions, the economic interdependence of the principal antagonists provided the structural underpinnings for a resolution of the conflict based on a transition to both liberal capitalism and political democracy. However, many civil conflicts have resisted negotiated resolution; many that ended were followed by authoritarian rather than democratic rule. What generalizations, if any, do these cases suggest?

The fundamental conundrum that a negotiated resolution of a prolonged civil conflict in which no side can achieve a decisive military victory must address is this: if a peace is to endure, it must be self-enforcing. It is unlikely that a third party can impose a resolution that is not in the interests of the contending parties; in that case an intervention by a third party must redefine the interests of the parties so that a cessation of conflict is in the interest of each. Moreover, each side must find it in their interest to stop fighting and to pursue peace not just at the time of negotiations but subsequently as well. In certain conditions, democratization, especially when accompanied by economic liberalization, may circumscribe the distributional outcomes of a cessation of hostilities such that the settlement proves self-enforcing.[7]

Scholars of civil wars distinguish between conflicts over identity issues such as national language and those over other matters. Some authors argue that because identity-based conflicts tend to be all-or-nothing struggles for indivisible stakes (control of the state, the right to name the sole national language, etc.), they should be harder to resolve by negotiated settlement than conflicts in which stakes are divisible, such as class-based conflicts. However, comparative empirical analyses have not found that to be the case. Mason and Fett (1996) found that ethnic conflicts are no less susceptible to negotiated settlement than nonethnic wars. According to Roy Licklider (1995), civil wars based on identity issues are no more intense and are just as likely to end in negotiated settlement as nonidentity wars, but those settlements are then more likely to break down.

---

[7] See the Appendix for a formal statement of these issues. In two related papers (Wood 1999a and 1999b), I develop this argument in detail.

Barbara Walter (1997) found that wars over ethnic identity are no less difficult to resolve than others and that outside guarantees are the key to an enduring settlement.

Perhaps the inconclusiveness of the literature reflects a tendency to combine two characteristics of civil conflicts that should be treated as distinct. By analyzing civil conflicts as ethnic or not, a second aspect is neglected: whether or not the principal antagonists are economically interdependent in such a way that a cessation of hostilities promises substantial benefits to both parties sufficient to create a structural basis for compromise. The former distinction remains salient, of course, but should not be confused with the latter: the parties to some ethnic conflicts are economically interdependent to a high degree; the parties to others are not. Indeed, in some cases I discuss later, a cessation of hostilities would be extremely costly to one or more parties.

Whether or not the structural basis of compromise is in place depends on the expected returns to continued conflict compared with the expected returns to compromise, as evaluated by each actor. In the case of indivisible stakes, compromise is difficult because neither party believes the returns would be adequate unless it can control *all* of the stakes. In conflicts over divisible stakes, however, some division of the postwar returns to compromise may lead both parties to prefer compromise to continued conflict.

When the conflict is over divisible stakes and the parties are economically interdependent, a range of mutually acceptable settlements may be possible.[8] Such interdependence enhances the returns to peace in contrast to conflicts over indivisible stakes. Key antagonists in the Salvadoran and South African conflicts were classes on whom war imposed not only the costs of conflict common to any war but also the costs of forgone benefits of production.

Moreover, the enhanced benefits to compromise in such conflicts provide significant resources with which to make "side payments" to what Stephen Stedman (1997) terms "spoilers," factions of one party or another that split from the principal group to try to wreck the agreement. The transfer of extensive land to the Zulu king and generous provisions for Afrikaner civil servants are examples of this.

Yet agreements negotiated at bargaining tables are often broken, so parties seek guarantees that the terms will be adhered to. In particular,

---

[8] For a formal statement of this argument, see Wood 1999a.

economic elites seek difficult-to-alter institutional constraints on post-transition redistribution that might significantly cut into their incomes or assets. Thus economic elites seek constitutional protection of the status quo distribution of private property rights, while insurgent representatives seek constitutional protection of the right to strike and attempt to prohibit constitutional restraints on future redistributive actions by the state. In polities where inequality is high, these issues are particularly salient because the median voter will tend to favor redistributive measures. In South Africa at the time of the transition to democracy, approximately three-quarters of the electorate had incomes below the mean.[9] Economic elites sought and won such constitutional provisions: not only was a right to private property included in the new Bill of Rights, any change in the provisions of the right (due process, adequate compensation, and so on) required the approval of a supra-majority of members of parliament. In El Salvador, the terms of the peace agreement (and the related constitutional changes) entailed an acceptance by the FMLN that the further land reform promised under the 1980 agrarian reform would not occur.

In the case of conflicts where there is economic interdependence, the institutions of a liberal market economy provide some discipline over post-transition populist redistribution. If populist initiatives threaten elite interests, the well-to-do can take their capital or their skills elsewhere.[10] So economic elites may accede to democratization if it occurs in the context of liberalized capital flows.[11] While it is also true that a liberal economy limits the ability of economic elites to benefit from monopolistic practices and exposes business to profit-limiting global competition, economic elites may be willing to accept these challenges as the price of restricting the redistributive capacities of the state. So when liberal rules govern the political economy, it matters less what political party is in power: market institutions restrict post-transition uncertainty about distributional outcomes. Economic elites may therefore seek to integrate domestic markets into the global economy during the negotiation period. This explains an otherwise puzzling fact of both transitions, the broad consensus among business across sectors in favor of economic liberalization

---

[9] Calculated from SALDRU 1993 data set, a survey of 8,848 households containing 43,974 individuals. See SALDRU 1994.

[10] See Wood 1999b.

[11] Thus the global spread of capital markets reinforces a previously mentioned aspect of the structural basis of compromise, the opportunity cost of forgone foreign investment as a result of civil war.

despite well-founded beliefs that not all firms in all sectors would be likely to weather increased competition.[12]

In identity-based conflicts where there is little economic interdependence, not only are there fewer gains to compromise but also fewer opportunities for limiting uncertainty about the consequences of compromise. In some cases, a basis for negotiated settlement may be to separate the parties into distinct nation-states. But in other cases, the two populations may be too closely entwined, one may control the principal assets of the country (making partition infeasible as the other party opposes partition because it would be left destitute), or one party may be adamantly opposed to separation for other (perhaps cultural) reasons.

In such instances, moderates may attempt to render the indivisible stakes divisible. In the case of identity issues, the negotiators may agree that the languages of *both* groups will be the national languages, as in Belgium, or that many languages will have equal official standing, as in the extreme case of eleven languages in South Africa. Negotiators may attempt to render power or prestige more divisible through power-sharing institutional innovations such as parliamentary dominance, proportional representation, federalism, or consociationalism.[13]

But such institutional innovations in the case of indivisible goods do not have the salient features that allow markets to limit uncertainty about post-transition outcomes: markets for divisible goods are decentralized mechanisms that operate through individual incentives. In the case of indivisible stakes (even if rendered more divisible), winner-take-all dynamics are difficult to avoid, and competitive markets are not sufficient to reliably reassure elites that post-transition distributional outcomes will lie within a reasonably small range.

In sharp contrast, where the insurgent forces possess divisible, highly valuable goods, such as diamonds and cocaine, the parties are *not* interdependent and civil conflicts are particularly difficult to resolve. Although the stakes are divisible, the parties are not mutually dependent, so the returns to cooperation may not be great. The costs of relinquishing at least partial control of the good may outweigh the benefits of peace.

Both indivisible stakes and the absence of economic interdependence

---

[12] Of course, in both cases sustained insurgency itself directly supported a more global outlook among economic elites who moved significant assets out of the country in response to the uncertain circumstances of the war.

[13] See Sisk 1996.

thus exacerbate the problem of post-transition uncertainty. Because constituents powerful enough to spoil the agreement may not accept such "splitting-the-difference" redefinitions of the state and nation (perhaps because of the reduced capacity to constrain uncertainty), the emergence of spoilers may be more likely than in conflicts where the parties are economically interdependent.[14] Postwar reconstruction assistance from international donors may provide side payments to help reconcile potential spoilers to a settlement, but in these cases such exogenous rewards to compromise are less effective than in cases where they reinforce a domestic structural basis of compromise.

Thus these two distinct dimensions – whether the parties perceive the stakes of the conflict to be divisible and whether their economic interdependence renders high returns to compromise – may illuminate why some civil conflicts are amenable to negotiated resolutions whereas others prove intractable despite significant international pressure. Perhaps ironically, protracted class-based conflicts in oligarchic societies – even where ethnic identities and racial divisions are highly salient, as in South Africa – are thus amenable to negotiated resolution once sustained insurgency erodes elite reliance on coercive institutions.

Conclusion

If the "long walk to freedom" (to borrow Nelson Mandela's phrase) in South Africa and El Salvador contrasts sharply with that in, say, Brazil, Costa Rica, and Spain, should we anticipate correspondingly distinct post-transition trajectories? Although a particular path to democracy does not, of course, automatically govern subsequent developments, the legacy of El Salvador's and South Africa's oligarchic past and the consequences of their "long walk" will not soon be erased. But the possibility of continued path dependency – countries that arrive at democracy from below face distinct obstacles to development and to the consolidation of democracy – will be the subject of another book. In the Epilogue I briefly speculate about these issues.

---

[14] For a different argument as to why spoilers frequently disrupt civil war negotiations, see Walter 1997. She notes that the problems posed by demobilization of armed forces (whatever the nature of the conflict) are likely to disrupt settlements.

Epilogue

THE LEGACY OF DEMOCRACY
FORGED FROM BELOW

We shed blood all these years in order to buy land at market prices?

        – Usulután *campesino*, 1992

Irish coffee is a drink made of whiskey in a tall glass. If you look at the bottom it is black, at the top it has a white cream with sprinkles of chocolate. And we're saying affirmative action programs, black economic empowerment programs, should not just produce sprinkles of chocolate. It must be directed at changing the social relations in society.

        – National Union of Mineworkers leader,
        March 1997

Just because democracy in El Salvador and South Africa was forged from below does not, of course, imply that the political transitions would result in a substantial redistribution of economic opportunity to the poor. In both cases, economic concessions won in negotiations were far from what the insurgent movements had hoped for at the height of their militancy: land reform would occur only under narrow rubrics; widespread nationalization of privately held assets was unconstitutional; and while democratic rule might result in stronger unions and strengthen allied political parties in the interests of workers, redistributive initiatives would be restrained by the threat of capital flight. Moreover, the terms of the transition in both cases left particular obstacles to the consolidation of democracy and the furthering of economic development.[1]

In both South Africa and El Salvador, evolving economic conditions in the aftermath of the transition threatened to blunt, if not reverse, even the

---

[1] For further analysis of the South African case, see Friedman 1995 and 1997.

209

COSATU march during wage negotiations, Cape Town, 1995. Banner reads (roughly), "Viva Cosatu. Umkohto We Siphure. Let us share in the fruits of our labours. Unity is our promise to free the land that workers shall . . . " Photograph by Benny Gool. © Benny Gool/Trace Images.

modest economic gains won at the negotiating table: growing unemployment in South Africa and the limited economic viability of land transferred under the terms of the peace agreement in El Salvador undermined the distributive impact of the new labor relations framework in South Africa and of the land redistribution in El Salvador. In short, competitive market pressures threatened to undo what the insurgents' bargainers had hoped to accomplish. Moreover, the promised institutional reforms proved difficult to realize, local authoritarian political cultures were resistant to national democratic reform, and reformed police forces faced steep uphill struggles against the traditional impunity of regime and economic elites.

In oligarchic countries, the canonical "dual transition" – the consolidation of democracy and the carrying out of extensive economic reform – is significantly complicated by the confluence of four legacies of this particular path to democracy: (1) its highly unequal distribution of wealth and life opportunities (particularly in the case of South Africa); (2) the substantial degree of social mobilization necessary for transitions from below to succeed; (3) the raised expectations of mobilized groups; and (4) a state whose police, judicial, and other institutions reflect past commitments to repression rather than accommodation of a plurality of interests and to the containment of social unrest rather than to the delivery of services meeting basic human needs. For key political actors – those whose militancy propelled the transition – trade liberalization and other liberal policies fall far short of and may be seen as obstacles to the types of economic reforms they expect. The fact that the antipathy of the insurgent rank and file to many of these market-based initiatives may be misplaced or exaggerated does little to ease the problem of disappointed expectations in the short run.

Thus, even where the dual transition is not threatened by overt defection by either erstwhile elites or the now enfranchised insurgents, the challenge of building social peace in the aftermath of democracy forged from below makes the transition to procedural democracy and enduring economic growth significantly more difficult. The tension between democratic consolidation and economic reform that Luiz Carlos Bresser Pereira, José María Maravall, and Adam Przeworski identified (1993) as present in all transitions is particularly acute where transitions are driven from below, given the higher level of organization and higher expectations of mobilized political actors.

If these fledgling democracies are to be consolidated, vibrant political competition between parties and other means of making the government accountable to citizens must be strengthened. In South Africa, political competition between parties seems likely to wane with the deepening of the ANC's formidable electoral dominance, suggesting the possibility of a long period of de facto single-party rule reminiscent of that of the Congress Party in India under Jawaharlal Nehru and his successors. Ongoing reshuffling of National Party leadership and the rapprochement of the IFP and the ANC are sobering developments from the point of view of democratic consolidation. National-list proportional representation and provisions that preclude members of Parliament from crossing the aisle to join the opposition will impede the development of opposition parties.[2] Moreover, the terms of the 1996 Constitution left apartheid-era "native authorities" for the most part in place, a significant failure to democratize rural authority.[3] Finally, the ability of the COSATU unions to constitute an

[2] Jung and Shapiro 1995.   [3] Mamdani 1996.

independent voice in policy matters is compromised by the erosion of union bargaining power due to persistent high unemployment and global competition and by the departure of key union leaders for government and private sector managerial positions.

In El Salvador, perhaps ironically, the prospects for a durable electoral opposition appear less bleak: although the historically antidemocratic party ARENA won not only the first but the second presidential election held after the transition, the FMLN emerged as the leading opposition party, becoming increasingly competitive with ARENA for local and national offices alike. But the inadequacy of campaign finance regulation and the winner-take-all structure of local government are impediments to democratic consolidation. Although after the March 2000 elections the FMLN held more seats in the Legislative Assembly than any other party and *campesino* activists enjoy freedoms of expression and association unprecedented in El Salvador, the consolidation of democracy will not be put to the test until ARENA loses a presidential election.

Appendix

A MODEL OF NEGOTIATED RESOLUTION OF CIVIL CONFLICTS

As argued in Chapter 8, a negotiated settlement of a civil conflict can endure only if each party finds the returns to compromise preferable to those of conflict. The informal model presented here explores the structural basis of compromise, particularly the role of expected post-settlement distributional outcomes in generating or blocking moves toward the negotiated resolution of civil conflict.[1] In addition, consideration of the model's simplifying assumptions illuminate the challenges that such negotiated resolutions must overcome.

Suppose that two parties, "the elites" and "the insurgents," engage with one another: each selects one of two strategies, to continue fighting ("fight") or to seek to resolve the war ("compromise"). The "payoffs" to combinations of the two strategies are given in Figure A.1, where the first entry represents the return to the row player and the second that to the column player for that combination of strategy choices. The substance of the payoffs is unimportant: all that matters is that actors do not knowingly choose lower payoffs over higher. To simplify the presentation, the payoffs are symmetrical, an assumption relaxed below.

At the onset of the conflict, fight is the dominant strategy for each party: it is preferred irrespective of what the other does. Thus the return to mutual conflict – fight-fight – is preferred by both to mutual compromise; initially, the payoffs in Figure A.1 are such that $\alpha > \gamma$ (and $\gamma < 1$). Formally, mutual conflict is the dominant strategy equilibrium, and the resulting outcome is Pareto superior to mutual compromise. Note that the interac-

---

[1] For a more formal treatment of the issues discussed here, see Wood 1999a and 1999b, which extend the approach in Wantchekon 1996 and Przeworski 1996.

213

	Elites	
	Compromise	Fight
Insurgents		
Compromise	γ,γ	$0,\alpha$
Fight	$\alpha,0$	$1,1$

Figure A.1 The logic of civil conflict and its resolution

tion is not a prisoner's dilemma as both parties hold mutual conflict to be superior to mutual peace.

During the course of a conflict, the benefits of mutual compromise may grow (at least by comparison with continued conflict), so γ may increase, until eventually $\gamma > 1$, making mutual compromise Pareto superior to mutual conflict. But as long as α remains larger than γ, mutual conflict remains the dominant strategy (and the payoffs describe a prisoner's dilemma). Strategically, the fact that mutual compromise is now Pareto superior to mutual conflict does not make a settlement possible, as mutual compromise is not an equilibrium outcome: the best response to the other's compromising is to fight.

In order for the conflict to end with a negotiated settlement rather than a victory, both sides must come to prefer peace to fighting – not unconditionally, but as long as the other side does as well. The interaction may take on the structure of what is commonly termed an assurance game (or coordination game) where both mutual peace and mutual war are self-enforcing outcomes requiring that $\alpha < \gamma$ and $\gamma > 1$ so that compromise is the best response to compromise, and mutual compromise is judged by each player to be superior to mutual conflict. Note that fight is still the best response to fight, so mutual conflict remains an equilibrium. The "ripeness" of a conflict for resolution is thus readily expressed by the transformation of the payoff matrix from one in which mutual peace is not self-enforcing to one in which it has the structure of the assurance game in which *if* peace could be attained, neither side would have an incentive to defect.[2]

But ripeness is not enough. Both parties must be induced to move *together* to a strategy of seeking peace; the reason is that the move is favored by each *only if the other makes the same shift.*

Above and beyond these conditions are those that become clear when

---

[2] Zartman 1989.

one abandons the game-theoretic assumption of common knowledge and the fiction of unitary actors and recognizes that the actors' beliefs are uncertain and that each "actor" comprises a group whose interests are heterogeneous. I develop each condition in turn.

First, even if both parties believe that the payoffs support a self-enforcing peace, one or the other, or both, may not know with certainty that the other shares this belief. For the outcome of mutual compromise to be reached, both sides must believe that not only their payoffs but also those of their opponent are in the required order. This is the dilemma of the would-be negotiator: not knowing whether the conflict has come to have the above logic and whether the opponent also shares that belief. The would-be negotiator needs to signal a credible commitment to the other side that the interaction is understood to have the assurance game structure. (Arguably, it is not enough for the two parties to *believe* that the conflict has taken on such a logic, but the conflict must indeed have that logic: if not, it is quite probable that one of the parties will discover its mistake and therefore believe a move back to the fight strategy would reap big rewards.) This uncertainty is compounded at the beginning of the process by the as yet undetermined nature of the bargaining: whether each prefers peace to war (if the other does as well) depends on the terms of peace, which introduces distributional issues into consideration. I return to this question (extending the above model) shortly.

Second and relatedly, the actors attempting a transition to peace are not single players but groups of people with a range of individual interests: the two "players" may not be cohesive single actors to the extent necessary for supporting the mutual compromise outcome (and the implementation of the peace agreement). If one or the other group is too divided, a splinter group may emerge and carry out armed actions that could threaten the entire process: the more internally heterogeneous the two actors, the more likely it is that some coalition within one or the other may benefit from defecting from the peace process. The compromises required by the peace agreement may themselves deepen existing differences within the elite or the insurgent groups. Thus spoiler groups may emerge particularly when those compromises have different implications for the different interests of the various constituencies of that "player."

The key issues are typically whether the military structures of each side will indeed demobilize and endure the resulting loss of influence, access to financial resources, and prestige within their group, and (in the case of class-based conflicts) whether sufficient assets can be transferred to the insurgents to make peace the best response to elite accommodation on the part of their membership base – without undermining the willingness of elites to compromise.

The transition from the fight-fight interaction to that of peace-peace is therefore highly problematic: the assurance-game logic is a necessary condition for the resolution of the conflict (unless, of course, mutual compromise is a dominant strategy for both parties), but it is not sufficient. To reassure the parties that the logic that brought them to negotiate will endure, peace agreements must provide "guarantees" that promote compliance.

Third parties can contribute to the resolution of such civil conflicts in four ways. First, they may provide additional incentives that reinforce the structure of the assurance game nationally or locally, raising the costs of defecting to "fight" (with the imposition of sanctions or the suspension of aid), reducing α, and contributing benefits that reward adherence to "peace" (with postwar financial assistance, for example), raising γ. Second, third parties may provide local coordination of the move between fight-fight and peace-peace in the form of mediation during negotiations over the peace agreement or cease-fire missions to assist in the physical separation of hitherto warring forces. Third, third parties may contribute to the transition by lessening the uncertainty on each side as to whether the other side in fact believes that the interaction is such that it would be better off with peace and is thus negotiating in good faith, and later by lessening the uncertainty that the other side is complying with the agreement. Fourth, third parties can smooth out differences between regions in the relative strengths of the two parties; by providing credible accountability for actions throughout the country, such parties can reduce the incentives for militants of the locally stronger side to carry out actions against the weaker that might lead to a vicious circle of retaliation and potentially the suspension of the settlement.

Expectations concerning the distributional outcomes of the postwar rules of the game form an essential part of the incentive structure. But the interests of the two parties may be very divergent, so they may find it difficult to agree on a particular set of institutions.[3] In particular, the benefits to compromising jointly may not be equally distributed. Suppose that the total benefits to be divided are 2γ (as in Figure A.1) and that a share β ($0 < \beta < 1$) of this total will be gained by the insurgents under the con-

---

[3] Przeworski 1996.

Appendix

	Elites	
	Compromise	Fight
Insurgents		
Compromise	$2\beta\gamma$, $2(1-\beta)\gamma$	$0,\alpha$
Fight	$\alpha,0$	$1,1$

Figure A.2   The distributional logic of conflict resolution

ditions of the negotiated peace (Figure A.2). The entry for mutual compromise in Figure A.2 is thus $2\beta\gamma$, $2(1 - \beta)\gamma$. Whether one party prefers compromise if the other party does now depends on both β and α. The coefficient β – the stakes of the game for the insurgents – depends on their expectations of the distribution of the returns to peace.[4] The structure of the interaction – more precisely, the structure of expected returns to the various combinations of strategies both during the transition and afterward – must be perceived by both sides to be that of an assurance game (*both* $2\beta\gamma$ and $2(1 - \beta)\gamma$ must exceed α).

Among the tasks of those who negotiate transitions to democratic rule is that of eliminating insofar as possible any incentive to defect by electoral losers. In oligarchic societies, economic elites must change their perception of the relationship between their interests and democratic rule (hitherto perceived as incompatible). Even if they come generally to prefer accommodation over conflict, they have an interest in the nature of the compromise. Although their willingness to compromise politically may reflect economic interests and political capabilities transformed by the insurgency, the conflict between their economic interests and those of the insurgents remains, formalized by β. Moreover, if the compromise is to endure, the distributional bargain must be heavily entrenched as a basic rule of the game to ensure that neither party has an incentive to defect from the agreement.

This illuminates the trade-off between political inclusion and economic compromise that was characteristic of the settlements in both South Africa and El Salvador: if both sides are to agree to the transition, β must be such

---

[4] The model thus assumes that negotiators do not negotiate behind a Rawlesian "veil of ignorance" concerning their interests. In these unequal societies where neither party has been able to defeat the other, negotiators seek to protect and further their interests in the negotiations. Although they may not be able to anticipate the precise consequences of particular institutional arrangements (Przeworski 1991: 87), in the cases considered here negotiators acted in light of the expected distributional consequences of various arrangements. See Friedman 1997.

that the rewards of peace exceed those of fighting for both parties; and each party must find ways of credibly precommitting to a range of values of β consistent with the other's accepting compromise. Elites accomplished this by conceding political democracy, addressing a long-held ground for grievance; the insurgents accomplished the analogous task by agreeing to a liberalized market economy with only minor changes in the distribution of property rights.

Note on Statistical Sources

All data for El Salvador, except where noted in the text, are from various issues of the quarterly publication *Revista Trimestral* of the Banco Central de Reserva, El Salvador's central bank. All data for South Africa, except where noted in the text, are from various issues of the South African Reserve Bank's *Quarterly Bulletin*, as well as the following publications of the Reserve Bank:

South Africa's National Accounts, 1946 to 1993. Pretoria: South African Reserve Bank, 1994.

South Africa's Balance of Payments 1946–1992. Pretoria: South African Reserve Bank, 1993.

Labour, Price and other Selected Economic Indicators of South Africa. Pretoria: South African Reserve Bank, 1994.

References

Acevedo, Carlos. 1991. "El Salvador's New Clothes: The Electoral Process 1982–1989." In *A Decade of War: El Salvador Confronts the Future*, edited by Anjali Sundaram and George Gelber, 19–37. New York: Monthly Review Press.

"Acuerdo de New York." 1991. Mimeo, n.p.

Adam, Heribert. 1971. *Modernizing Racial Domination: South Africa's Political Dynamics*. Berkeley: University of California Press.

Adler, Glenn, and Eddie Webster. 1995. "Challenging Transition Theory: The Labor Movement, Radical Reform, and Transition to Democracy in South Africa." *Politics and Society* 23(1): 75–106.

African National Congress (ANC). 1949. "'Programme of Action': Statement of Policy Adopted at the ANC Annual Conference, December 17, 1949." Reprinted in *From Protest to Challenge: A Documentary History of African Politics in South Africa, 1882–1990*, vol. 2: *Hope and Challenge 1935–1952*, edited by Thomas Karis and Gail Gerhart, 337–9. Pretoria: Unisa Press.

African National Congress (ANC). 1952. "Letter replying to letter from the prime minister's office and statement of intention to launch defiance campaign, from Dr. J. S. Moroka and W. M. Sisulu to Prime Minister D. F. Malan, February 11, 1952." Reprinted in *From Protest to Challenge: A Documentary History of African Politics in South Africa, 1882–1990*, vol. 2: *Hope and Challenge 1935–1952*, edited by Thomas Karis and Gail Gerhart, 480–2. Pretoria: Unisa Press.

Aglietta, Michael. 1979. *A Theory of Capitalist Regulation*. Translated by David Fernbach. London: New Left Books.

Alesina, Alberto, and Roberto Perotti. 1996. "Income Distribution, Political Instability, and Investment." *European Economic Review* 40: 1203–28.

Almond, Gabriel, and Sidney Verba. 1963. *The Civic Culture: Political Attitudes and Democracy in Five Nations*. Princeton, N.J.: Princeton University Press.

Anderson, Thomas. 1971. *Matanza: El Salvador's Communist Revolt of 1932*. Lincoln, Nebr.: University of Nebraska Press.

Anglo American Corporation of South Africa Limited (AAC). 1986a. "Managing in Political Uncertainty: Operating Management Guidelines." Typescript.

Anglo American Corporation of South Africa Limited (AAC). 1986b. Statement by Gavin Relly, Chairman for release on June 13, 1986. Typescript.

Atkinson, Doreen. 1994. "Brokering a Miracle? The Multiparty Negotiating Forum." *South African Review* 7: 13–43.

Aubey, Robert T. 1969. "Entrepreneurial Formation in El Salvador." *Explorations in Entrepreneurial History* 6(3): 268–85.

Azpuru, Dinorah. 1999. "Peace and Democratization in Guatemala: Two Parallel Processes." In *Comparative Peace Processes in Latin America*, edited by Cynthia J. Arnson, 97–126. Washington, D.C.: Woodrow Wilson International Center for Scholars.

Bacevich, A. J., James D. Hallums, Richard H. White, and Thomas F. Young. 1988. "American Military Policy in Small Wars: The Case of El Salvador." Paper presented at John F. Kennedy School of Government, Harvard University.

Baloyra-Herp, Enrique A. 1982. *El Salvador in Transition*. Chapel Hill: University of North Carolina Press.

Barro, Robert J. 1997. *Determinants of Economic Growth: A Cross-Country Empirical Study*. Cambridge, Mass.: MIT Press.

Bénabou, Roland. 1997. "Inequality and Growth." *National Bureau of Economic Research Macroeconomic Annual* 1997: 11–74.

Beretta, Gianni. 1989. "Joaquín Villalobos: Los puntos sobre las ies." *Pensamiento Propio* 7(57): 13–17.

Bermeo, Nancy. 1997. "Myths of Moderation: Confrontation and Conflict during Democratic Transitions." *Comparative Politics* 29(3): 305–22.

Bernhard, Michael. 1993. "Civil Society and Democratic Transition in East Central Europe." *Political Science Quarterly* 108(2): 307–26.

Bernstein, Ann, and Bobby Godsell. 1988. "The Incrementalists." In *A Future South Africa: Visions, Strategies, and Realities*, edited by Peter L. Berger and Bobby Godsell, 164–99. Boulder, Colo.: Westview Press.

Bhaskar, V., and Andrew Glyn. 1995. "Investment and Profitability: The Evidence from the Advanced Capitalist Countries." In *Macroeconomic Policy after the Conservative Era: Studies in Investment, Saving and Finance*, edited by Gerald A. Epstein and Herbert M. Gintis. Cambridge: Cambridge University Press, 175–96.

Blanchflower, David G., and Andrew J. Oswald. 1994. *The Wage Curve*. Cambridge, Mass.: MIT Press.

Bollinger, William. N.d. "Organized Labor in El Salvador: A Historical Overview." Occasional Papers Series 13. Los Angeles, Calif.: Interamerican Research Centure.

Bowles, Samuel. 1985. "The Production Process in a Competitive Economy: Walrasian, Marxian, and Neo-Hobbesian Models." *American Economic Review* 76(1): 16–36.

Bowles, Samuel. 1995. "Choice of Technology, Sectoral Priorities and Employment: The Challenge of Job Creation in the South African Economy." Unpublished report to the Presidential Labour Market Commission, December 1.

Boyce, James K., ed. 1996. *Economic Policy for Building Peace: The Lessons of El Salvador*. Boulder, Colo.: Lynne Rienner.

References

Bratton, Michael, and Nicholas van de Walle. 1997. *Democratic Experiments in Africa: Regime Transitions in Comparative Perspective*. Cambridge: Cambridge University Press.

Bresser Pereira, Luis Carlos, José María Maravall, and Adam Przeworski. 1993. *Economic Reforms in New Democracies*. Cambridge: Cambridge University Press.

Brockett, Charles D. 1988. *Land, Power, and Poverty: Agrarian Transformation and Political Conflict in Central America*. Boston: Unwin Hyman.

Brockett, Charles D. 1995. "A Protest-Cycle Resolution of the Repression/Popular-Protest Paradox." In *Repertoires and Cycles of Collective Action*, edited by Mark Traugott, 117–44. Durham, N.C.: Duke University Press.

Browning, David. 1971. *El Salvador: Landscape and Society*. Oxford: Oxford University Press.

Browning, David. 1983. "Agrarian Reform in El Salvador." *Journal of Latin American Studies* 15: 399–426.

Buergenthal, T. 1994. "The United Nations Truth Commission for El Salvador." *Vanderbilt Journal of Transnational Law* 27(3): 497–544.

Bulmer-Thomas, Victor. 1983. "Economic Development over the Long Run – Central America since 1920." *Journal of Latin American Studies* 15: 269–94.

Bulmer-Thomas, Victor. 1987. *The Political Economy of Central America since 1920*. New York: Cambridge University Press.

Bundy, Colin. 1979. *The Rise and Fall of the South African Peasantry*. Berkeley: University of California Press.

Burton, Michael, Richard Gunther, and John Higley. 1992. "Introduction: Elite Transformations and Democratic Regimes." In *Elites and Democratic Consolidation in Latin America and Southern Europe*, edited by John Higley and Richard Gunther, 1–37. Cambridge: Cambridge University Press.

Byrne, Hugh. 1996. *El Salvador's Civil War: A Study of Revolution*. Boulder, Colo.: Lynne Rienner.

Cabarrús, Carlos Rafael. 1983. *Génesis de una revolución*. Mexico: Ediciones de la casa, Centro de Investigaciones y Estudios Superiores en Antropología Social.

Cardenal, Rodolfo. 1985. *Historia de una esperanza: vida de Rutilio Grande*. San Salvador: UCA Editores.

Cardoso, Fernando H. 1986. "Entrepreneurs and the Transition Process: The Brazilian Case." In *Transitions from Authoritarian Rule: Comparative Perspectives*, edited by G. O'Donnell, P. Schmitter, and L. Whitehead, 137–53. Baltimore, Md.: Johns Hopkins University Press.

Chapman, T. Neal, and Murray B. Hofmeyr. 1994. "Business Statesman of the Year Award." Address to the Harvard Business School Club of South Africa.

Charney, Craig. 1994. "Political Violence, Local Elites, and Democratic Transition: Business and the Peace Process in South Africa." Paper presented at the Annual Meeting of the American Political Science Association, Atlanta, Georgia.

Clark, Peter K. 1979. "Investment in the 1970s: Theory, Performance and Prediction." *Brookings Papers on Economic Activity*, 1(1979): 73–124.

Coleman, Max, and David Webster. 1986. "Repression and Detentions in South Africa." In *South Africa Review III*, edited by the South African Research Service, 110–36. Johannesburg: Raven Press.

Colindres, Eduardo. 1976. "La Tenencia de la Tierra en El Salvador." *Estudios Centroamericanos* 31(335–6): 463–72.

Colindres, Eduardo. 1977. *Fundamentos Económicos de la Burguesía Salvadoreña*. San Salvador: UCA Editores.

Collier, Ruth Berins. 1999. *Paths toward Democracy: The Working Class and Elites in Western Europe and South America*. Cambridge: Cambridge University Press.

Collier, Ruth Berins. Forthcoming. "Democratic Transition." In *Encyclopedia of Democratic Thought*, edited by Paul Barry Clark and Joe Foweraker. London: Routledge.

Collier, Ruth Berins, and James Mahoney. 1997. "Adding Collective Actors to Collective Outcomes." *Comparative Politics* 29(3): 285–303.

Commission on the Truth for El Salvador. 1993. "From Madness to Hope: The 12-Year War in El Salvador." Report of the Commission on the Truth for El Salvador. New York: United Nations.

Consultative Business Movement National Team (CBM). 1993. *Managing Change: A Guide to the Role of Business in Transition*. Cape Town: Creda Press.

Davies, Robert. 1989. "After Cuito Cuanavale: The New Regional Conjuncture and the Sanctions Question." In *Sanctions against Apartheid*, edited by Mark Orkin, 198–206. Cape Town: David Philip.

de Sebastián, Luis. 1979. "El Camino Económico Hacia la Democracia." *Estudios Centroamericános* 34(372/3): 947–60.

de Soto, Alvaro, and Graciana del Castillo. 1994. "Obstacles to Peacebuilding." *Foreign Policy* 94: 69–83.

de Villiers, René. 1971. "Afrikaner Nationalism." In *The Oxford History of South Africa*, vol. 2, *South Africa 1870–1966*, edited by Monica Wilson and Leonard Thompson, 365–423. Oxford: Clarendon Press.

del Castillo, Graciana. 1997. "The Arms-for-Land Deal in El Salvador." In *Keeping the Peace: Multi-dimensional UN Operations in Cambodia and El Salvador*, edited by Michael W. Doyle, Ian Johnstone, and Robert C. Orr, 342–65. Cambridge: Cambridge University Press.

Dirección General de Estadística y Censos. 1974. *Tercer Censo Nacional Agropecuario, 1971*. San Salvador: Dirección General de Estadística y Censos.

Diskin, Martin. 1989. "El Salvador: Reform Prevents Change." In *Searching for Agrarian Reform in Latin America*, edited by William C. Thiesenhusen, 429–50. Boston: Unwin Hyman.

Dunkerley, James. 1988. *Power in the Isthmus: A Political History of Modern Central America*. London: Verso.

Du Preez, Max, Gavin Evans, and Rosemary Grealy. 1988. *The Broederstroom Encounter*. Johannesburg: Consultative Business Movement.

Durham, William H. 1979. *Scarcity and Survival in Central America: The Ecological Origins of the Soccer War*. Stanford, Calif.: Stanford University Press.

Ebrahim, Hassen. 1998. *The Soul of a Nation: Constitution-Making in South Africa*. Cape Town: Oxford University Press.

Economic Commission for Latin America and the Caribbean (ECLAC). 1993. "Economic Consequences of Peace in El Salvador" (August 30).

References

Eguizábal, Cristina. 1992. "Parties, Programs, and Politics in El Salvador." In *Political Parties and Democracy in the United States and Central America*, edited by Louis W. Goodman, William M. LeoGrande, and Johanna Mendelson Forman, 135–60. Boulder, Colo.: Westview Press.

Ellis, Stephen, and Tsepo Sechaba. 1992. *Comrades against Apartheid: The ANC and the South African Communist Party*. London: James Currey.

Evans, Ivan. 1997. *Bureaucracy and Race: Native Administration in South Africa*. Berkeley: University of California Press.

Facultad Latinoamericana de Ciencias Sociales-Programa El Salvador (FLACSO). 1995. *El Proceso Electoral 1994*. San Salvador.

Fallon, Peter. 1992. *An Analysis of Employment and Wage Behavior in South Africa*. World Bank Informal Discussion Papers on Aspects of the Economy of South Africa, Discussion Paper 3. Washington, D.C.: World Bank Southern Africa Department.

Fallon, Peter, and Luiz A. Pereira de Silva. 1994. *South Africa: Economic Performance and Policies*. World Bank Informal Discussion Papers on Aspects of the Economy of South Africa, Discussion Paper 7. Washington, D.C.: World Bank Southern Africa Department.

Fedderke, Johannes, Raphael H. J. De Kadt, and John M. Luiz. N.d. "Indicators of Political Liberty, Property Rights and Political Instability in South Africa, 1935–1997." Unpublished Paper. Johannesburg: University of the Witwatersrand.

Fedderke, J. W., R. H. J. de Kadt, J. M. Luiz. N.d.a. "Growth and Institutions: A Study of the Link between Political Institutions and Economic Growth in South Africa – A Time-Series Study, 1935–1997." Unpublished paper. Johannesburg: University of the Witwatersrand.

Fedderke, J. W., R. H. J. de Kadt, J. M. Luiz. N.d.b. "Indicators of Political Liberty, Property Rights and Political Instability in South Africa: 1935–1997." Typescript.

Fedderke, Johannes, and W. Liu. N.d. "Modelling the Determinants of Capital Flow and Capital Flight: With an Application to South African Data from 1960–1995". Unpublished paper. Johannesburg: University of the Witwatersrand.

Fedderke, J. W., and W. Liu. N.d. "South African Capital Flows and Capital Flight over the 1960–1995 period." Typescript.

Federated Chamber of Industries (FCI). 1986. "Business Charter of Social, Economic and Political Rights" and "Action Programme of South African Business." Reprinted in *The Innes Labour Brief* 1(4), 1990: 68–74.

Feldstein, Martin. 1982. "Inflation, Tax Rules and Investment: Some Econometric Evidence." *Econometrica* 50: 825–62.

Foley, Michael W., with George R. Vickers and Geoff Thale. 1997. *Land, Peace, and Participation: The Development of Post-War Agricultural Policy in El Salvador and the Role of the World Bank*. Washington, D.C.: World Bank.

Food and Agriculture Organization of the United Nations (FAO). 1992. *FAO Yearbook: Production*, vol. 46. FAO Statistics Series, 112. Rome.

Food and Agriculture Organization of the United Nations (FAO). 1995. *FAO Yearbook: Production*, vol. 49. FAO Statistics Series, 130. Rome.

Frente Farabundo Martí para la Liberación Nacional (FMLN). 1989. "Hacia una revolución democrática en El Salvador." *Pensamiento Propio* 4(60): 1–8.

Frente Farabundo Martí para la Liberación Nacional (FMLN). 1990. "Position of the FMLN on Ending Militarism, Reaching a Cease-Fire and Advancing to an Unarmed Democracy." August 17.

Friedman, Steven. 1987. *Building Tomorrow Today: African Workers in Trade Unions 1970–1984*. Johannesburg: Raven Press.

Friedman, Steven, ed. 1993a. *The Long Journey: South Africa's Quest for a Negotiated Settlement*. Johannesburg: Raven Press.

Friedman, Steven. 1993b. "South Africa's Reluctant Transition." *Journal of Democracy* 4(2): 56–69.

Friedman, Steven. 1995. "South Africa: Divided in a Special Way." In *Politics in Developing Countries*, edited by Larry Diamond, J. J. Linz, and S. M. Lipset, 531–81. Boulder, Colo.: Lynne Rienner.

Friedman, Steven. 1997. "Too Little Knowledge Is a Dangerous Thing: South Africa's Bargained Transition, Democratic Prospects and John Rawls's 'Veil of Ignorance.'" Unpublished Paper. Johannesburg: Center for Policy Studies.

Fundación Salvadoreña para el Desarrollo Económico y Social (FUSADES). 1989. *Boletin Económico y Social* 46.

Funkhouser, Edward. 1992. "Mass Emigration, Remittances, and Economic Adjustment: The Case of El Salvador in the 1980s." In *Immigration in the Work Force: Economic Consequences for the United States and Source Areas*, edited by G. J. Borjas and R. B. Freeman, 135–75. Chicago: University of Chicago Press.

Geddes, Barbara. 1999. "What Do We Know about Democratization after Twenty Years?" *Annual Review of Political Science* 2: 115–44.

Gelb, Stephen. 1991. "South Africa's Economic Crisis: An Overview." In *South Africa's Economic Crisis*, edited by Stephen Gelb, 1–32. London: Zed Books.

Gerhart, Gail M. 1978. *Black Power in South Africa: The Evolution of an Ideology*. Berkeley: University of California Press.

Gibb, T., and F. Smythe. 1990. "El Salvador: Is Peace Possible?" Washington, D.C.: Washington Office on Latin America, April.

Giliomee, Hermann. 1997. "Surrender without Defeat: Afrikaners and the South African Miracle." Paper presented at the Centre for African Studies Seminar, February 26, University of Cape Town.

Gobierno de El Salvador. 1992. *Acuerdos de Chapultepec*. San Salvador: Secretaria Nacional de Comunicaciones.

Goodwin, Jeff, and James M. Jasper. 1999. "Caught in a Winding, Snarling Vine: The Structural Bias of Political Process Theory." *Sociological Forum* 14(1): 27–54.

Goodwin, Jeff, and Theda Skocpol. 1989. "Explaining Revolutions in the Third World." *Politics and Society* 17(4): 489–509.

Goodwyn, Lawrence. 1991. *Breaking the Barrier: The Rise of Solidarity in Poland*. New York: Oxford University Press.

References

Gordon, David. 1980. "Stages of Accumulation and Long Economic Cycles." In *Processes of the World-System*, edited by T. Hopkins and I. Wallerstein, 9–45. Beverly Hills, Calif.: Sage.

Gordon, David, Richard Edwards, and Michael Reich. 1994. "Long Swings and Stages of Capitalism." In *Social Structures of Accumulation*, edited by David M. Kotz, Terence McDonough, and Michael Reich, 11–28. Cambridge: Cambridge University Press.

Gordon, Sara R. 1983. "La Transformación Agraria en El Salvador: Un Conflicto Interburgués." *Estudios Sociales Centroamericanos* 36: 13–37.

Greenberg, Stanley B. 1980. *Race and State in Capitalist Development*. New Haven, Conn.: Yale University Press.

Haggard, Stephan, and Robert Kaufman. 1995. *The Political Economy of Democratic Transitions*. Princeton, N.J.: Princeton University Press.

Hamill, James. 1994. "The Crossing of the Rubicon: South Africa's Post-Apartheid Political Process 1990–1992." *International Relations* 12(3): 9–37.

Harberger, A. C. 1993. "Measuring the Components of Economic Growth in El Salvador." San Salvador: FUSADES. Mimeo.

Hatfield, Mark O., Jim Leach, and George Miller. 1990. "Bankrolling Failure: United States Policy in El Salvador and the Urgent Need for Reform." Washington, D.C.: U.S. Congress, Arms Control and Foreign Policy Caucus.

Herbst, Jeffrey. 1997–8. "Prospects for Elite-Driven Democracy in South Africa." *Political Science Quarterly* 112(4): 595–615.

Heye, Christopher. 1995. "Expectations and Investment: An Econometric Defense of Animal Spirits." In *Macroeconomic Policy after the Conservative Era: Studies in Investment, Saving and Finance*, edited by Gerald A. Epstein and Herbert M. Gintis, 197–223. Cambridge: Cambridge University Press.

Hirsch, Alan. 1989. "Sanctions, Loans and the South African Economy." In *Sanctions against Apartheid*, edited by Mark Orkin, 270–84. Johannesburg: David Philip.

Hofmeyr, Julian. 1994. *An Analysis of African Wage Movements in South Africa*. Research Monograph 9. Durban: Economic Research Unit, University of Natal.

Holiday, David. 1997. "Guatemala's Long Road to Peace." *Current History* 96(607): 68–74.

Holiday, David, and William Stanley. 1993. "Building the Peace: Preliminary Lessons from El Salvador." *Journal of International Affairs* 46(2): 415–38.

Huntington, Samuel. 1991. *The Third Wave: Democratization in the Late Twentieth Century*. Norman: University of Oklahoma Press.

Innes, Duncan. 1989. "Multinational Companies and Disinvestment." In *Sanctions against Apartheid*, edited by Mark Orkin, 226–39. Johannesburg: David Philip.

Innes Labour Brief. 1990. "Debating Business Strategies." *Innes Labour Brief* 1(4): 39–44.

Johnson, Kenneth. 1993. "Between Revolution and Democracy: Business Elites and the State in El Salvador during the 1980s." Ph.D. diss., Tulane University.

Johnson, R. W. 1996a. "The 1994 Election: Outcome and Analysis." In *Launching Democracy in South Africa: The First Open Election, April 1994*, edited by

R. W. Johnson and Lawrence Schlemmer, 301–22. New Haven, Conn.: Yale University Press.

Johnstone, F. A. 1970. "White Prosperity and White Supremacy in South Africa Today." *African Affairs* 69: 124–40.

Joint Group. 1994. *Report of the Joint Group for the Investigation of Illegal Armed Groups with Political Motivation in El Salvador.* San Salvador, July 28. Mimeo.

Jung, Courtney, and Ian Shapiro. 1995. "South Africa's Negotiated Transition: Democracy, Opposition and the New Constitutional Order." *Politics and Society* 23(3): 269–308.

Kaempfer, William H., Anton D. Lowenberg, H. Naci Mocan, and Kudret Topyan. 1995. "International Sanctions and Anti-Apartheid Politics in South Africa: An Empirical Investigation." *Journal for Studies in Economics and Econometrics* 19(1): 1–27.

Kaimowitz, David. 1990. "The Political Economies of Central America: Foreign Aid and Labour Remittances." *Development and Change* 20(10): 637–55.

Karis, Thomas, and Gail Gerhart. 1977a. "Challenge and Violence 1953–1964." In *From Protest to Challenge: A Documentary History of African Politics in South Africa 1882–1964*, vol. 3, edited by Thomas Karin and Gwendolen M. Carter. Stanford, Calif.: Hoover Institution Press.

Karis, Thomas, and Gail Gerhart. 1977b. *From Protest to Challenge: A Documentary History of African Politics in South Africa 1882–1964*, vol. 3: *Challenge and Violence 1953–1964*. Stanford, Calif.: Hoover Institution Press.

Karis, Thomas, and Gail Gerhart. 1997. *From Protest to Challenge: A Documentary History of African Politics in South Africa, 1882–1990*, vol. 5: *Nadir and Resurgence, 1964–1979*. Stanford, Calif.: Hoover Institution Press.

Karl, Terry Lynn. 1985. "After La Palma: The Prospects for Democratization in El Salvador." *World Policy Journal* 2(2): 305–30.

Karl, Terry Lynn. 1986a. "Imposing Consent?: Electoralism vs. Democratization in El Salvador." In *Elections and Democratization in Latin America*, edited by P. Drake and E. Silva, 9–36. San Diego: Center for Iberian and Latin American Studies, University of California.

Karl, Terry Lynn. 1986b. "Petroleum and Political Pacts: The Transition to Democracy in Venezuela." In *Transitions from Authoritarian Rule: Latin America*, edited by Guillermo O'Donnell et al., 196–219. Baltimore, Md.: Johns Hopkins University Press.

Karl, Terry Lynn. 1989. "Negotiations or Total War: Salvador Samayoa Interviewed by Terry Karl." *World Policy Journal* 6(2): 321–55.

Karl, Terry Lynn. 1990. "Dilemmas of Democratization." *Comparative Politics* 23(1): 1–21.

Karl, Terry Lynn. 1992. "El Salvador's Negotiated Revolution." *Foreign Affairs* 71(2): 147–64.

Kentridge, Matthew. 1993. "Turning the Tanker: The Economic Debate in South Africa." Social Contract Series. Johannesburg: Center for Policy Studies.

Kitschelt, Herbert P. 1992. "Political Regime Change: Structure and Process-Driven Explanations?" *American Political Science Review* 86(4): 1028–34.

References

Klug, Heinz. 1995. "Extending Democracy in South Africa." In *Associations and Democracy*, edited by Josh Cohen and Joel Rogers, 214–35. London: Verso.

Knight, Jack. 1992. *Institutions and Social Conflict*. Cambridge: Cambridge University Press.

Kuper, Leo. 1971. "African Nationalism in South Africa, 1910–1964." In *The Oxford History of South Africa*, vol. 2: *1870–1966*, edited by M. Wilson and L. Thompson, 424–76. Oxford: Clarendon Press.

Legassick, Martin. 1974. "South Africa: Capital Accumulation and Violence." *Economy and Society* 3: 253–91.

Lernoux, Penny. 1980. *Cry of the People*. Garden City, N.Y.: Doubleday.

Lewis, David. 1997. "Black Workers and Trade Unions." In *From Protest to Challenge: A Documentary History of African Politics in South Africa, 1882–1990*, vol. 5, edited by Karis and Gerhart, 189–220. Stanford, Calif.: Hoover Institution Press.

Licklider, Roy. 1995. "The Consequences of Negotiated Settlements in Civil Wars, 1945–1993." *American Political Science Review* 89(3): 681–90.

Lindo-Fuentes, Hector. 1990. *Weak Foundations: The Economy of El Salvador in the Nineteenth Century*. Berkeley: University of California Press.

Lipset, Seymour Martin. 1960. *Political Man: The Social Bases of Politics*. New York: Doubleday.

Lipton, Merle. 1985. *Capitalism and Apartheid: South Africa, 1910–84*. Totowa, N.J.: Rowman & Allanheld.

Lodge, Tom. 1983. *Black Politics in South Africa since 1945*. London: Longman Group.

López Vallecillos, Italo. 1979. "Rasgos Sociales y Tendencias Políticas en El Salvador 1969–1979." *Estudios Centroamericános* 34(372/3): 863–84.

Lowenberg, Anton. 1997. "Why South Africa's Apartheid Economy Failed." *Contemporary Economic Policy* 15: 62–72.

Lungo Uclés, Mario. 1996. *El Salvador in the Eighties. Counterinsurgency and Revolution*. Edited with an introduction by Arthur Schmidt. Translated by Amelia F. Shogan. Philadelphia: Temple University Press.

McCleary, Rachel M. 1996. "Guatemala: Expectations for Peace." *Current History* 95(598, February): 88–92.

McCleary, Rachel M. 1997. "Guatemala's Postwar Prospects." *Journal of Democracy* 8(2, April): 129–43.

McClintock, Cynthia. 1998. *Revolutionary Movements in Latin America*. Washington, D.C.: U.S. Institute of Peace Press.

Mamdani, Mahmood. 1996. *Citizen and Subject: Contemporary Africa and the Legacy of Late Colonialism*. Princeton, N.J.: Princeton University Press.

Mandela, Nelson R. 1964. "Statement during the Rivonia trial, by Nelson R. Mandela, April 20, 1964." In *From Protest to Challenge: A Documentary History of African Politics in South Africa 1882–1964*, vol. 2: *Hope and Challenge 1935–1952*, edited by Thomas Karis and Gwendolan M. Carter, 771–96. Stanford, Calif.: Hoover Institution Press.

Maree, Johann. 1987. "Overview: Emergence of the Independent Trade Union Movement." In *The Independent Trade Unions, 1974–1984: Ten Years of the South*

African Labour Bulletin, edited by Johann Maree, 1–11. Johannesburg: Ravan Press.

Marx, Anthony W. 1992. *Lessons of Struggle: South African Internal Opposition, 1960–1990*. New York: Oxford University Press.

Marx, Anthony W. 1998. *Making Race and Nation: A Comparison of South Africa, the United States and Brazil*. New York: Cambridge University Press.

Marx, Karl. 1964 [1937]. *Class Struggles in France – 1848–1850*. New York: International.

Mason, T. David, and Patrick J. Fett. 1996. "How Civil Wars End: A Rational Choice Approach." *Journal of Conflict Resolution* 40(4): 546–68.

Mayer, Enrique, and Elio Masferrer. 1979. "La Población Indígena de América en 1978." *América Indígena* 39(2): 217–337.

Melvin, Michael, and Kok-Hui Tan. 1996. "Foreign Exchange Market Bid-Ask Spreads and the Market Price of Social Unrest." *Oxford Economic Papers* 48: 329–41.

Miles, Sara, and Bob Ostertag. 1989. "D'Aubuisson's New Arena." *NACLA Report on the Americas* 23(2): 14.

Montgomery, Tommie Sue. 1995. *Revolution in El Salvador: From Civil Strife to Civil Peace*. 2d ed. Boulder, Colo.: Westview Press.

Moore, Barrington Jr. 1966. *Social Origins of Dictatorships and Democracy*. Boston: Beacon Press.

Moorsom, Richard. 1989. "Foreign Trade and Sanctions." In *Sanctions against Apartheid*, edited by Mark Orkin, 253–69. Johannesburg: David Philip.

Morris, M. L. 1976. "The Development of Capitalism in South African Agriculture: Class Struggle in the Countryside." *Economy and Society* 5(3): 292–343.

Munck, Gerardo L. 1993. "Beyond Electoralism in El Salvador: Conflict Resolution through Negotiated Compromise." *Third World Quarterly* 14(1): 75–93.

Murray, Kevin, Ellen Coletti, and Jack Spence. 1994. *Rescuing Reconstruction: The Debate on Post-War Economic Recovery in El Salvador*. Cambridge: Hemisphere Initiatives.

National Peace Convention. 1991. *National Peace Accord*. Pamphlet.

Nattrass, Jill. 1981. *The South African Economy: Its Growth and Change*. Cape Town: Oxford University Press.

Nattrass, Nicoli. 1990. "Economic Power and Profits in Post-war Manufacturing." In *The Political Economy of South Africa*, edited by N. Nattrass and E. Ardington, 107–28. Oxford: Oxford University Press.

Nattrass, Nicoli. 1991. "Controversies about Capitalism and Apartheid in South Africa: An Economic Perspective." *Journal of Southern African Studies* 17(4): 654–77.

Nattrass, Nicoli. 1999. "The Truth and Reconciliation Commission on Business and Apartheid: A Critical Evaluation." *African Affairs* 98: 373–91.

North, Douglass C. 1981. *Structure and Change in Economic History*. New York: Norton.

Norton, Chris. 1991. "The Hard Right: ARENA Comes to Power." In *A Decade of War: El Salvador Confronts the Future*, edited by Anjali Sundaram and George Gelber, 196–215. New York: Monthly Review Press.

References

O'Donnell, Guillermo, and Philippe C. Schmitter. 1986. *Transitions from Authoritarian Rule: Tentative Conclusions about Uncertain Democracies.* Baltimore, Md.: Johns Hopkins Press.

O'Meara, Dan. 1983. *Volks-Kapitalisme: Class, Capital and Ideology in the Development of Afrikaner Nationalism 1934–1948.* Johannesburg: Raven Press.

O'Meara, Dan. 1996. *Forty Lost Years: The Apartheid State and the Politics of the National Party, 1948–1994.* Columbus: Ohio State University Press.

Overseas Development Council. 1994. "Informe Preliminar del Equipo Nacional de El Salvador." Unpublished report. San Salvador.

Padayachee, Vishnu. 1988. "Private International Banks, the Debt Crisis and the Apartheid State, 1982–1985." *African Affairs* 87(348, July): 361–76.

Paige, Jeffrey M. 1987. "Coffee and Politics in Central America." In *Crises in the Caribbean Basin,* edited by Richard Tardanico, 141–90. Newbury Park: Sage.

Paige, Jeffrey M. 1993. "Coffee and Power in El Salvador." *Latin American Research Review* 28: 7–40.

Paige, Jeffrey M. 1997. *Coffee and Power: Revolution and the Rise of Democracy in Central America.* Cambridge, Mass.: Harvard University Press.

Paus, Eva. 1996. "Exports and the Consolidation of Peace." In *Economic Policy for Building Peace: The Lessons of El Salvador,* edited by James K. Boyce, 247–78. Boulder: Lynne Rienner.

Payne, Leigh A. 1995. "Brazilian Business and the Democratic Transition: New Attitudes and Influence." In *Business and Democracy in Latin America,* edited by E. Bartell and L. A. Payne, 217–56. Pittsburgh: University of Pittsburgh Press.

Payne, Leigh A., and Ernest Bartell. 1995. "Bringing Business Back In: Business-State Relations and Democratic Stability in Latin America." In *Business and Democracy in Latin America,* edited by Ernest Bartell and Leigh A. Payne, 257–90. Pittsburgh: University of Pittsburgh Press.

Pearce, Jenny. 1986. *Promised Land: Peasant Rebellion in Chalatenango, El Salvador.* London: Latin American Review.

Pelupessy, Wim. 1991. "Agrarian Reform in El Salvador." In *A Decade of War: El Salvador Confronts the Future,* edited by A. Sundaram and G. Gelber, 38–57. New York: Monthly Review Press.

Pérez Brignoli, Héctor. 1995. "Indians, Communists, and Peasants: The 1932 Rebellion." In *Coffee, Society and Power in Latin America,* edited by William Roseberry, Lowell Gudmundson, and Mario Samper Kutschbac, 232–61. Baltimore, Md.: Johns Hopkins University Press.

Persson, Torsten, and Guido Tabellini. 1992. "Growth, Distribution, and Politics." In *Political Economy, Growth and Business Cycles,* edited by Alex Cukierman, Zvi Hercowitz, and Leonardo Leiderman, 3–22. Cambridge, Mass.: MIT Press.

Peterson, Anna L. 1997. *Martyrdom and the Politics of Religion: Progressive Catholicism in El Salvador's Civil War.* Albany: State University of New York Press.

Plummer, Alfred. 1971. *Bronterre: A Political Biography of Bronterre O'Brien, 1804–1864.* London: George Allen and Unwin.

Popkin, Margaret. 1994. *Justice Delayed: The Slow Pace of Judicial Reform in El Salvador.* Washington, D.C.: Office on Latin America and Hemisphere Initiatives.

Posel, Deborah. 1991. *The Making of Apartheid 1948–1961*. Oxford: Clarendon Press.

Poznanski, Kazimierz A. 1996. *Poland's Protracted Transition: Institutional Change and Economic Growth, 1970–1994*. Cambridge: Cambridge University Press.

Price, Robert M. 1991. *The Apartheid State in Crisis: Political Transformation in South Africa 1975–1990*. New York: Oxford University Press.

Prinsloo, J. W., and H. Smith. 1996. "Developments in Fixed Capital Stock." *Quarterly Bulletin December 1996*, 31–44. Pretoria: South African Reserve Bank.

Przeworski, Adam. 1986. "Some Problems in the Study of the Transition to Democracy." In *Transitions from Authoritarian Rule: Comparative Perspectives*, edited by Guillermo O'Donnell, Philippe C. Schmitter, and Laurence Whitehead, 47–63. Baltimore, Md.: Johns Hopkins University Press.

Przeworski, Adam. 1991. *Democracy and the Market*. New York: Cambridge University Press.

Przeworski, Adam. 1996. "Democracy as an Equilibrium." New York University Department of Politics. Manuscript.

Przeworski, Adam, and Fernando Limongi. 1993. "Political Regimes and Economic Growth." *Journal of Economic Perspectives* 7: 51–70.

Przeworski, Adam, and Michael Wallerstein. 1988. "Structural Dependence of the State on Capital." *American Political Science Review* 82(1): 13–29.

Romer, Paul. 1986. "Increasing Returns and Long-Run Growth." *Journal of Political Economy* 94: 1002–37.

Romer, Paul. 1994. "The Origins of Endogenous Growth." *Journal of Economic Perspectives* 8(1): 3–22.

Roseberry, William. 1991. "La Falta de Brazos: Land and Labor in the Coffee Economies of Nineteenth-Century Latin America." *Theory and Society* 20: 351–81.

Rothchild, David. 1997. *Managing Ethnic Conflict in Africa: Pressures and Incentives for Cooperation*. Washington, D.C.: Brookings Institution Press.

Rueschemeyer, Dietrich, Evelyne Huber Stephens, and John D. Stephens. 1992. *Capitalist Development and Democracy*. Chicago: University of Chicago Press.

Rustow, Dankwart A. 1970. "Transitions to Democracy: Towards a Dynamic Model." *Comparative Politics* 2(3): 337–63.

Salazar Candell, Roberto. 1993. "El Salvador: Política Industrial, Comportamiento Empresarial y Orientaciones para la Transformación Industrial." *Revista Económica Social* 33: 235–70.

Saul, John S. 1986. "The Crisis Deepens." In *The Crisis in South Africa*, edited by John Saul and Stephen Gelb, 211–45. New York: Monthly Review Press.

Saul, John S., and Stephen Gelb. 1981. "The Crisis in South Africa: Class Defense, Class Revolution." In *The Crisis in South Africa*, 1986, edited by John Saul and Stephen Gelb, 53–210. New York: Monthly Review Press.

Saunders, Christopher. 1988. *The Making of the South African Past*. Cape Town: David Philip.

Schwarz, Benjamin C. 1991 *American Counterinsurgency Doctrine and El Salvador: The Frustrations of Reform and the Illusions of Nation Building*. Santa Monica, Calif.: Rand.

References

Secretaria de Reconstrucción Nacional (SRN). 1992a. "Plan de Reconstrucción Nacional (Fase de Contingencia)." San Salvador, February.

Secretaria de Reconstrucción Nacional (SRN). 1992b. "Programa de Apoya a la Reinserción de los Ex-combatientes del FMLN." San Salvador, September 8.

Segovia, Alexander. 1996a. "Domestic Resource Mobilization." In *Economic Policy for Building Peace: The Lessons of El Salvador*, edited by James K. Boyce, 107–28. Boulder, Colo.: Lynne Rienner.

Seidman, Gay W. 1994. *Manufacturing Militance: Workers' Movements in Brazil and South Africa, 1970–1985*. Berkeley: University of California Press.

Seligson, Mitchell A. 1995. "Thirty Years of Transformation in the Agrarian Structure of El Salvador, 1961–1991." *Latin American Research Review* 30(3): 43–75.

Sevilla, Manuel. 1985. *La Concentración Económica en El Salvador*. Managua: Instituto Investigaciones Económicas y Sociales.

Simkins, Charles. 1994. "A New Deal? The Implications of the Interim Constitution for Business." *Optima* (April): 41–4.

Sisk, Timothy D. 1995. *Democratization in South Africa: The Elusive Social Contact*. Princeton, N.J.: Princeton University Press.

Sisk, Timothy D. 1996. *Power Sharing and International Mediation in Ethnic Conflicts*. New York: Carnegie.

Snyder, Richard. 1992. "Explaining Transitions from Neopatrimonial Dictatorships." *Contemporary Politics* 24(4, July): 379–99.

South African Labour Development Research Unit (SALDRU). 1994. *South Africans Rich and Poor: Baseline Household Statistics*. Cape Town: University of Cape Town.

South African Institute of Race Relations (SAIRR). 1959–60. *A Survey of Race Relations in South Africa*. Johannesburg.

South African Institute of Race Relations (SAIRR). 1963. *A Survey of Race Relations in South Africa, 1962*. Johannesburg.

Southall, Roger J. 1983. *South Africa's Transkei: The Political Economy of an Independent Bantustan*. New York: Monthly Review Press.

Sparks, Allister. 1995. *Tomorrow Is Another Country*. Chicago: University of Chicago Press.

Spence, Jack, et al. 1998. "Promise and Reality: Implementation of the Guatemala Peace Accords." Cambridge, Mass.: Hemisphere Initiatives.

Spence, Jack, David Dye, and George Vickers. 1994. *El Salvador: Elections of the Century*. Cambridge, Mass.: Hemisphere Initiatives, July.

Spence, Jack, and George Vickers. 1994a. *A Negotiated Revolution? A Two-Year Progress Report on the Salvadoran Peace Accords*. Cambridge, Mass.: Hemisphere Initiatives.

Spence, Jack, and George Vickers. 1994b. *Toward a Level Playing Field: A Report on the Post-War Salvadoran Electoral Process*. Cambridge, Mass.: Hemisphere Initiatives.

Spence, Jack, George Vickers, and David Dye. 1995. *The Salvadoran Peace Accords and Democratization: A Three Year Progress Report and Recommendations*. Cambridge, Mass.: Hemisphere Initiatives.

Stanley, William. 1995. "International Tutelage and Domestic Political Will: Lessons from El Salvador's Civilian Police Project." *Studies in Comparative International Development*, May 1995.

Stanley, William. 1996. *The Protection Racket State: Elite Politics, Military Extortion, and Civil War in El Salvador.* Philadelphia: Temple University Press.

Stanley, William, and David Holiday. 1997. "Peace Mission Strategy and Domestic Actors: UN Mediation, Verification, and Institution-building in El Salvador." *International Peacekeeping* 4(2, Summer): 22–49.

Stanley, William, and David Holiday. 1999. "Everyone Participates, No One Is Responsible: Peace Implementation in Guatemala." Paper contributed to the Stanford University Center for International Security and Cooperation/ International Peace Academy, Project on Peace Plan Implementation, August.

Stedman, Stephen John. 1997. "Spoiler Problems in Peace Processes." *International Security* 22(2): 5–53.

Stephens, Evelyne Huber. 1989. "Capitalist Development and Democracy in South America." *Politics and Society* 17(3): 281–352.

Stiglitz, Joseph, and Carl Shapiro. 1984. "Unemployment as a Worker Discipline Device." *American Economic Review* 74(3): 433–44.

Stokes, Gale. 1993. *The Walls Came Tumbling Down: The Collapse of Communism in Eastern Europe.* New York: Oxford University Press.

Stolcke, Verena. 1995. "The Labors of Coffee in Latin America: The Hidden Charm of Family Labor and Self-Provisioning." In *Coffee, Society and Power in Latin America*, edited by William Roseberry, Lowell Gudmundson, and Mario Samper Kutschbach, 65–93. Baltimore, Md.: Johns Hopkins University Press.

Talbot, John M. 1995. "The Regulation of the World Coffee Market: Tropical Commodities and the Limits of Globalization." In *Food and Agrarian Orders in the World Economy*, edited by Philip McMichael, 139–68. Westport, Conn.: Praeger.

Taylor, Charles, and Michael Hudson. 1972. *World Handbook of Political and Social Indicators.* 2d ed. New Haven, Conn.: Yale University Press.

Taylor, Charles, and David Jodice. 1983. *World Handbook of Political and Social Indicators.* 3d ed. New Haven, Conn.: Yale University Press.

Therborn, Goran. 1979. "The Rule of Capital and the Rise of Democracy." *New Left Review*. Verso Press.

Thompson, Leonard M. 1960. *The Unification of South Africa 1902–1910.* London: Oxford University Press.

Thompson, Leonard M. 1971. "The Compromise of Union." In *The Oxford History of South Africa*, vol. 2: *1870–1966*, edited by M. Wilson and L. Thompson, 325–64. Oxford: Clarendon Press.

Thompson, Leonard M. 1995. *A History of South Africa.* New Haven, Conn.: Yale University Press.

Tilly, Charles. 1985. "War Making and State Making as Organized Crime." In *Bringing the State Back In*, edited by Peter Evans, Dietrich Rueschemeyer, and Theda Skocpol, 169–91. New York: Cambridge University Press.

References

Torchia, Andrew. 1988. "The Business of Business: An Analysis of Political Behavior of the South African Manufacturing Sector under the Nationalists." *Journal of Southern African Studies* 14(3): 421–45.

Trapido, Stanley. 1971. "South Africa in a Comparative Study of Industrialization." *Journal of Development Studies* 7(3): 309–20.

Trapido, Stanley. 1978. "Landlord and Tenant in a Colonial Economy: The Transvaal 1880–1910." *Journal of Southern African Studies* 5: 26–58.

Trudeau, Robert H. 1993. *Guatemalan Politics: The Popular Struggle for Democracy.* Boulder, Colo.: Lynne Rienner.

Tucker, Bob, and Bruce R. Scott. 1992. *South Africa: Prospects for Successful Transition.* Kenwyn: Juta.

United Nations Conference on Trade and Development (UNCTAD). 1992. *International Trade Statistics Yearbook.*

United Nations Development Programme (UNDP). 1993. *Launching New Protagonists in Salvadoran Agriculture: The Agricultural Training Programme for Ex-Combatants of the FMLN.* San Salvador, December.

United Nations Development Programme (UNDP). 1994. "Programa de apoyo a la reinserción económica de líderes y mandos medios del FMLN." San Salvador, March (Proyectos ELS/93/006 y ELS/93/012; "Informe de Avances y Evaluación").

United States, General Accounting Office (U.S. GAO). 1993. *Foreign Assistance: U.S. Support for Caribbean Basin Assembly Industries.* Washington, D.C., December.

van Onselen, Charles. 1996. *The Seed Is Mine: The Life of Kas Maine, A South African Sharecropper 1894–1985.* New York: Hill and Wang.

van Onselen, Charles. 1997. "Paternalism and Violence on the Maize Farms of the South-Western Transvaal 1900–1950." In *White Farms, Black Labor: The State and Agrarian Change in Southern Africa, 1910–1950,* edited by Alan H. Jeeves and Jonathan Crush, 192–213. Portsmouth, N.H.: Heinemann.

Vickers, George. 1992. "El Salvador: A Negotiated Revolution." *Report on the Americas* (North American Congress on Latin America), 25(5): 4–8.

Vilas, Carlos M. 1995. *Between Earthquakes and Volcanoes: Market, State, and the Revolutions in Central America.* New York: Monthly Review Press.

Walter, Barbara. 1997. "The Critical Barrier to Civil War Settlement." *International Organization* 51(3): 335–64.

Walter, Knut, and Phillip J. Williams. 1993. "The Military and Democratization in El Salvador." *Journal of Interamerican Studies and World Affairs* 35: 39–88.

Wantchekon, Leonard. 1996. "Political Coordination and Democratic Stability." Paper presented at New York University School of Law, February 21.

Weeks, John. 1986. "An Interpretation of the Central American Crisis." *Latin American Research Review* 21(3): 31–54.

Weiss Fagen, Patricia. 1996. "El Salvador: Lessons in Peace Consolidation." In *Beyond Sovereignty: Collectively Defending Democracy in the Americas,* edited by Tom Farer, 213–37. Baltimore, Md.: Johns Hopkins University Press.

Whitfield, Teresa. 1994. *Paying the Price: Ignacio Ellacuria and the Murdered Jesuits of El Salvador.* Philadelphia: Temple University Press.

Whitfield, Teresa. 1999. "The Role of the United Nations in El Salvador and Guatemala: A Preliminary Comparison." In *Comparative Peace Processes in Latin America*, edited by Cynthia J. Arnson, 257–90. Washington, D.C.: Woodrow Wilson International Center for Scholars.

Williams, Robert G. 1986. *Export Agriculture and the Crisis in Central America*. Chapel Hill: University of North Carolina Press.

Williams, Robert G. 1994. *States and Social Evolution: Coffee and the Rise of National Governments in Central America*. Chapel Hill: University of North Carolina Press.

Williamson, Oliver E. 1985. *The Economic Institutions of Capitalism: Firms Markets, Relational Contracting*. New York: The Free Press.

Wilson, Francis. 1971. "Farming, 1866–1966." In *The Oxford History of South Africa*, vol. 2: *1870–1966*, edited by M. Wilson and L. Thompson, 103–71. Oxford: Clarendon Press.

Wilson, Francis. 1972. *Labour in South African Gold Mines*. Cambridge: Cambridge University Press.

Wintrobe, Ronald. 1998. *The Political Economy of Dictatorship*. Cambridge: Cambridge University Press.

Wise, Michael. 1986. *Agrarian Reform in El Salvador: Process and Progress*. San Salvador: USAID.

Wolf, Daniel. 1992. "ARENA in the Arena: Factors in the Accommodation of the Salvadoran Right to Pluralism and the Broadening of the Political System." *LASA Forum* 23: 10–18.

Wood, Elisabeth Jean. 1995. "Agrarian Social Relations and Democratization: The Negotiated Resolution of the Civil War in El Salvador." Ph.D. diss., Stanford University.

Wood, Elisabeth J. 1996. "The Peace Accords and Postwar Reconstruction." In *Economic Policy for Building Peace: The Lessons of El Salvador*, edited by James K. Boyce, 73–106. Boulder, Colo.: Lynne Rienner.

Wood, Elisabeth Jean. 1999a. "Civil War Settlement: Modeling the Bases of Compromise." Paper presented at the Annual Meeting of the American Political Science Association, Atlanta, September 2–5.

Wood, Elisabeth Jean. 1999b. "The Stakes of the Game: The Politics of Redistribution in Democracies Forged from Below." Paper presented at the Annual Meeting of the American Political Science Association, Atlanta, September 2–5.

Wood, Elisabeth Jean. 2000. "Redrawing Boundaries: Insurrection, Class, and Citizenship in Rural El Salvador." Unpublished book manuscript.

Wood, Elisabeth Jean, and Alexander Segovia. 1995. "Macroeconomic Policy and the Salvadoran Peace Accords." *World Development* 23(12): 2079–2101.

World Bank. 1994a. *El Salvador: The Challenge of Poverty Alleviation*. World Bank Report 12315-ES. Washington, D.C., June 9.

World Bank. 1994b. *World Development Report 1994*. New York: Oxford University Press.

Yashar, Deborah J. 1996. "Indigenous Protest and Democracy in Latin America." In *Constructing Democratic Governance: Latin America and the Caribbean in the*

References

1990s, edited by Jorge I. Dominguez and Abraham F. Lowenthal, 87–105. Baltimore, Md.: Johns Hopkins University Press.

Yudelman, David. 1983. *The Emergence of Modern South Africa*. Westport, Conn.: Greenwood Press.

Zartman, William I. 1989. *Ripe for Resolution: Conflict and Intervention in Africa*. 2d ed. New York: Oxford University Press.

Zielinski, Jakub. 1995. "The Polish Transition to Democracy: A Game-Theoretic Approach." *Archives européennes de sociologie* 36: 135–58.

Index

Index

Index

Index

Index

Webster, Eddie, 17
Western Province General Workers Union (WPGWU), 133, 137
Wiehahn Commission (SA), 136–8, 167, 176, 178
Witwatersrand Native Labour Association (WNLA, SA), 115, 116

WNLA, *see* Witwatersrand Native Labour Association
WPGWU, *see* Western Province General Workers Union

Youth League (ANC), 126, 128

CPSIA information can be obtained
at www.ICGtesting.com
Printed in the USA
FFOW04n0231281214
9884FF